# Chance, Phenomenology
and Aesthetics

Also Available at Bloomsbury

*Heidegger's Style: On Philosophical Anthropology and Aesthetics*,
Markus Weidler
*Heidegger and the Problem of Phenomena*, Fredrik Westerlund
*Understanding Derrida, Understanding Modernism*, Jean-Michel Rabaté
*Hermeneutics and Phenomenology: Figures and Themes,* ed. Saulius Geniusas
and Paul Fairfield
*Hegel's Political Aesthetics: Art in Modern Society*, ed. Stefan Bird-Pollan
and Vladimir Marchenkov

# Chance, Phenomenology and Aesthetics

*Heidegger, Derrida and Contingency in Twentieth-Century Art*

Ian Andrews

BLOOMSBURY ACADEMIC
LONDON • NEW YORK • OXFORD • NEW DELHI • SYDNEY

BLOOMSBURY ACADEMIC
Bloomsbury Publishing Plc
50 Bedford Square, London, WC1B 3DP, UK
1385 Broadway, New York, NY 10018, USA
29 Earlsfort Terrace, Dublin 2, Ireland

BLOOMSBURY, BLOOMSBURY ACADEMIC and the Diana logo
are trademarks of Bloomsbury Publishing Plc

First published in Great Britain 2021
This paperback edition published in 2022

Copyright © Ian Andrews, 2021

Ian Andrews has asserted his right under the Copyright, Designs and
Patents Act, 1988, to be identified as Author of this work.

For legal purposes the Acknowledgements on p. viii constitute
an extension of this copyright page.

Cover design by Charlotte Daniels
Cover image © Ian Andrews

All rights reserved. No part of this publication may be reproduced or
transmitted in any form or by any means, electronic or mechanical,
including photocopying, recording, or any information storage or retrieval
system, without prior permission in writing from the publishers.

Bloomsbury Publishing Plc does not have any control over, or responsibility
for, any third-party websites referred to or in this book. All internet addresses
given in this book were correct at the time of going to press. The author and
publisher regret any inconvenience caused if addresses have changed or sites
have ceased to exist, but can accept no responsibility for any such changes.

A catalogue record for this book is available from the British Library.

Library of Congress Cataloging-in-Publication Data

Names: Andrews, Ian (Media Artist), author.
Title: Chance, phenomenology and aesthetics: Heidegger, Derrida and
contingency in twentieth century art / Ian Andrews.
Description: London; New York: Bloomsbury Academic, 2020. | Includes
bibliographical references and index.
Identifiers: LCCN 2020029903 | ISBN 9781350148468 (hb) | ISBN 9781350187122
(paperback) | ISBN 9781350148475 (epdf) | ISBN 9781350148482 (ebook)
Subjects: LCSH: Art–Philosophy. | Aesthetics. | Chance. | Heidegger,
Martin, 1889-1976. | Husserl, Edmund, 1859-1938. | Derrida, Jacques. | Cage, John.
Classification: LCC BH39 .A5775 2020 | DDC 111/.85–dc23
LC record available at https://lccn.loc.gov/2020029903

ISBN: HB: 978-1-3501-4846-8
PB: 978-1-3501-8712-2
ePDF: 978-1-3501-4847-5
eBook: 978-1-3501-4848-2

Typeset by Deanta Global Publishing Services, Chennai, India

To find out more about our authors and books visit www.bloomsbury.com
and sign up for our newsletters.

*To Tamara Larsson. My guiding star.*

# Contents

| | |
|---|---|
| Acknowledgements | viii |
| List of Abbreviations | ix |
| | |
| Introduction | 1 |
| 1 The spot on the wall | 11 |
| 2 Sound and phenomenology: Pierre Schaeffer's sonic research | 31 |
| 3 Chance as *epochē* : John Cage and non-intentionality | 49 |
| 4 Twisting free from aesthetics and the will | 71 |
| 5 Purposive purposelessness | 93 |
| 6 Fluxus and the flux | 113 |
| 7 The spark of contingency: Photography, cinema and temporality | 135 |
| 8 Poethics | 159 |
| | |
| Notes | 177 |
| Bibliography | 200 |
| Index | 214 |

# Acknowledgements

I offer the greatest thanks to Professor Norie Neumark, for essential guidance and support, and to Dr Martin Harrison, who rigorously challenged my ideas at the deepest level. I owe a deep gratitude to my parents who patiently proofread early drafts of chapters, and Annelies Larsson for invaluable assistance with English translation of German texts. I am thankful for various conversations with friends and colleges: Sophia Learner, Greg Shapley, Garry Bradbury, Sarah Last, Michael Graeve, Margie Borschke, Mark Titmarsh, Ruark Lewis, Geoffrey Barnard, John Hopkins, Billy Gruner, Brad Miller, Justin Clemens and Adam Nash. I thank Barbara Bolt and Francisco López for their kind responses to my questions. I thank Tom Ellard for inviting me to lecture on the subjects which informed Chapter 7. This book would not have been possible without the patient efforts of Liza Thompson, Lisa Goodrum, Lucy Russell, Rennie Alphonsa, Giles Herman and others at Bloomsbury Press.

A shorter and significantly different version of Chapter 2, 'Sound and Phenomenology', has been published as 'Sonic Practice as Research: The Problem of Aesthetics' in *New Scholar* Vol. 2. No. 1. 2013. A reduced version of Chapter 7, 'Poethics', has been published in *Parrhesia: A Journal of Critical Philosophy* as part of the conference proceedings of the Australian Society for Continental Philosophy Conference at Deakin University in Melbourne in 2017.

# Abbreviations

## Heidegger's works

BPP      *The Basic Problems of Phenomenology*, trans. Albert Hofstadter (Bloomington: Indiana University Press, 1988).

BQP      *Basic Questions of Philosophy: Selected 'Problems' of 'logic'*, trans. Richard Rojcewicz and André Schuwer (Bloomington: Indiana University Press, 1994).

BT      *Being and Time*, trans. John Macquarrie and Edward Robinson (Oxford: Blackwell, 1962).

BW      *Basic Writings: From Being and Time (1927) to The Task of Thinking (1964)*, edited, with general introduction and introductions to each selection by David Farrell Krell (San Francisco: Harper San Francisco, c1993).

DOT      *Discourse on Thinking: A Translation of Gelassenheit*, trans. John M. Anderson and E. Hans Freund (New York: Harper & Row, 1969).

EP      *The End of Philosophy*, trans. Joan Stambaugh (Chicago: University of Chicago Press, 2003).

FCM      *The Fundamental Concepts of Metaphysics: World, Finitude, Solitude*, trans. William McNeill and Nicholas Walker (Bloomington: Indiana University Press, 1995).

G      *Gelassenheit*, 2nd edn (Pfullingen: Neske, 1960).

GA 5      *Holzwege* (Frankfurt: Vittorio Klostermann, 1977) 'Der Ursprung des Kunstwerkes' (1935–6), 1–74. 'Die Zeit des Weltbildes' (1938), 75–113.

| | |
|---|---|
| GA 6.1 | *Nietzsche I* (Frankfurt: Vittorio Klostermann, 1996). 'Der Wille zur Macht als Kunst' (1936–7). |
| GA 7 | *Vorträge und Aufsätze*, 10th edn (Stuttgart: Klett-Cotta, 2004). 'Die Frage nach der Technik' (1949), 9–40. 'Wissenschaft un Besinnung' (1954), 41–66. 'Überwindung der Metaphysik' (1936–46), 67–95. |
| GA 9 | *Wegmarken* (1919–58, Frankfurt: Vittorio Klostermann, 1967). |
| GA 13 | *Aus der Erfahrung des Denkens 1910-1976* (Frankfurt: Vittorio Klostermann, 2002). |
| GA 24 | *Die Grundprobleme der Phänomenologie* (Frankfurt: Vittorio Klostermann, 1975). |
| GA 29/30 | *Die Grundbegriffe der Metaphysik: Welt, Enlichkeit, Einsamkeit*, ed. Friedrich-Wilhelm von Herrmann (Frankfurt: Vittorio Klostermann, 1983). |
| GA 39 | *Hölderlin's Hymnen 'Germanien' und 'Der Rhein'* (Frankfurt: Vittorio Klostermann, 1980). |
| GA 40 | *Einführung in die Metaphysik*, 6th edn (Tübingen: Max Niemeyer Verlag, 1998). |
| GA 45 | *Grundfragen der Philosophie: Ausgewählt 'Problem' der 'Logik'* (Frankfurt: Vittorio Klostermann, 1984). |
| GA 56/57 | *Zur Bestimmung der Philosophie* (Frankfurt: Vittorio Klostermann, 1987). |
| HH | *Hölderlin's Hymns 'Germania and the Rhein'*, trans. William McNeill and Julia Ireland (Bloomington, Indiana University Press, 2014). |
| IM | *An Introduction to Metaphysics*, trans. Gregory Fried and Richard Polt (New York and London: Yale University Press, 2000). |
| N I | *Nietzsche: vol. I: The Will to Power as Art*, trans. David Farrell Krell (San Francisco: Harper and Row, 1979). |
| PR | *The Principle of Reason*, trans. Reginald Lilly (Bloomington: Indiana University Press, 1991). |

| | |
|---|---|
| SG | *Der Satz vom Grund* [GA 10], 9th edn (Stuttgart: Klett-Cotta, 2006). |
| SZ | *Sein und Zeit* [GA 2] (Tübingen: Max Niemeyer, 1957). |
| TDP | *Towards the Definition of Philosophy: With a Transcript of the Lecture Course 'On the Nature of the University and Academic Study'*, trans. Ted Sadler (New Brunswick: Athlone Press, 2000). |

## Husserl's works

| | |
|---|---|
| CM | *Cartesian Meditations: An Introduction to Phenomenology*, trans. Dorion Cairns (Dordrecht: Kluwer Academic, 1995). |
| Ideas I | *Ideas: General Introduction to Pure Phenomenology I (Ideas I)*, trans W. R. Boyce Gibson (London: George Allen & Unwin, 1969). |
| Hua I | *Husserliana I: Cartesianische Meditationen und Pariser Vorträge* (The Hague: Martinus Nijhoff, 1950). |
| Hua III/1 | *Husserliana III/1: Ideen zu Einer Reinen Phänomenologie und Phänomenologischen Philosophie* (The Hague: Martinus Nijhoff, 1976). |
| Hua X | *Husserliana X: Vorlesungen zur Phänomenologie des Inneren Zeitbewusstseins,* |
| LI I | *Logical Investigations*, Vol. 1, trans. J. N. Findlay (London: Routledge, 2001). |
| LI II | *Logical Investigations*, Vol. 2, trans. J. N. Findlay (London: Routledge, 2001). |
| LU II | *Logische Untersuchungen*, Zweiter Theil (Halle: Max Niemeyer, 1901). |
| PCIT | *On the Phenomenology of the Consciousness of Internal Time (1893–1917)*, trans. John Barnett Brough (Dordrecht: Springer, 1991). |

| | |
|---|---|
| PIT | *The Phenomenology of Internal Time-Consciousness*, trans. Calvin O. Schrag, ed. Martin Heidegger (Bloomington and London: Indiana University Press, 1964). |

## Derrida's works

| | |
|---|---|
| E | 'Economimesis', trans. R. Klein. *Diacritics* 11, no. 2, The Ghost of Theology: Reading of Kant and Hegel (Summer, 1981): 2–25. |
| FL | 'Force of Law: The "Mystical Foundation of Authority"', trans. Mary Quaintance. *Cardozo Law Review,* 11 (1990): 920–1045. |
| LInc | *Limited Inc*, trans. Samuel Weber and Jeffrey Mehlman (Evanston: Northwestern University Press, 1988). |
| MC | 'My Chances/Mes Chances: A Rendezvous with Some Epicurean Stereophonies'. In *Taking Chances: Derrida, Psychoanalysis, and Literature*, edited by Joseph Smith and William Kerrigan, 1–32 (Baltimore: Johns Hopkins University Press, 1984). |
| OG | *Of Grammatology*, trans. Gayatri Chakravorty Spivak (Baltimore: Johns Hopkins University Press, 1976). |
| Pos | *Positions*, trans. Alan Bass (Chicago: University of Chicago Press, 1981). |
| SP | *Speech and Phenomena, and Other Essays on Husserl's Theory of Signs*, trans. David B. Allison (Evanston: Northwestern University Press, 1973). |
| TP | *The Truth in Painting*, trans. Geoff Bennington and Ian McLeod (Chicago: University of Chicago Press, 1987). |

# Introduction

In the twentieth century, beginning with the work of Marcel Duchamp, artists have often attempted to suspend decision making in the creation of the work of art, establishing a distance between intention and outcome. In the visual arts, chance and rule-based procedures feature in the dada procedures of Duchamp, Hans Arp and Tristan Tzara, the surrealist ventures into 'objective chance', the Fluxus game-works and events of George Brecht and Dick Higgins, the post-minimalist process art of Sol LeWitt, Adrian Piper, Robert Morris, John Baldessari, Ed Ruscha, Vito Acconci, Douglas Huebler, Dan Graham, Hanne Darboven and Hans Haacke, and in the relational documentation of encounters and social networks in the work of On Kawara, Sophie Calle and Stephen Willats. In music chance, contingency systems and indeterminacy have been employed by John Cage, La Monte Young, Christian Wolff, Morton Feldman, Earl Brown, Richard Maxfield, Toshi Ichiyanagi, Alvin Lucier, Robert Ashley, Cornelius Cardew, Gavin Bryars, Brian Eno and 'glitch'/'microsound' practices. In literature, rule-based systems have been used by the Oulipo, Cage, Jackson Mac Low, Brion Gysin, William S. Burroughs, language poetry and conceptual poetry (including algorithmic computer poetry). Aleatory and rule-based procedures occur in the cinema of the English landscape film, structural film, Christian Marclay and Eve Sussman. In dance, chance and game-like rules have been employed by choreographers such as Merce Cunningham, Simone Forti, Ann Halprin, Elaine Summers and Ruth Emerson. This, of course, is only a partial list, and many of these artists worked, or continue to work, across a number of media and disciplines. We often see rule-based procedures combined with the utilization of 'found' material, which – extending from the readymade to the collage – constitutes a suspension of intention to a certain extent. Many of these works, particularly in the area of sound and music, additionally attempt to frame phenomena in the here and now.

In this book I wish to take a chance on giving chance a chance – to defend chance in the realms of both art and philosophy. What I am referring to is not chance as a phenomenon: the objective chance of André Breton and the surrealists, or the uncanny coincidences inventoried in *Das Gesetz der Serie* (*The Law of Seriality*) by Paul Kammerer – the Austrian biologist much admired by the dadaists. Rather, this book is concerned with what has been called by John Cage the 'chance operation' – this means substituting some kind of aleatory system or methodologically distanced set of procedures for a conscious or unconscious (spontaneous) process of subjective decision making. A better name, perhaps, would be 'non-intentionality' were it not for its proximity, and potential confusion, with the phenomenological term 'intentionality', which means something quite different from, but is not unrelated to, 'intention'.

The central question in this study is, why should artists suspend intention in the practice of making works of art? Further, since many of the art practices involving aleatory operations aim for some sort of direct access to the real, what is this access? What do these works give us? This study proposes that the non-intentional operation in art functions as a quasi-phenomenological reduction, a radical estrangement, or shift in attitude, in order to encounter phenomena, language and the structure of experience, from a (non-anthropocentric) perspective and enables an encounter with the unforeseen. By enabling an event of unforeseeable otherness, these practices disrupt our horizons of expectation, shatter our predelineatory frameworks and force us to reconfigure our relation to the real in terms of everyday experience.

Serious inquiry into non-intention in art tends to get shut down very quickly. Chance operations are often seen as a somewhat obsolete remnant of a failed avant-garde ambition to fuse art and life, or they are regarded as a form of mysticism that involves a quasi-religious calling upon oracles. However, when more thoughtful criticism of non-intentional procedures is offered, it regularly reproduces either one of the two sedimented standpoints. The first insists that the erasure of self or ego in the creative act violates the traditional model of expression where the work of art is said to reveal an outward manifestation of the inner feelings and sensibilities of the artist. According to such a view, the work of art produced by chance operations would lack authorial authenticity. The second view contends that the surrendering of intention disempowers the human agency of the artist and thus prevents the work of art from intervening in the ethico-political sphere. We could call the first attitude 'aestheticism' and the second 'representationalism'. In short, in both of these ways, any inquiry into non-intentional strategies tends to get closed down by what I would call 'the hegemony of intention'.

Aestheticism is dominated by the idea of expression which would hold that the work of art materializes and delivers the inner subjective feelings of the artist to a beholder who presumably experiences the same emotions in its presence. In aestheticism, art remains alienated from discourse and maintains no epistemological status. In contemporary art, this model has been largely displaced by a critical anti-aesthetic tradition of representationalism (although there are signs of aestheticism's re-emergence in line with the 'affective turn' taking place in the humanities and social sciences). According to representationalism, the work of art is an inessential conduit for a truth or a political ideology. Once the work's message has been received, the concrete materiality of the work is rendered redundant. Central to the representational model is the idea that the work of art is a product of a self-conscious logical argument, always prior to the fabrication of the work. Of course, these constitute extreme positions that rarely see the light of day within the specialized field of contemporary art discourse. In non-specialized art commentary, however, one often encounters a fusion of both positions: where art might be seen as both the beautiful product of artistic expression and the provider of a message. Yet, even within the more specialized fields of critical art discourse, representationalism and aestheticism tend to govern thinking on art from a distance.

More than any other thinker, Martin Heidegger sets out a way of thinking the work of art outside of the modern Cartesian framework to which both of these arguments essentially belong. He wishes to preserve an autonomous power for art which is not held hostage to the vague and ineffable experience of aesthetics or the instrumental thinking of representationalism. In Heidegger's conception of the encounter with the work of art, knowing is associated with both willing resoluteness and a non-willing letting, where the act of artistic creation is thought more as an event in which phenomena are 'let' to emerge, rather than a strictly voluntary act – whether that act is spontaneous or calculated. Heidegger retrieves the Greek terms *technē* and *poiēsis* which link the production of art to an ontological-phenomenological, epistemological, modality prior to a productionist conception of the work of art (and a productionist interpretation of being). Art, in Heidegger's view, constitutes a kind of letting (*Lassen*) that is prior to, and counter to, the metaphysical idea of production (the forming of matter in accordance with a preconceived idea, or image, in the mind). In accordance with this view, making art, rather than being thought as 'creation', is thought in terms of letting something already existing emerge from out of concealment. In a very broad sense, Heidegger's thinking on art would seem to be amenable to an autopoietic mode of production.

Heidegger's meditation on the work of art, despite its undeniable complexity, poses some difficulties for contemporary thinking on art. First of all, Heidegger, in contrast to Hans-Georg Gadamer, has little knowledge of modern art – apart from an interest in Vincent Van Gogh, Paul Klee and the Basque sculptor Eduardo Chillida. More importantly – and this presents great problems for this study – Heidegger insists that truth – the meaning of being, or the truth of being – is 'out there' waiting to be unconcealed by the work of art. It is my view that we must reserve a deep suspicion towards any claim which insists that works of art – including avant-garde works which deliver us over to the here and now – bring us unto contact with the truth of naked reality, or things as they really are. For Derrida, this idea constitutes the metaphysical privileging of presence as truth's self-showing and the effacement of the trace in the experience of being. As Richard Rorty argues, the world is out there but truths about it – descriptions about it – are not.[1] The world does not give us truth about its intrinsic nature, and, according to Rorty, it is a mistake to think that the world, or the self, even *has* an intrinsic nature. Rather, truth is something made and put together in a vocabulary. For Derrida, truth – along with 'meaning' and 'being' – is a constituted textual effect. This is not to say that there is no truth. Rather, truth depends on the possibility of repetition which at the same time prevents it from becoming something 'in-itself', independent of the play of signifiers within discursive frameworks.

Certainly, there is good reason to deflect Heidegger's meditation on the work of art away from the pre-Socratic notion of truth as unconcealment, as *alētheia*, where truth, as something given, is unveiled. However, I think it would serve us well to keep in play a certain notion of the given, which stems from Jean-Luc Nancy's reading of Heidegger, 'in which being gives itself essentially as the action of sense',[2] where what is given does not consist of facts but rather the making sense of being by letting be the action which is essentially being itself. In what I see as his most productive reflections on the work of art, Heidegger proposes that the work of art enables an estrangement which renders the mundane, and the everyday, extraordinary. Letting allows the work to jolt us and produce a shift of attention which disrupts the normal grid of interpretation and pre-constituting power relations, and enables a different relation to the world, and a different language game. In such a way, I would propose that the work of art is an event that troubles self-evidence, opening up the most obvious and most simple, but, at the same time, the work puts its own status, as work and thing, into question.

The 'letting' that Heidegger proposes in 'The Origin of the Work of Art', and the non-willing thinking that he strives for in the later works, can be seen as a basic phenomenological disposition that suspends the imposition of interpretive bias. But this does not mean that we come to some pure relation to the real and its truth uncontaminated by presuppositions and mediations. In fact, what comes into view are the very presuppositions and constructions by which we constitute the real in our experience of it. My contention is that this 'letting be' finds consonance with John Cage's suspension of taste and memory, carried out by the deployment of the chance operation. According to this abstention, at a certain point in the process of the work, it is essential that there occurs a letting go of intention, after which all subsequent willing is suspended. Yet, this is no simple passive abandonment of will. We always find the intention to make a work; to first conceive of the system; to determine its mapping onto material elements; to determine its scope and rules and so on. Moreover, what we encounter is the decision to stand behind the work, to take responsibility; a certain steadfast resolve to continue at all costs regardless of outcomes.

Since, for Heidegger, both representational thinking and aestheticism belong to what he calls the domain of the will, to engage in a new way of thinking the work of art also means to engage in questions of thinking non-willingly. Derrida, to some extent, follows Heidegger's footsteps when it comes to the critique of the will. Of course, it would be a mistake to equate Derrida's 'undecidables' quite simply with non-intention. Yet Derrida's writing – from the early (post-)phenomenological texts to the later writing on justice – implicitly (and sometimes explicitly) undermines the dominant metaphysical idea of intention as a subject's 'wanting-to-say', that is, it questions the idea of a subjectively internal, non-linguistic, pre-existing volitional sense which gets expressed into language. Rather than subjective intention functioning as the basis for communication, Derrida argues that the accidental is structural to all formation of meaning. More originary than meaning, the trace and spacing have, at best, a secondary relation to a subject's intention. For Derrida, chance is always part of the system of writing which cannot be thought without instability and play. Without contingency nothing moves; nothing gets itself done.

Don Ihde observes, in running through variations in the exploration of the possible, that the practice of art and the practice of phenomenology share a similarity. When we consider works which intend to bring us to some commerce with the here and now, with what is often called direct experience, I believe that phenomenology is one of the most valuable tools we have. It would be a mistake to think that aleatory or system-based works of art, which engage with phenomena *as* phenomena and which frame the real in the here and now, simply hand us over to the raw flux (the real is not simply given in naked perception). Rather, they elucidate the very structures that make experience possible (and impossible), through an engagement in the play between the implicit and explicit structures of experience. The challenge, in the wake of Husserl and Derrida, is to think experience differently without reproducing a naive concept of experience, or positing a self-identical, self-sufficient transcendental ego or, for that matter, simply dismissing experience in the name of a more original discursivity.

Chapter 1 functions as an introduction to chance-related procedures in mid-twentieth-century avant-garde art. My main purpose here is to distinguish the mechanical chance operation and the use of the formal constraint from other related practices: in particular, automatism and other projective procedures which function as stimulants to the imagination. I begin with surrealist pure psychic automatism, outlining its development towards the 'plastic automatism' of action painting in New York which I then oppose to the dadaist 'mechanical' chance operations of Marcel Duchamp, Tristan Tzara and Jean Arp, and those of John Cage, comparing these, in turn, to the literary use of the formal constraint in the French group Oulipo.

Through chance operations, Cage radically expands the scope of musical listening to encompass all sounds. Because the investigation of the sonic world would not only seem to engage in a direct encounter with phenomena but, further, paves the way to conceiving phenomena in non-visualist, non-objectivist terms, it would seem to provide a unique phenomenological starting point and bridge the disciplines of phenomenology, art and aesthetics. However, this approach is not without its problems. In Chapter 2 I set out to show that Pierre Schaeffer's phenomenological method of sonic research, based on Husserl's eidetic reduction, results, ultimately, in a categorizing of sound according to aesthetic presuppositions.

As opposed to Schaeffer's exclusionary methodology, Cage's approach, in a different phenomenological attitude, democratizes sonic phenomena by letting them be. In Chapter 3 I look at the philosophical implications of Cage's chance operations and indeterminacy along with other procedural strategies. I contend that Cage's indeterminate operations function as a kind of phenomenological bracketing: an abstention (*epochē*) which lets sounds be by suspending aesthetic values of taste, and giving us a certain access to the experience of listening. This chapter works through some of the problematic issues raised by Cage's chance operations and indeterminacy, and looks at how they are addressed by post-Cagean composition, sound art and process art.

Deepening this idea of letting in the chance operation, Chapter 4 traces Heidegger's meditation on the work of art carried out in the 1930s. Here I examine Heidegger's rejection of subjective aesthetic experience, and attempt to flesh out the relation between the idea of the work of art as an event in which phenomena are let to emerge and Heidegger's twisting free from the domain of the will as a consequence of his confrontation with the thought of Nietzsche – which paves the way for Heidegger's mature conceptions of non-willing thinking and *Gelassenheit* in the 1940s and 1950s. This chapter establishes the transitional beginnings of Heidegger's mature conception of the will as non-willing and its relation to the letting that the work of art enables.

Following on from this, Chapter 5 explores certain consonances in the thought of Cage, Meister Eckhart and the later Heidegger. Both Cage and Heidegger develop a philosophy of letting originating in Eckhart's theology which, for Heidegger, opens the question of how we may think outside of the domain of the will and the principle of sufficient reason, and, for Cage, opens onto the question of how the acceptance of chance leads to a self-alteration that changes one's relation to the world. Eckhart's stricture of detachment forms the basis of two of Cage's well-known catchphrases: 'art is the imitation of nature in her manner of operation', and [art is] 'purposeful purposelessness'. Utilizing Derrida's deconstruction of Kant's *Critique of Judgment* in *The Truth in Painting* and 'Economimesis', I thresh out Cage's phrases in relation to both their proximity and distance from Kant's third *Critique*. Although it is certain that Cage holds to a certain aesthetics of the beautiful, and although Kant offers what is, indeed, a radical theory of how the subject comes to grips with contingency, Cage's aesthetics resists the subjectivism and anthropocentrism that is ultimately secured by the Kantian framework dominated by intention, reason and the ideal.

Returning to phenomenology in Chapter 6, I break with what I see as Cage's naive and conservative, modernist, approach that is characterized by the privilege of the unique and unrepeatable encounter with phenomena, brought nearer by an aesthetic tuning of the sensory faculties. I question the limits of such a way of thinking the work, concentrating upon the capacity for Fluxus works to put into question the metaphysical distinction between so-called primary and secondary experience (discursivity). Utilizing the work of Husserl and Derrida, I examine the role that Fluxus works play in a deconstruction of experience. Here I consider George Brecht's Fluxus event scores in terms of the part they play in the interrupting and re-configuring of experience, enabling the comprehension of an anonymous field of constitutive elements, both present and absent, sensory and textual.

In a way that is structurally similar to the *epochē*, the photographic apparatus, as a mechanical mediating technology, has the capacity to produce images automatically without human subjective control. In this way, the camera, when used as a passive recording agent, performs an operation that is structurally similar to the *epochē* of the chance operation. The idea that the mechanical and indexical nature of the photographic image ties it to a relation with contingency informs the work of a diverse range of artists in the 1960s and 1970s. This particular ontology of the photographic image and the relation of both the static image and the moving image to time are examined in Chapter 7 along the lines of Derrida's notion of hauntology and Heidegger's fundamental attunement of profound boredom.

One of the most tenacious arguments against aleatory art is that it puts at risk political and ethical responsibility. Finally, in Chapter 8, I examine how, in non-intentional work, intention can ethically fold back into the work, particularly in work involving words, where ethico-political responsibility would seem to be critically at stake. Here I compare Derrida's non-voluntaristic notion of iterability with what Joan Retallack calls the 'poethical'. Because the structure of iterability prevents authorial intention functioning as the guarantor of meaning, this prevents a distinct line being drawn between the univocity of rational 'transparent' discourse and the equivocality of poetic forms of discourse.

The point of this study is not to champion a specific art movement or set of practices. Rather, I am concerned with inquiring into the rationale of chance and aleatory procedures and measuring them up against a thread of continental philosophy which would seem to be open to this way of thinking. This is not a comprehensive survey of chance procedures in art. As a matter of economy, I have focused on the early to mid-twentieth-century avant-garde, and particularly on artists and practices within the magnetic field of John Cage. This is certainly not to say that this period exclusively constitutes exemplary instances of aleatory practices. Yet it is a period in which inquiry into chance and aleatory procedures flourished. What seems remarkable is the distinct absence of women specifically using chance as part of their practices. This may well have to do with a reluctance on the part of women to suspend control and decision making when the granting of sovereignty has historically been denied to women. However, in the twentieth century, and particularly in the twenty-first century, we have seen a substantial number of female artists employing collage as a practice – a practice which is essentially inflected by chance.

# 1

# The spot on the wall

This book presents a defence for the deployment of the aleatory or chance operation in the work of art. In other words, it seeks to give chance a chance, to rescue its image from some of the standard derisions it has been forced to endure. I will propose that the work of chance is neither frivolous buffoonery, nor clownish anti-art. I will argue that its rationale has serious philosophical implications. It may be that following this line of thought through philosophy and the discourse of art, we may discover that, in the end, chance was never on trial at all. Rather, it is art, or the standardized conceptions of art, that needs to be revised. Aleatory procedures in art will always attract bad press from, on the one hand, those who believe that the work of art is essentially a manifestation of the feelings or innate sensibilities of the artist, or from, on the other hand, those who believe that art is an act of commentary and that the work of art is merely a carrier for ideas and external truths, political or otherwise. The exploration of the use of chance in art opens up a theoretical space that puts into question the role of intention in art and thought. The question shifts to asking: What is the place of intention in art? Why does intention, as either rational, calculating, conceptual reasoning, or as irrational, intuitive, expression, dominate all conceptions of art, the activity of the artist and the work of art? My first task will first be to delimit the chance operation – or what might more properly be described as 'the mechanical aleatory procedure' – in the history of art and determine the differences between it and other allied procedures. This will take the form of a kind of potted history where I examine the practices and their rationales and determine, in a brief way, how these rationales come into proximity with various theoretical currents in the twentieth century.

Chance came to be deployed as an artistic strategy in its most pure form in the early twentieth century with the avant-garde movements of dada and surrealism. However, the roots of chance as an aid to artistic practice go much further back. Max Ernst's essay on frottage begins with a quote from Leonardo da Vinci, from his *Treatise on Painting* – a text that was much admired by the surrealists.

> It is not to be despised, in my opinion, if, after gazing fixedly at the spot on the wall, the coals in the grate, the clouds, the flowing stream, if one remembers some of their aspects; and if you look at them carefully you will discover some quite admirable inventions. Of these the genius of the painter may take full advantage, to compose battles of animals and of men, of landscapes or monsters, of devils and other fantastic things which bring you honor. In these confused things genius becomes aware of new inventions, but it is necessary to know well (how to draw) all the parts that one ignores, such as the parts of animals and the aspects of landscape, rocks, and vegetation.[1]

Leonardo advocates a technique that finds, in certain physical ephemera, textures and patinas – such as aged or smeared walls, stones and veined marble – the subjects which the artist aspires to capture, such as landscapes, battles and animals. He recounts Botticelli's example where an artist throws a paint-soaked sponge against the wall and sees, in the pattern produced, a landscape. This story replicates another – said to be apocryphal – from Pliny, where a painter, frustrated by his attempts to capture the foam at the mouth of a dog, finally throws his sponge in disgust at the failed rendering and, by chance, the result delivers everything he had been striving to achieve. Pliny goes on to say that, in this case, chance comes to represent nature in art, and reflects that the painting of the dog is due to an equal result of chance and art – or we might say chance and technics. This conception, no doubt, comes from Agathon's saying reproduced by Aristotle: 'art (*technē*) is beloved of chance (*tuche*), and chance of art.'[2]

The story of the sponge can easily be read as a practical way to reproduce ephemera such as the foam at a dog's, or horse's, mouth. Here chance might be utilized in order to depict the chaotic, the random, the contingent. The sponge, one could say, generates noise. But in Leonardo's handling of the story of the sponge something else comes into play. The chance procedure is regarded as a stimulant to the imagination. In the chaotic forms, images suggest themselves to the artist. However, what the artist sees in the noise is what the artist wishes to see. E. H. Gombrich describes this process as an 'interaction between making and matching, suggestion and projection'.[3] For an artist like Alexander Cozens – who took Leonardo's advice quite seriously, integrating it into his 'blotting method' – what he and his pupils wished to see in the random application of ink were landscapes, and in particular, landscapes depicted in the manner of Claude Lorrain. Gombrich compares this process to the psychiatric diagnostic tool developed by Hermann Rorschach. Known as a 'projective' test, the Rorschach test suggests certain objects to the patient who projects unconscious images onto the shapes. The patient attempts to find meaning in contingency; signification in the a-semiotic. Rorschach's procedure belongs to the history of what is known as 'kleksography' – the art of discovering images in inkblots – which begins with the work of the German romantic poet and spiritualist Justinus Kerner with the publication of his *Kleksographien*, a volume of poetry and inkblots, in 1857. Kerner developed his poetry out of the images and in this way the chance element functioned as a stimulant to his imagination.

## Surrealism and automatism

Ernst's deployment of frottage (and other techniques such as *grattage*) is, as Georges Hugnet points out, 'not exactly the aesthetic exploitation of a spot on the wall in the manner of Leonardo,' but it still remains very close.[4] However, instead of matching the perceived images to conscious and determinant images in the mind, the objective of Ernst's frottage is to uncover images stored in the unconscious (if we believe this to be possible). The method involves, as Ernst puts it, 'excluding all conscious mental guidance (of reason, taste, morals), reducing to the extreme the active part of that one whom we have called, up to now, the "author" of the work'.[5] This process certainly involves chance, but to a much greater extent it is aligned with the surrealist technique of 'pure psychic automatism'. This practice, which is typified by the method of automatic writing, presents one way in which the artist may gain access to the resources of the unconscious. For André Breton, the unconscious does not falsify; it cannot be controlled, and it is innately free from the biases imposed by the conscious mind (rationality). The plethora of surrealist chance techniques are variously said to project, reflect or appeal to the unconscious.

In the first surrealist manifesto, Breton appeals to Pierre Reverdy's definition of poetic metaphor in order to get to the heart of the surrealist image:

> The image is a pure creation of the mind. It cannot be born from a comparison but from a juxtaposition of two more or less distant realities.
>
> The more the relationship between the two juxtaposed realities is distant and true the stronger the image will be – the greater its emotional power and poetic reality.[6]

Although he accepts Reverdy's conception of metaphor, Breton objects that

> it does not seem possible to bring together, voluntarily, what he calls 'two distant realities' [such as Lautreamont's chance meeting of an umbrella and sewing machine on a dissection table]. The juxtaposition is made or not made, and that is the long and the short of it.[7]

The upshot of this is that, for Breton, surrealist images cannot emerge out of consciousness. They cannot be evoked at will, nor, once they have emerged from the unconscious, can they be suppressed. They cannot be imagined since imagination is a reflective and voluntary activity. They can only be discovered, found or encountered. In surrealist automatism it is not just reason, rationality, discursive consciousness that need to be bypassed, but any conscious imaginative or reflective process. Breton is well aware that the unconscious cannot be made to bend to the will of consciousness, and that it will not give up its contents on demand or respond to a direct programmatic interrogation.

Breton views Reverdy's two distant realities as resembling the poles of an electrical power source between which constitute a potential difference – or 'voltage' in the more common usage. The spark is what is generated by this difference. The greater the difference, the larger the spark. The conjunction of the two poles – which always remains a difference and not a sublation – produces a meaning, while not directly violating reason to produce the irrational or the illogical. The meaning can, nevertheless, only be observable by reason but cannot be its product (which the irrational certainly can). Although, at times, described as a higher reality, surreality would better be described as a widened reality: a reality that, in phenomenological terms, includes for the human subject not just correlates of consciousness but correlates of the unconscious.

Of the various surrealist techniques, it is automatic writing, dream reports and mediumistic, quasi-spiritualist, experiments that constitute a dialogue with interiority. Although some of these techniques may resemble the séance, automatism does not transcend the consciousness/unconscious of the individual subject, and as such can be said to constitute an atheist resistance to any religious or spiritualist externality where the voice or word emits from some supersensible realm of the dead. (Avital Ronell reminds us that the French word for psychoanalytic session is *séance*.)[8] At the same time, by contrast, surrealist games introduce chance procedures which are essentially external to any singular individual consciousness, operating in an intersubjective manner.

## Automatism and abstract expressionism

In the late 1930s the ideas of surrealist automatism begin to drift across the Atlantic and begin to inform the practices of the New York school and abstract expressionism. These artists embraced particular aspects of automatism such as its prescriptions for limiting the control enforced by rational consciousness over artistic production. As Robert Motherwell relates, they took the central aim of surrealism as proposed in Breton's definition in the first surrealist manifesto, in Motherwell's words, 'to make a work automatically without *a priori* aesthetic or moral conditions'.[9] At the same time, however, while distrusting the literariness of surrealism, and what they saw as its clichés and romanticism – typified by the work and promotional activity of Salvador Dali, the most visible of the surrealists at the time – the New York artists ultimately began to question the role of the unconscious in automatism.

The precepts of surrealist automatism arrived in New York from at least two different directions. The Byelorussian, John Graham (Ivan Gratianovitch Dombrowski)[10] – an early mentor for Motherwell and Pollock – brought the core ideas of surrealist automatism, and the techniques of automatic writing, from Paris (where he was allegedly acquainted with Breton). Graham published a monograph on art entitled *System and Dialectics of Art*, which, rather than proscribing a Hegelian dialectics, offered his meditations on the purpose and origin of art in a question and answer format. Like Breton, Graham regards the unconscious as a vast archive of all previous experiences available to be tapped by the artist. The purpose of art, as Graham sees it, is to restore lost access to the unconscious. As he puts it,

> Human beings lost to a great extent or never possessed the access to the wisdom stored in the unconscious. The unconscious mind is the power house, the creative agent. The conscious mind is the clearing house or a controlling agent.[11]

For Graham, the personal technique, which he calls 'automatic *ecriture*', is one of three necessary elements in the production of the work of art.

Another stream for the ideas of automatism was introduced by the Chilean painter Roberto Matta Echaurren who set up a group of 'automatic painters' including Pollock, Motherwell, Peter Busa, William Baziotes and Gerome Kamrowski. The formation of this group, as Motherwell claims, marked the real beginning of abstract expressionism.[12] Although highly critical of what they viewed as surrealism's clichéd images, this group of artists met regularly to develop methods of painting utilizing automatic principles sometimes resulting in collaborative paintings.[13] These automatic practices were informed, to various degrees, by existentialism, ideas concerning the Jungian collective unconscious, Gestalt theory, the process philosophy of Alfred North Whitehead, the American pragmatism of John Dewey and William James, Chinese Daoism and Japanese Zen Buddhism. It was through the combination of these various currents that abstract expressionists began to rethink the role of the unconscious in what came to be known as action painting. Although Motherwell, in the 1950s, was quick to defend the role of the unconscious in automatic painting – against vulgar assertions that implied that the action painter's activity consisted simply of not knowing what they are doing, making paintings in their sleep, or in a state of intoxication – he had already by 1944 begun to cast doubt on the automatism of surrealism:

> The fundamental criticism of automatism is that the unconscious cannot be *directed*, that it presents none of the possible choices which, when taken, constitute any expression's form. To give oneself over completely to the unconscious is to become a slave.[14]

The unconscious is not accessible by the will, nor can it be directed by the will. Paradoxically then, for Motherwell, 'the retreat into the unconscious is in a sense the desire to maintain a "pure ego", [where, in contrast] everything in the conscious world is held to be contaminating'.[15]

Against the literary models of surrealism, Motherwell favoured what he calls a 'plastic automatism' which had absolutely nothing to do with delving into the unconscious. Motherwell's model is instead physiological. In this way, the painters of the New York school slowly extracted themselves from the surrealist idea of 'pure psychic automatism', towards a more physical automatism based on the experimental exploration of material properties and actions. It became clear that, like Leonardo's spot on the wall, or the Rorschach inkblots, an automatism that worked with the imagination (conscious or unconscious) could not help producing the clichés that were the product of a received Freudian stock of subjects and images, images which would be, in turn, further legitimized by the subsequent application of psychoanalytic theory. Here projection could be seen to be at work producing consciously sexual and transgressive images.[16] Writers retrieved, not so much the raw unconscious, but the literary tropes and images of Lautreamont, de Nerval and Sade. Painters, through the techniques of frottage and grattage, tended to finesse the raw forms into the explicitly monstrous and sexually ambiguous.

David Lomas, in an extensive study of surrealist automatism, challenges Breton's conviction that automatic texts constitute the direct transcription of the author's unconscious. Against this conception, which he calls surrealism's 'jargon of authenticity', Lomas proposes that automatic writing, when it comes down to it, engages in a simulation which draws upon the differential possibilities of language itself – its techniques introducing a certain randomness which produces 'lexical decomposition'.[17] Lomas points to Michael Riffaterre's analysis of surrealist texts which argues that, rather than being transcriptions of the unconscious as a pure presence, the texts produce 'the automatism effect'.[18] According to Lomas, Riffaterre demonstrates that the narrative disruptions and semantic incompatibilities present in the text have their origin in external intertextual sources always withheld from the reader. Riffaterre contends: 'it does not really matter whether automatic texts are genuine or not. Their literariness does not reside in their recording of unconscious thought, but rather in their appearance of doing so.'[19]

It is important to note that Lomas's designation of automatism as simulation is not meant in any derogatory sense. Rather, he sees this reconceptualization as a way out of an impossible aporia where the authenticity of any text of automatic writing remains always indeterminate since the originating material is, in principle, inaccessible to the author as well as the reader. Since the authenticity of automatic writing can never be established – and we must remember that Breton militantly denounced all fakes and pastiches – it is more productive to consider these texts – positively – Lomas argues, as products of randomness.

## Plastic automatism

With plastic automatism, which Motherwell compares to Monet's term 'organic automatism',[20] we see an emphasis on process and the breaking down of mind/body dualism. While various theoretical currents circulated within the milieu of abstract expressionism, Daniel Belgrad astutely points out that contemporary critics of abstract expressionism tended to read its rationale solely through the optics of the prevailing existentialism of the 1940s and 1950s (introduced to American audiences by the *Partisan Review* in 1946). Under the influence of existentialism, critics such as Harold Rosenberg – who incidentally coined the term 'action painting' – contributed to narrowing the theoretical scope of abstract expressionism to a programme valourizing the direct expression of the life-world of the artist:

> A painting that is an act is inseparable from the biography of the artist. The painting itself is a 'moment' in the unadulterated mixture of his life. . . . The act-painting is of the same metaphysical substance as the artist's existence.[21]

Involving dramatic choice, the adoption of a freely chosen project against the meaningless absurd determinism of the physical world, the American take on existentialism is significantly voluntaristic and, as Belgrad observes, Rosenberg was at the time highly critical of second-generation abstract expressionist Helen Frankenthaler precisely for what he saw as her reluctance to assert her will over the paint.[22] In this way, the existentialist conception of abstract expressionism tended to downplay its aleatory and automatic procedures in favour of voluntaristic self-expression. However, a very different, more radical picture of abstract expressionism emerges, when we consider the diverse 'field theories' employed by the artists (those mentioned earlier), described by Belgrad, as broadly positing 'the existence of a continuous field of energy prior to any experience of individuality'.[23]

The most radical aspect of abstract expressionist automatism would seem to have been its program of breaking down any absolute distinction between body and mind. It became less a question of a mind directing a body to produce, as best it can, images formed in the mind, and more an act closer to what Maurice Merleau-Ponty calls embodied or incarnate consciousness. In this context the word 'plastic' also refers to a certain interaction between the body of the artist and the paint (materials). Drawing upon Motherwell's utilization of the term 'plastic', Belgrad speaks of a 'plastic dialogue', whose notion of plasticity should be thought, in the way that William James thought it, as a 'quality of relative resistance'.[24]

James's notion of plasticity, as 'the possession of a structure weak enough to yield to an influence, but strong enough not to yield all at once',[25] has a remarkable similarity to the way the term 'plasticity' is thought by Catherine Malabou. In Malabou's terms, this notion of plasticity cannot be thought in isolation from habit. In speaking of the 'plastic individual' in Hegel, Malabou proposes that habit, 'a process whereby the psychic and the somatic are translated into one another, is a genuine plasticity',[26] and habit is 'the plastic operation which makes the body into an instrument'.[27] Here we encounter habit in a positive rather than a negative sense. What inhabits Pollock's practice is *practice*, in the sense of sustained repetition in order to engender and nurture good habits. Pollock's paintings are the result of a practiced corporeality. All painting is, of course, a practiced practice in this sense, but Pollock's methods take this idea to the extreme limit where self-consciousness is put entirely out of action and an automatic 'second nature' effectively takes over. Chance operations are, in a certain sense, the polar opposite of this appeal to second nature. While there is certainly no room for self-conscious reflection in either automatism or the chance operation, only the latter effectively breaks with the habitual.

## Mechanical chance

With the publication of Motherwell's *The Dada Painters and Poets* in 1951, a younger generation of artists (Allan Kaprow, George Brecht, Robert Rauschenberg and Jasper Johns) began to come under the influence of dada, and there began, in the latter half of the 1950s, a renewed interest in chance procedures as distinct from automatism. In his pamphlet 'Chance Imagery' (1957/66)[28] the Fluxus artist George Brecht wonders whether we should admit automatism as a chance process. If the chance operation can be defined as the putting into action of consciously unknown or unlooked-for causes, then, he surmises, automatism is by this definition a chance process. Yet, throughout the essay, Brecht seems less than happy with this conclusion. There is a tension between what he describes as automatism, on the one hand, and what he calls 'mechanical' chance procedures on the other. Brecht initially sees the work of Jackson Pollock as the focal point in the development of chance procedures in art. The method of dripping paint employed by Pollock certainly, to a large extent, relinquishes much of the conscious control and decision making of the artist. Although we might object that plastic automatism relies on built-up habits of learned behaviour, bodily thinking or unconscious expressivity, Brecht finds that there is enough randomness in the behaviour of the materials after their application to justify Pollock's methods as a species of chance operation. However, in an after-note written eight years after 'Chance Imagery', Brecht makes an abrupt departure from the procedure of automatism, stating that, when the article was written, he had only recently met John Cage, and thus, 'had not yet seen clearly that the most important implications of chance lay in his work rather than in Pollock's'.[29] Ultimately, Brecht favours the mechanical chance procedures which develop out of dada rather than automatism, which has its roots in surrealism.

Hans Richter, in his personal memoir of the dada period, notes two divergent philosophies when it came to the use of chance in dada artworks. One direction involves achieving a balance between, as Richter phrases it, 'chance and anti-chance', a balance between volition and non-volition. The blending of intention and non-intention is epitomized, as Richter observes, by Jean (Hans) Arp in a number of generically titled, torn paper collages (*Selon les lois du hasard* – 1916 – *Collage with Squares Arranged According to the Laws of Chance* – c. 1971 – *Nach dem Gesetz des Zufalls* – 1920). Although the titles suggest the following of a strict method of the chance operation, the grid-like structure of these works reflect a method where chance is only deployed as the starting point of the compositional process.[30] In these works Arp obviously let the torn pieces of paper fall onto the canvas randomly, but, contrary to anecdotal accounts which relate that the artist immediately pasted down the scraps where they fell, it seems that while the orientation of the scraps may have been preserved, their positions were altered in a conscious and determinate way to form the final composition. An example of the other direction can be seen in Tristan Tzara's instruction to make a dadaist poem by randomly drawing words out of a bag or hat, in order to repurpose poetry from its literary use as an 'instrument of expression'.[31] In contrast to Arp, Tzara demanded the absolute acceptance of chance. As Richter puts it, he 'attributed importance exclusively to the Unknown'.[32]

In perhaps the earliest instance of dada chance determination, Marcel Duchamp incorporated chance and gravity into his *Trois Stoppages-Etalon* (*Three Standard Stoppages*), 1913–14, by taking three one-metre-long threads which were held straight and horizontal and dropped from a height of one metre. The threads were allowed to fall onto three blank canvases. They were then fixed to the canvases with varnish preserving the contours that occurred as the result of their fall. The result in each case is a 'deformed metre', a 'canned metre' embodying, for Duchamp, 'canned chance'.[33] In another experiment, Duchamp combined '*adress*', skill in aiming, with the inadequacy of the equipment used, when he fired nine shots of matchsticks dipped in paint from a toy cannon to form the flattened perspective points of the nine malic moulds in his *The Large Glass* (*The Bride Stripped Bare by Her Bachelors, Even*) 1915–23. For Duchamp, chance functions as a way of neutralizing taste; of making it indifferent. As he relates to Pierre Cabanne, 'I had to beware of its [the object – readymade] "look". . . . You have to approach something with an indifference, as if you have no aesthetic emotion. The choice of readymades is always based on visual indifference and at the same time, on the total absence of good or bad taste.'[34] Taste is, according to Duchamp, 'a habit'. It is the 'repetition of something already accepted'.[35]

For some artists the rigour of the chance operation is the rigour – no matter how simple the procedure – to adhere completely to the process. To disallow the outcome of a chance operation, or to modify its results – even one of its outcomes – would compromise the process, for it would reintroduce the volitional activity of the artist and consequently allow aesthetic decisions based on judgements of taste into the work. In mechanical chance operations the artist must first put in place a system, or a set of rules, which maps occurrences onto artistic outcomes, and these decisions must be predetermined. Here, certainly decision comes into play. Duchamp decided that he would use three strings, that they would be one metre in length, that the dimensions of the canvas would be such and such and that the straight edge of the stoppage would be on a certain side of the fallen string. Yet all of these decisions are at least one step removed from any possible aesthetic determination. The Fluxus artist Dick Higgins formulated the strategy of placing 'the material at one remove from the composer'[36] – an idea very similar to George Brecht's notion of the 'irrelevant process', where the chance outcome is the result of the combination of two or more unrelated events. For Brecht, 'bias in the selection of elements for a chance-image can be avoided by using a method of selection of those elements which is independent of the characteristics of interest in the elements themselves.'[37]

In order for the total displacement of aesthetic values to occur authentically, all decisions relating to the system must be predetermined. According to this logic, decisions on, or modifications to, the structure must not occur during or after the process has been initiated. Cage – whose preferred chance procedure involved the tossing of coins according to the strictures of the *I Ching* – emphatically states:

> That is precisely the first thing the *I Ching* teaches us: acceptance. It essentially advances the lesson: if we want to use chance operations, then we must accept the results. We have no right to use it if we are determined to criticize the results and seek a better answer.[38]

This necessity of rigour in the chance operation also applies to many forms of process art. In two essays published in the late 1960s, Sol Le Witt makes this clear. In 'Paragraphs on Conceptual Art', he writes:

> To work with a plan that is pre-set is one way of avoiding subjectivity.... The plan would design the work.... In each case, however, the artist would select the basic form and rules that would govern the solution of the problem. After that the fewer decisions made in the course of completing the work, the better.[39]

And in 'Sentences on Conceptual Art':

> The process is mechanical and should not be tampered with. It should run its course.[40]

## The formal constraint

Raymond Queneau is highly critical of what he sees as the false freedom of surrealist automatism and rejects the deployment of chance and the aleatory in the creation of literary works. Queneau was, for a brief time, a member of the surrealist group but left in 1930 with George Bataille, Michel Leiris and other members who came to be known as the 'dissident surrealists'. In 1960 Queneau co-founded the French avant-garde literary group Oulipo (*Ouvroir de Littérature Potentielle*) with mathematician François le Lionnais. In short, the project of the Oulipo was and still remains the unlimited generation of poetic literary texts through the use of the formal systematic constraint. The constraint could be a particular mathematical formula mapped to certain instructions, such as the S+7 method where every noun in the text is replaced with the seventh noun that follows its place in a dictionary. Queneau's objections to chance and the aleatory are essentially objections to Breton and other surrealist's theories of automatism and the practice of automatic writing. Regardless of whether such writing emerges directly from consciousness or the unconscious, the surrealist methods promote the spontaneous which, for the Oulipo, constitutes a false freedom which is really a form of enslavement. Although the methods may be used to stimulate the imagination or to produce the spark which divulges the content of the unconscious, Queneau insists that the decisions involved are essentially arbitrary and subjective.

> Another entirety false idea in fashion nowadays is the equivalence which is established between inspiration, exploration of the subconscious, and liberation; between chance, automatism, and freedom. Now the Inspiration that consists in blind obedience to every impulse is in reality a sort of slavery. The classical playwright who writes his tragedy observing a certain number of familiar rules is freer than the poet who writes that which comes into his head and who is the slave of other rules of which he is ignorant.[41]

The constraint, on the other hand, inserts a mathematical procedure between the volition of the artist and the written word. However, one cannot help noticing that the formal restraint resembles the mechanical chance operation (of Duchamp, Tzara, Arp, etc.) in the sense that the operation inserts an impermeable barrier between the subjective or representational will of the artist and the resulting work. It is thus necessary to radically distinguish the constraint and the chance operation from many of the surrealist methods: objective chance, the exquisite corpse, question-answer games, frottage-grattage-decalcomania and, most significantly, automatism in all its forms. Even Breton's objective chance (*hasard objectif*) presupposes unconscious causation, in opposition to the idea of chance as sheer randomness: a causation which is either too complex or trivial to warrant any inquiry into it.

Queneau insists on what he calls *voluntary*, or *conscious*, approach to literature, by which he means, not that *writing* should be spontaneous or rational, but that the *formal constraint* must be consciously predetermined and voluntarily enforced. For Queneau, surrealist chance (automatism) posits a certain freedom: the freedom to choose or decide based on a whim or fancy, according to the slimmest criteria. Spontaneity and feeling are linked to freedom, but this constitutes a freedom that Queneau does not trust. There is, however, another category of freedom which Queneau does not comment on: the freedom *from* decision. This is the liberatory movement away from individual subjectivity. On this count, the chance operation falls on the side of the constraint. Although Queneau theorizes the formal constraint as 'anti-chance', it is, for the most part, the mechanical chance operation seen from the reverse perspective. Here emphasis is put on the *decision* to put a system in place in order to *suspend* decision. That is, to suspend decision for as long as the constraint is in place. However, there still remains one major difference between the Oulipian constraint and the mechanical chance operation: the method of the constraint is algorithmic and motivated, while the chance operation is mechanical and, very often, unmotivated. For the Oulipo, the constraint is not merely a means to an end; it must also illustrate a principle: one which allows the reader to generate the unprinted potential lines of poetry for themselves: one of the axioms of the Oulipo is that the constraint is not a mere means but a 'principle'.[42]

Does it matter greatly if the method is motivated or unmotivated? I will take up this issue in Chapter 3. For now, the point I wish to make is that the constraint is any method that puts out of action the spontaneous and arbitrary in the creation of the work of art. Of course, it is possible to argue that even automatic writing involves some degree of the use of a constraint: for instance, the speed of the process. And it could also be argued that frottage or the throwing of a sponge produces images which bypass volition, conscious or unconscious. But is not all writing, painting, speaking, infected with some small degree of the formal constraint (rules of form or genre as Queneau notes earlier), or of (chance) elements which fall outside of the artist's control? Any method, in order to function as a constraint, must be effectively constraining and rigorously applied. In this way the Oulipian constraint and the chance operations of Duchamp and Cage perform a suspension of volition that resembles phenomenological bracketing.

## Chance as *epochē*

What is at stake in Brecht's analysis is the imperative to avoid human or subjective bias in the procedure. Brecht's preferred method of avoiding bias is, as we have seen, what he calls the 'irrelevant process': where there is no logical or formal connection between the systematic procedure – the set of rules to be followed – and the manipulation of materials – the ways in which they can be altered. Any decision making by the artist in the creative process must be, according to this process, at least at one remove from the material. Why should the artist seek to avoid subjective bias in the selection of elements? Brecht makes it sound as if the goal is to achieve scientific objectivity such as in producing an uncontaminated data set. Why should the artist seek to sidestep subjectivity? Is it to reinstate some kind of objectivity? I would suggest that the reasons for the elimination of bias could be better thought through phenomenologically rather than empirically. Both the utilization of chance operations in the creation of the work of art and the phenomenological investigation into phenomena as objects of consciousness involve a radical shift in perspective. In Husserl's phenomenology, the shift is achieved through the bracketing which functions in order to suspend, or put out of play, any epistemological or metaphysical presuppositions – or more generally, any taken-for-granted beliefs in regard to the nature of experience. It suspends what Husserl calls the 'natural attitude', the default (pre-phenomenological) mode of attention. The natural attitude is our spontaneous or naive (but not in any derogatory sense) belief in the world, or in the way we take the world as given. This bracketing is called 'the *epochē*' and forms an important part of Husserl's transcendental-phenomenological reduction. It is essentially a change in attitude adopted by the phenomenologist that precedes any phenomenological descriptive work. Put simply, in phenomenological observation and description, when the *epochē* is applied, the experience of the world is reduced to the experience of phenomena.

In chance operations, what is bracketed are, specifically, aesthetic judgements of taste which might determine the selection, placement, order and the like of elements, as well as any imposition of values. But, further, what occurs is a radical suspension of the creative act itself in terms of the traditional (modern) idea of expression – where something, supposedly, inner, originary, original and deeply felt is pressed outward: ex-pressed. On a more mundane level what is also suspended in the chance operation is technique and the habitual 'second nature' which builds up along with the mastery (through constant practice) of a craft – a certain expertise. In the chance operation and other mechanical, systematic or procedural approaches, a set of rules are put in place in order to put these judgements of taste, expressive whims and habits of training, out of action. Likewise, Husserlian phenomenology puts out of play a number of presuppositions or naive standpoints.

The chance operation, or any other constraint functioning in the creative process of the work of art, functions primarily as an *epochē*. It may not conform exactly to the phenomenological *epochē*, but it shares many of its characteristics. An important consideration, however, is that the *epochē* in chance operations is effectively imposed by the establishment of a fixed system, and not by the volitional and spontaneous adjustment that Husserl's phenomenological method requires. In this sense, it makes the adjustment much more achievable. The major difference between the phenomenological reduction and the artistic constraint is that the latter does not involve reflection on the part of the subject. Automatism, on the other hand, is quite different. We could say that it involves the deployment of an *epochē*, but what is suspended is logical instrumental consciousness in order to plumb the depths of the unconscious. In Automatic writing the *epochē* which suspends order and logic, bypassing the censoring ego, as Breton claims, is put in place merely by the speed of transcription. The mechanical chance operation, suspending presuppositions and reflective judgements, allows us to look at the world with new eyes, or, in Cage's case, to listen to the world with new ears.

## The paradox of non-intention

A common objection to the idea of non-intentionality in art is that the process of making art can never be entirely non-intentional, since there is always the decision to begin the work in the first place. Thus, many commentators have pointed to what they see as an irresolvable paradox of non-intention, where the desire to erase intention must surely be considered to be an intention itself. Seth Kim-Cohen calls into question the viability of chance operations as an artistic procedure, citing Christoph Cox's observation regarding the apparent paradox of the intention of non-intention. Kim-Cohen suggests that artistic expression and intention are ultimately unavoidable because one must always consciously make a decision how to begin. Moreover, Kim-Cohen maintains that if we accept the various 'death of the author' positions of Roland Barthes and Michel Foucault, then the problem of avoiding authorship would seem to become a 'non-problem' and consequently the necessity to 'absent' the volition of the artist from the process disappears.[43] However, this would seem to require the artist to be able to continue making art, according to self-conscious conceptual intention or aesthetic volition, while, at the same time, remaining secure in the knowledge – perhaps with a certain amount of irony – that such operations are largely mythical. But there are several other problems with this argument. Obviously, it would be untenable to propose that there could be an absence of intention in the process of formulating and instituting any non-intentional procedure or process. However, non-intention is not some absolute position opposed to intention. It is never a totalizing monolithic law that governs the whole production of a work, a series or a career – or the artist's life for that matter. Rather, non-intention operates – or intention is put out of action – at decisive stages in the making of the work. These are precisely, in Cage's work, the points at which aesthetic-subjective decisions are most likely to be called upon. It would be wrong to think of non-intentional operations in terms of an absencing or negation of intention. Rather, as I have proposed, non-intentionality forms a quasi-phenomenological *epochē*: a temporary suspension; a holding-off; a bracketing. Intention is never subject to radical doubt. In Husserl's phenomenology, after the *epochē* we return to the natural attitude, to the world conceived in such a way. After the chance operation we return to intention and decision. There is never a point at which the very concept of intention is undermined. Intention is simply put out of play. What Cage's use of non-intentional procedures has in common with phenomenology – and in particular Heidegger's version of it – is that it involves a 'letting' that in the most basic terms suspends an 'ought'. In other words, Cage's 'letting sounds be' puts out of action any presuppositional idea or desiderata of how he might think they *ought* to sound. In other words, it's an aesthetic, or more properly, anti-aesthetic version of a phenomenological reduction.[44] At the heart of the non-intentional operation is a certain acceptance. One accepts the outcomes without revision. In terms of acceptance, non-intention should be seen in the same way that the Oulipo view the constraint, as an affirmation rather than a negation.

Further, the holding-off of intention is structured by resolve and conviction, and these terms bear a relation to intention. First, there is resolve, by which I mean the determination to see the process through to the end: to not relinquish the suspension of intention within the process, to let things play out – here we might think of Heidegger's term *Entschlossenheit* ('open resoluteness'). Then – linked to acceptance – is the author's *conviction* to stand by the work, to not review the results, to not jettison the work and start again, to not take it light-heartedly or as a joke and to guard it against any theatricality. We might say, in Heidegger's terms: to 'preserve' the work. It's not that this idea of the experimental operation wants to kill off the subject or silence the ego. There is no suggestion of playing with the idea that we can occupy a transcendent place beyond and outside the subject in some other realm. Rather, the objective is to see what can happen, what other possibilities open up, when the everyday subjective, and calculating, voluntarism is temporarily put out of action. In this sense it should be seen as a decentering of the subject: the opening up of a way of access to beings that loses its anthropological privilege – a radical shift in position. Joan Retallack describes this as a redirection, or reconfiguration of the 'geometry of attention'.[45] It's not that we can simply dispense with all presuppositions. Rather we can gain a perspective that makes us aware of them. William S. Burroughs calls them the 'prerecordings'. This notion hooks up with Bourdieu's institutional encodings that condition our actions, Foucault's theorization of discursive formations, as well as Derrida's idea of the trace (writing pre-conditioning speech) as a '"delayed transmission" of difference (a "prerecorded" or "delayed" broadcast in French is *une émission différée*)'.[46]

Automatism, when it functions as a stimulant for the imagination, even if it could be said to provoke the unconscious to reveal its contents through free association, ends up being another version of Leonardo's spot on the wall. When projection comes into play the automatic technique cannot be relied on to effectively exclude any aesthetic or moral concern. The New York artists succeeded in directing automatism away from the imagination towards an organic corporeal automatism. But in this form of plastic automatism the artist inhabits a process which is essentially different from, and at odds with, the mechanical chance operation and its 'irrelevant process'. If we were to map the variety of chance and automatic practices in art, we could place Pollock at one extreme and Duchamp and Cage at the other. What then divides these procedures is that on the one side (Pollock's) habit is related to plasticity (Malabou) and is seen as a positive value, while on the other side (Cage) habit is seen in negative terms as something to be bypassed in order to reach the unknown. Cage, of course, was very dismissive of Pollock's work, and in an interview with Irving Sandier in 1966 responds: 'I wanted them [Pollock's paintings] to change my way of seeing not my way of feeling.'[47] 'Automatic art, in fact, has never interested me, because it is a way of falling back, resting on one's memories and feelings subconsciously, is it not? And I have done my utmost to free people from that.'[48]

What Cage desires is the open work that leads to a new perspective on the world. The essential difference between Pollock and Cage is that in Pollock's practice habit is something to be nurtured, developed, exercised and built up. For Cage, habit is something to be bypassed, bracketed, exorcized or demolished. These polar positions correspond to what are two distinct traditions in Western philosophy. The positive sense of habit develops in a tradition that begins with Aristotle, runs through Aquinas, Spinoza, Leibniz and Hume, through to Ravaisson, Bergson and Deleuze and, most recently, Malabou. It can also be seen in the phenomenology of Paul Ricoeur and Merleau-Ponty, and the American pragmatism of John Dewey and William James. The negative perspective on habit is located in the writing of Augustine, Meister Eckhart, Kierkegaard, Kant and, to varying extent, Husserl, Heidegger and Derrida. In the first (positive) tradition, habit is conceived as the conservation of change essential for adaptability. In the second (negative) tradition, habit is viewed as that which is resistant to, and inhibits, change.

I do not regard it as a matter of choosing sides in a debate between the virtues of habit and the shortcomings of habit. My aim here is to delimit the field of artistic practice that I wish to make the centre of my inquiry. I do not wish to raise aleatory practices over plastic autonomy and corporeal habit. My point here is to emphasize their difference – a difference that I feel becomes muddied in Brecht's 'Chance Imagery'. However, the central object of this inquiry is the strategy of using the mechanical operation, procedure or constraint, in order to escape the mechanical nature of habitual life.

2

# Sound and phenomenology
## Pierre Schaeffer's sonic research

There is little doubt that sound art and certain avant-garde experimental music practices offer a unique perspective in terms of their attempts, in various ways, to frame the here and now of spatial and temporal experience. Since the 1980s, a theoretical discourse in association with these practices has dramatically grown. It is a discourse which seeks to unsettle the traditional ontological privilege of the visual in Western philosophy and explore various aspects of auditory phenomena and culture. Possibly the first text to broach these issues in a direct way was Don Ihde's *Listening and the Voice: Phenomenologies of Sound*, published in 1976. As Ihde contends, 'The examination of sound begins with a phenomenology.'[1] In other words, a phenomenological discipline of some sort would seem to provide a good starting point because it enquires not only into sound as phenomena but, simultaneously, into the act of listening. But what kind of phenomenology should this be, and in what direction should it proceed? Ihde outlines two types, or what, in his way of thinking, constitute two phases of phenomenology. The first is the transcendental phenomenology of Husserl. The second is the hermeneutic-existential phenomenology of Heidegger. Ihde suggests that Heidegger's phenomenology functions not only historically as the continuation and deepening of Husserl's phenomenology but further as a methodological extension, where the taking up of Husserl's methodological framework functions as the initial starting point. Ihde designates Husserl's direction as 'first phenomenology': a descriptive science of experience concerned with explicating the directedness of consciousness and how, in terms of the subject/object distinction, things (and their meaning) are constituted. Heidegger's phenomenology is correspondingly designated as 'second phenomenology': not only characterized by the more outwardly directed exploration of limits and horizons but, further, involving a painstaking dismantling of the sedimented traditions of thought (Heidegger's *destruktion* of the Western history of ontology).[2] Since, as Ihde sees it, first phenomenology and second phenomenology belong together, the enquiry into sound requires both. The enquiry begins with first phenomenology and its abstraction into essences, but then proceeds towards existential-hermeneutic questioning which calls into question the ingrained conceptions that underlie the very process of abstraction that was embarked upon in the first stage. My own enquiry here will – with various modifications – extend this model to include what could be called 'third phenomenology': Derrida's deconstruction of Husserl's phenomenology and delimitation of Heidegger's nostalgic privileging of early Greek inceptional thought, the meaning of being and the transcendental signified, or master word, of *Ereignis* (the event of propriation or owning). It would be a grave mistake to think that Derrida simply shows phenomenology to the door. Derrida reactivates Husserl's thought in a certain way, employing its resources, not simply against itself but in order to constantly challenge the primacy and centrality of phonocentrism, logocentrism and ontotheology in Western metaphysics. A central component of Derrida's thought is the continuation of the phenomenological-hermeneutic critique of the domain of the will carried out in the work of Heidegger.

What has tended to dominate the discourse of sound in the arts is a particular focus on a phenomenology loosely based on Husserlian methods. This is often, at best, an investigation carried out in terms of a first phenomenology concerned with immediacy, presence and essences, and, at worst, a mixture, or conflation, of empirical, psychological and aesthetic ideas with phenomenological motives. What has emerged out of these writings is a form of essentialism that Seth Kim-Cohen astutely identifies as the 'sound-in-itself' tendency. This tendency is underwritten by what has been called the 'acousmatic reduction', which, put simply, excludes all visual stimuli and causal associations in order to direct attention to the purely aural as sound object. On the other hand, I would argue that Kim-Cohen's insistence that any phenomenological approach into the nature of sound constitutes a 'dead end' simply imposes a new dogmatism. Instead, I propose that Husserl's most radical discoveries, and the transformation of these by Heidegger and Derrida, offer a very rich set of resources for any philosophical investigation into sound.[3]

## Sound and vision

Within the metaphysical tradition, since Plato, sound has been regarded as a deficient mode of being. In contrast to the visual and tactile thing, sound has been, due to its invisible, ephemeral and non-enduring nature, historically cast as secondary and derivative. Consequently, sound has traditionally been excluded from what counts as knowledge, and from what are thought of as real objects of knowledge: those that can be seen and touched. With Plato, Frances Dyson observes, 'immateriality, invisibility ephemerality become ontological orphans', and what develops is 'an epistemology where objects of knowledge are ideal, subsistent, immaterial forms that embody eternal order, intelligibility, and meaning'.[4] With the development of this metaphysical ocularcentrism, sound comes to be thought as an attribute, or quality, of a thing, rather than as constituting a certain idea of thingness in itself. The exception, for Plato, is, of course, the voice which, being closest to the living breath (*pneuma*) of the soul – because of its immediacy, directness and plenitude – assumes primacy over the (more material) written word. Dyson proposes that the voice, however, also suffers a process of 'abstraction and desonorization'.[5] The 'grain' of the voice recedes to the background and the immaterial ideal content of a subject's meaning-intention, as a silent inner voice, occupies the central ground of metaphysical epistemology. Dyson's critique of visualism is heavily indebted to Ihde, who argues that the latent visualist tradition of philosophy consists of 'at least two interwoven factors'.[6] These are, for Ihde, reduction *to* vision, where knowing is identified with seeing and images, and the corresponding metaphorics of light and clarity; and reduction *of* vision, where the visual itself is reduced and, correspondingly, what is regarded as real is thought in terms of an abstract extended object, as representation in the mind (e.g. in Cartesian subjectivism).

Dyson recognizes the possibility for a kind of sonic thinking that, based on a-specular aural, rather than visual metaphors, would have the potential to 'resist philosophical interrogation' and rhetorically contribute to 'rendering the cracks in Western metaphysics more apparent'.[7] As Dyson claims, the otherness of the body and the otherness of aurality 'both resist the categorical imperatives of Western epistemology, both refuse the boundaries and divisions, the subject-object dichotomies, the ontological identities *that* epistemology seeks to impose'.[8] The phenomenon of sound, having no discreet identity, consisting of flows that have no edges, seems to promise a rather different phenomenological starting point than visually apprehended objects – one which would seem to resist the metaphysical conception of objectification and presents, as Ihde puts it, 'material for a recovery of the richness of primary experience that is now forgotten or covered over in the too tightly interpreted visualist traditions'.[9] That is, in short, to examine the possibilities for, and limitations of, a philosophy of listening, encompassing a phenomenology of sound. It would seem that sonic practices are uniquely placed by enabling (i) a direct encounter with the flux of phenomena and (ii) being a way of conceiving phenomena in non-visualist, non-objectivist terms.

Concern with the phenomenon of sound, as the material element of music, becomes the focus of two pioneering composers in the mid-twentieth century: Pierre Schaeffer and John Cage. In both of these approaches we can see an initial equivalence between the aim of phenomenological observation and description – to see through to what gives itself in perception – and the questioning of the nature of sound initiated by a quest for an expanded aesthetics of music. Schaeffer's conception of *musique concrète* utilized the technology of audio recording to capture and isolate sounds in order to engage in research into the nature of sonority and develop a form of music based on concrete sound material rather than the abstract arrangement of tones. Cage, in a similar way, wished to discover the richness of the aural world and alert his audience's listening to the sounds of everyday existence. As Cage often puts it, his objective was 'to let sounds be themselves'. What is at stake here is the possibility for an ontological disclosure of the nature of sound through music and/or art. For Schaeffer, this consists of a laborious analysis of aural phenomena in order to establish the natural laws – culturally universal, or pre-cultural – that would inform a new and expanded conception of musical composition. For Cage, on the other hand, research into sounds has the objective of 'changing' the listener, so as to sharpen their senses, or open their audition to the everyday life-world. These investigations into the nature of sound divide into two distinct approaches. The first, characterized by Schaeffer, employs, to a certain extent, the methodology of Husserl's phenomenology in order to observe the conscious act of listening and thus discover the fundamental and universal ground for musicality within sonority. The second, epitomized by Cage, calls for a renewed investigation into the sonic universe in order to hear the world and thus learn to live in such a way that one becomes more attentive to our day-to-day immersed state of being with sounds: a position more consonant with the ontological direction of Heidegger's hermeneutical phenomenology. Both directions seek to overturn the tradition which has historically assigned the sonic to a secondary status with regard to the visual. Both seek, in different ways, to question the nature of sound in ontico-ontological terms and, hardly surprisingly, both begin their inquiry from within the discipline of music. In this chapter I will test the limits of first phenomenology in the investigation of sound and demonstrate that the Husserlian eidetic reduction, in the form of the acousmatic reduction, as it is deployed by Schaeffer's sonic research, is essentially a reduction to aesthetics.

## Sound-in-itself

Commenting on the differences between German academic discourse on sound art and its English equivalent, Andreas Engström and Åsa Stjerna have noted that 'In the English literature, sound art is often connected to sound's inner aesthetical qualities'.[10] They observe that 'The focus of sound can also be exemplified with what Christoph Cox sees as a neo-modernist trend in the arts, namely sound art's focus on the "sound-in-itself"'.[11] While Cox regards the sound-in-itself tendency in a positive light, the same cannot be said of Kim-Cohen, by far the most outspoken critic of Minimalist inspired phenomenological approaches to sound. Kim-Cohen addresses his criticism to what he sees as an adjacency between (i) the medium-specific intrinsic concerns for painting, of Clement Greenberg, (ii) the exclusive concern with the immanent features of sound in Schaeffer and (iii) the insistence of the value of sound-in-itself of Cage.[12] He contrasts this to 'the conceptual turn' initiated by Duchamp,[13] 'suggested by the gallery art of the sixties, one that ignores the prepositional question, which is at its core a perceptual question – what to look at, or listen to – and focuses instead on the textual and intertextual nature of sound'.[14] As far as Kim-Cohen is concerned the discourses around sound art seemed to have missed the conceptual turn that occurred in the visual arts. He writes:

> There is a sense among practitioners and theorists alike that sound knows what it is: sound is sound. I will try to reduce this resistance by returning

attention to works and ideas stubbornly received in the untenable space of the blinking ear. The aim is to rehear them, rethink them, reexperience them starting from a non-essentialist perspective in which the thought of *sound-in-itself* is literally unthinkable. Against sound's self-confidence – the confidence in the constitution of the sonic self – I propose a rethinking of definitions, a reinscription of boundaries, a reimagination of ontology: a conceptual turn toward a non-cochlear sonic art.[15]

The rather unwieldy term 'non-cochlear sonic art' is, of course, the aural equivalent to Duchamp's notion of 'non-retinal' painting. It signifies a turn to an intellectual encounter rather than visceral plastic celebration. Just as non-retinal painting does not occur at the site of the look, a non-cochlear sound art, for Kim-Cohen, transcends the space of listening. But this does not mean that sound and vision are disqualified from the work of art, as he makes clear: 'A conceptual sonic art would necessarily engage both the non-cochlear and the cochlear, and the constituting trace of each in the other.'[16] I would argue that the sound-in-itself tendency, although its aims would appear to be phenomenological, is ultimately a reduction of sound *qua* art (as sound art), and sound in the world, to form.

## Acousmatic listening

The primary procedure for elimination of visual bias in sonic research is Schaeffer's conception of 'acousmatic listening', which has its origin in his insistence that to objectively evaluate a given sound one must disregard the existence of its source, since identification with the source would carry visualist presuppositions. The term 'acousmatic' derives from Pythagoras's pedagogical requirement that initiates receive his teachings through acoustic means only: their teacher visually obscured behind a screen or curtain. These pupils were termed *akousmatikoi*. The acousmatic tradition philosophically seeks to overturn the traditional ontological hierarchy, where the visual faculty is privileged over the aural faculty, restoring to listening a sense of the unique existence of sound as phenomena that is not governed by, and subsumed under, the legislation of visual objects. Since the visual-material object or phenomenon is most usually considered as the originating source or cause of the sound event, Schaeffer insists on a listening (and compositional) practice that would actively obscure any cause–effect relation of the visual-material object and the produced sound. A sound, in *musique concrète*, is thus isolated from its world, and with this transition becomes 'for itself' – in Schaeffer's terminology, a 'sound object'. Acousmatic listening is often referred to – following Husserl's methodology of the phenomenological reduction – as reduced listening. Whereas the phenomenological reduction puts out of play any concern with the question of the existence of the object or phenomenon under investigation, reduced listening suspends any concern with the material cause of the sonic object. Schaeffer's concept of the *objet sonore* forms the basis of Metz's conceptions of sound as object. Metz conceives the term 'aural object' to describe an object that consists of sound and can only be encountered through audition: 'an infra-object, an object that is only aural'.[17]

Observing that Schaeffer's intrinsic investigations into sound, and his theorization of the sound object, remain reasonably faithful to Husserl's phenomenology, Brian Kane isolates two aspects of Schaeffer's 'hybrid discipline' which cannot be satisfactorily accounted for without a consideration of Husserl's influence. These are: '(i) that a phenomenological investigation into listening will disclose the original ground of our musical practices; (ii) that the correlate of this investigation is the discovery of an objective, yet ideal, entity – i.e. the sound object'.[18] Following Husserl's objections to the naive factuality of empiricism and the subjective problems of psychology, Kane observes that Schaeffer similarly wished to overcome the scientifically dominated acoustic basis of music and the subjective and cultural criterion of habitual musical practice.

## Phenomenology

Before examining the proximity of Schaeffer's sonic research to Husserl's phenomenology, it is essential to understand the primary motivation of phenomenological research which is to provide, with all scientific rigour, a 'first philosophy' that would constitute the ground for both philosophy and the sciences. In order to discover the laws of a primordial science, Husserl rejects both the empiricism of the natural sciences – where such a determination would be derived inductively from facts given in the external world – particularly realism (or physicalism) and the empiricism of psychologism. The problem with realism is that only something that can be attributed physical characteristics is recognized as real. Thus, something like consciousness is either simply denied any reality, or it is naturalized or physicalized. The problem with psychologism is that it is an empirical science based on induction from individual experiences, where the Real is posited in '*individual* form', 'as having spatio-temporal existence', in contingent 'matters of fact' (*Tatsächlichkeit*) (*Hua III/1* 12, *Ideas I*, 52–3 §2; Husserl's emphasis), whereas knowledge, for Husserl, demands an essential universality that transcends individual contingent situations. Husserl also distanced himself from neo-Kantian epistemology and its associated philosophies of value and culture, along with the idea of philosophy as a world view that, from the phenomenological point of view, dogmatically relies upon unwarranted fundamental axioms. If phenomenology is to be an *a priori* science, it cannot derive its truth from the theoretical and must, as Husserl insists, be free from all untested philosophical ideas. As Husserl maintains, 'In these studies we stand bodily aloof from all theories, and by "theories" we here mean anticipatory ideas of every kind' (*Hua III/1* 62, *Ideas I* 105 §30).

To engage in a more originary or primordial scientific approach to philosophy, phenomenology turns its attention to the self-giving evidence of 'the things themselves' as they appear to living consciousness. Husserl's 'principle of all principles', by which, he says, no theory can lead us astray, insists that 'every primordial dator Intuition is a source of authority (*Rechtsquelle*) for knowledge, that whatever presents itself in "intuition" in primordial form (as it were in its bodily reality), is simply to be accepted as it gives itself to be, though only within the bounds in which it then presents itself' (*Hua III/1* 52, *Ideas I* 92 §24). Husserl is not concerned with the facts of the physical object but with *how* things appear to us in consciousness. Phenomenology is a science of *eidetic* being that aims at establishing knowledge, not of individual facts ('that-ness') but essential ideal universality ('what-ness'). It thus seeks to derive fundamental principles from a reduction that excludes matters of fact from the *eidos*. Husserl thus calls this reduction the 'eidetic reduction' (*Hua III/1* 5, *Ideas I* 44, Introduction). This requires a new method of philosophical inquiry, one which is characterized by '*a new way of looking at things*' (*Hua III/1* 5, *Ideas I* 43, Husserl's emphasis). We can see how Kane is able to claim a strong correspondence between Husserl's goals for phenomenology and Schaeffer's desire to discover the fundamentals of a new and culturally neutral form of music by way of a direct appeal to the sounds themselves. Both sonic research and phenomenology call for patient-detailed and rigorous investigations into the matters themselves, often calling upon the combined efforts of a number of researchers. Husserl, as is often noted, expressed his preference for beginning with the 'small change' of *minutiae*, rather than the 'big bills' of grand claims.[19] Schaeffer, as well, was quite aware that the discovery of the fundamental laws of musicality could only come after a long and patient research into sonority.

## The phenomenological reduction

Phenomenological reduction, put simply, is the methodological readjustment of viewpoint. As Jacques Taminiaux observes, Husserl's 'reduction' undergoes a number of metamorphoses in his writings.[20] Moreover, as Husserl proposes in *Ideas I*, when we speak of '*the* phenomenological reduction', we are speaking of a number of different methodological steps of '"disconnexion" or "bracketing"', taking the form of a 'graded reduction' (*Hua III/1* 73, *Ideas I* 114 §33, Husserl's emphasis). As Taminiaux shows, the methodological procedure of the phenomenological reduction combines a 'negative move [which] consists in suspending what blocks the way to the phenomena' and a positive return, 'a *reductio* – to the specific mode of appearing of the phenomenon'.[21] Husserl's negative move is the *epochē* – from the Greek term meaning 'a holding back', or 'abstention'. With the *epochē*, the question of, or the belief in, the existence of the external world is put into suspension. That is not to say that the existence of the external world is simply denied or plunged into doubt. Rather, the *epochē* is an abstention from any position taking in terms of either *for* or *against* existence. However, the natural standpoint is not disputed but rather carried along with the reduction, although it is put out of play. As Husserl says, '*we make "no use" of it*' (*Hua III/1* 65, *Ideas I* 108 §31, Husserl's emphasis). Similarly, the methodology of acousmatic listening functions in Schaeffer's sonic research as a phenomenological *epochē*. First, by removing all reference to a sound's physical source, determinations about the sound that are uncontaminated by visual and contextual relations can be made. Thus, as Schaeffer argues, it 'gives back to the ear alone the entire responsibility of a perception that ordinarily rests on other sensible witnesses'.[22] The acousmatic condition performs what Husserl calls an eidetic reduction, where any spatio-temporal factual information, or in Schaeffer's terms, 'any relation with what is visible, touchable, measurable',[23] about the sound is disregarded in favour of concentration on the essence of the sound-in-itself, in other words, what remains the same after all the variants have been stripped away. What we arrive at in this eidetic reduction is what Schaeffer calls the sound object. Second, the acousmatic *epochē* is enforced by means of the technological intervention of recording technology. The tape recorder, by reproducing the sound disconnected from its source, functions in a similar way to Pythagoras's curtain. But further, like Husserl's phenomenological *epochē*, the acousmatic abstention puts out of play any question regarding the existence of the phenomena. By disregarding any questions of spatio-temporal existence, the original sound event and the sound recording played back through loudspeakers are regarded as more or less ontologically equivalent.[24] This recalls André Bazin's argument that the arts of registration (photography, cinema sound recording) are processes that exclude the hand of man and are hence natural or, at least, pre-cultural. And as natural phenomena, Bazin argues for – if not the absolute ontological equivalence of the film image to the pro-filmic event (all the elements that are placed, or that fall, before the camera's field of view) – at the very least their inseparability. Thus, in the acousmatic situation, Schaeffer argues, 'the differences separating direct listening (through a curtain) and indirect listening (through a speaker) in the end become negligible'.[25] Further, for Husserl, the phenomena under investigation are not considered in terms of their individuality as existent things but rather as correlates of acts of consciousness. What becomes the object of observation is not the actual thing itself but, rather, how things appear to us, or are heard by us, in consciousness. This Husserl calls 'ideation', or the 'essential seeing' (*Wesensschau*) of the eidetic reduction.

## Reduced listening and the eidetic reduction

The aim of reduced listening – aided by the acousmatic abstention – is to locate the essential (and universal) form – the sound object – within arbitrary sound material. What it seeks to observe, through such a listening, is the act of listening itself. Moreover, it seeks to isolate something essential in the sound object as it occurs in consciousness in order to be led to pure musicality. The method that Schaeffer uses in his *solfège*[26] corresponds to Husserl's method of 'essential seeing' by way of, as Kane points out, 'free variation', in which the phenomenological investigator is able to run through the multiplicity of variants – multiple viewpoints or adumbrations (*Abschattungen*)[27] – of an object in direct givenness, or in the imagination or *Phantasy* – in order to establish the essential form or *eidos*: the 'what' that remains the same throughout the variations. Rather than performing the free variation of a sound in the imagination, Schaeffer utilized sound reproduction technology – first phonograph recordings, then, at a later stage, tape recordings – to isolate and replay sounds in order to run through the variants. The recorded sound thus takes the place of the fantasized sound in the imagination. But, one can sense an objection here: If the sound is captured on tape, does it not remain much the same on each subsequent playback? How does one run through the variations that would be the aural equivalent of viewing an object from different angles – in front, behind and so on? One way in which free variation occurs takes place entirely within the consciousness of the listener. Although the sound signal (its physical phenomena as movement of air) does not vary – to any significant degree – in each repeated playback, the listener is able to direct herself towards different aspects of the sound. Although the sound is acoustically the same, it is heard differently in consciousness each time. As Schaeffer explains, 'since these repetitions are brought about in physically identical conditions, we become aware of the variations in our listening and better understand what is in general termed its "subjectivity."'[28] Another method of free variation relies on external modification of the sound signal. The sound event can be recorded from different positions resulting in multiple recordings of a single event listened to alternatively, or a single recording can be submitted to transformations such as variations in playback speed, direction, volume, filtering or editing. By comparing the unaltered version with the altered, the listener is able to progressively identify the essential sonority that remains the same in each version. Like Husserl's method of eidetic variation, the original sound – the sound as it was first perceived – is taken as a model or guide which gives direction and acts as the point of departure for the production of variants. At different points the variants overlap and within this region of coincidence the general essence can be found. But one runs into boundaries where the variation is taken too far and the general form loses its identity and so, at some stage, the attempt at comparison has to be abandoned and a new sonic object is found in the altered version. For Schaeffer, this is the point where a new sonorous object is given.

Running through the multiplicity of variations takes place, for Husserl, in a purely passive way that results in a synthetic unity. Thus, as Klaus Held observes, the limits or edges, where unity can no longer be found in the variations, are not invented by consciousness; rather, consciousness, in a passive way, 'bumps into them'.[29] Held claims, however, that Husserl never really answers the question of how these limits are set. Thus, Husserl finds it necessary to specify a second stage to the reduction that consists of an active identification of the *eidos* as ideally identical. Only by 'retaining-in-grasp' all the variations can the invariant general essence be seen 'purely for itself'.[30] The purely identical can be seen for itself because it is, as Husserl claims, '*passively preconstituted*', but in order to be isolated 'seeing of the *eidos* rests in the *active intuitive apprehension* of what is preconstituted'.[31] Without retaining 'in grasp' we are only left with the last variation imagined. It is around this idea of the passively preconstituted sound object that Schaeffer's *solfège* experiences difficulty.

## From sound object to musical object

Schaeffer's sound object is, in Husserl's terms, an 'intentional object'. By the term 'intentionality' Husserl stresses that every perception is a perception of something. The intentional object is thus the correlation in consciousness of the perception of something as a 'what'. The term, at least in English, seems to carry a strong voluntarist connotation, but it would be wrong to think it in that way. Intentionality is, rather, a 'directing towards' very much like the directing of attention towards something. '*Attention*ality' might be a better word (if it were a word). Further, intentionality, as we shall see in Chapter 6, is the very structure of experience. The sound object is not a material object and it is certainly not, as Schaeffer stresses, the magnetic tape on which the sound is recorded; rather, it is only an object relative to our listening. The sonic object is, as Schaeffer says, 'a function of an intention of listening'.[32] Within Schaeffer's research methodology, the sound object occupies the lowest stage of investigation. Through the system of *solfège*, sound objects are to be further reduced to become musical objects that are infused with meaning.

Carlos Palombini observes that the aim of *musique concrète* was to discover 'musicality' from research into sonority.[33] In other words, Schaeffer's research into the nature of sound had the aim of developing a new theory of music out of the sonic material. Traditionally composition proceeds from the abstract – a musical idea in the composer's mind – towards the concrete (the complex reality of sounds in space). Schaeffer's great insight was to reverse this process, moving from the contingent and particular of found sounds, or noise, towards the abstraction of form. *Musique concrète* begins with the act of listening rather than notation of imagined tones (which only comes at the final stage). Yet, can such an approach 'discover' musicality without first presupposing a concept of musicality? Moreover, Schaeffer wishes to replace the traditional 'theory of music' that he sees as based on the science of acoustics, with a method that finds new musical structures in the perceptual structures of listening. In order to achieve this, Schaeffer formulates five stages of musical research which make up his programme for a generalized music theory: typology, morphology characterology, analysis and synthesis. The levels of typology – the sorting of sound objects into types – and morphology – describing the sound objects in terms of form – belong to the lower order of the sonorous. The levels of analysis – the estimation of the possibilities for the emergence of musical values (according to new criteria) in the sound material – and synthesis – the bringing together of criteria and the formation of rules for musical objects – belong to the higher order of the transition to the musical. Through what Schaeffer calls 'musical invention', morphology leads to analysis; and through 'musicianly invention', typology leads towards synthesis. Underlying these terms is the foundational concept in Schaeffer's music theory which he calls, by way of a neologism, 'aucology'. As Michel Chion defines it,

> The subject of aucology is the study of mechanisms of listening, properties of sound objects and their musical potential in the natural perceptual field of the ear. Concentrating on the problem of the musical functions of sound characteristics, aucology relates to *acoustics* in more or less the same way as *phonology* relates to *phonetics*.[34]

Aucology thus corresponds to a phenomenological eidetic listening in the Husserlian sense. It seeks to find a pathway between the lower sonorous level of the sound object and the higher level of the musical object. But it must do so without any recourse to the referential musical codes that, in traditional music, occupy a place between the two levels. The question, then, is how to proceed from the lower levels of the sound object to the higher levels of musicality; to develop a 'natural' musical language, without imposing any presuppositions from cultural conventions but rather finding musicality in the natural structures of perception. In proceeding from the sonorous level directly to higher level of musicality, bypassing the intermediate level of cultural codes, the role of aucology, as Chion observes, is to 'prepare the ground for the reclaiming of musical meaning'.[35] This transition must occur, as Schaeffer insists, 'in accordance with the logic of the material'.[36] Schaeffer's experimental music theory would seem to present, as Chion notes, a 'difficult situation'.

> A severe discipline, then, this aucology which examines the object for its musical potential, but must always remain at the outer limits of music. For it starts out from below, from the sonorous, and no preconceived musical organization from above can in accordance with its own rules hold out a hand to help it haul itself up to the heights where meaning is enthroned.[37]

In order to circumvent these difficulties, Schaeffer introduces what might be described as a compromise. He designates by the term 'suitable object' sound objects that seem more appropriate than others for the development of musicality. Although, as Chion observes, Schaeffer's suitable objects are 'objects which are judged "good enough", without being thought of as "musical" beforehand',[38] is not the very distinction between suitable and non-suitable objects subject, in some way, to the imposition of presupposed musical values? Cage argues that if we accept Schaeffer's methodology of 'solfeggio [*solfège*]',[39] 'We put ourselves in the position of accepting certain sounds but not others', and, in contrast to Schaeffer, claims: 'I have never put in my head any idea about perfecting sounds, nor any commitment to bettering the sonorous race. I simply keep my ears open.'[40]

## Phenomenology's latent aesthetics

Does not the quest to find musicality in itself function as a goal that, in a certain way, brings theoretical presuppositions into the primary realm of immediate lived-experience? Although cultural, or at least monocultural, ideas of musical language are put out of action, does not a certain conception of music – what it is to be 'musical' in the first place – operate from the beginning and enter into the investigation at the lowest level? Does not Schaeffer's preconception of the musical object bring into every investigation a musical aestheticizing *will* that, rather than letting the phenomena give itself from itself, orders sound according to an aesthetic privilege to form? The relation of form to presence in phenomenology is questioned by Derrida in the 1967 essay 'Form and Meaning: A Note on the Phenomenology of Language',[41] where he contends that although Husserl attempts to free his concept of form from Platonic-Aristotelian philosophy, his work remains caught within metaphysics because it ultimately presents form as presence itself. That is, the way that things (beings, all that is) give themselves is, in Husserl's phenomenology, ultimately subjugated to a quasi-aesthetic notion of form. The imposition of form, according to Derrida, determines and limits the sense of being in terms of presence within the closure of metaphysics. In marginal remarks in the essay Derrida alludes to a latent aesthetics that runs through Husserl's phenomenology. The metaphysical imposition of form, Derrida insists, 'cannot fail to effectuate a certain subjection to the look', and 'this putting-on-view' could be shown to 'permit a movement between the project of formal ontology' and 'the latent theory of the work of art' (*SP* 108–9). In a methodology similar to *Speech and Phenomena*, Derrida traces, in Husserl's text (predominantly *Ideas I* §124), the idealizing movement from a silent pre-expressive stratum of sense to meaningful expressive speech. The universal and conceptual form that speech expresses must, for Husserl, '*repeat or reproduce* a sense content' that is already silently present in perception (*SP* 115, Derrida's emphasis). From this point of view, Derrida remarks, 'we could question the entire aesthetics latent in phenomenology' (*SP* 115, note 8). Similarly, Schaeffer's search for an a-cultural, universal musical meaning rests on this relation between form and meaning. If Husserl's phenomenology limits or reduces being to form, in the process of ideation, by isolating the *eidos* that underlies lived-experience and gives meaning to speech in a pre-expressive wanting-to-mean, can it be likened to aesthetics?

Husserl says very little about art and aesthetics, but, in his letter to Hofmannsthal, he admits to an analogy between the phenomenological attitude and aesthetic consciousness.[42] And in his discussion of phantasy and the neutrality modification (the more scientific term for the abstention of the *epochē*), in *Ideas I* §111, Dürer's engraving *Knight, Death and the Devil* is employed as an example. Both aesthetic experience and the phenomenological reduction, according to Husserl, put the belief in the existence of the external world into suspension. Husserl describes the natural standpoint where one is immersed in the world as naively '*"interested" in the world*' (*Hua I* 73, *CM* 35 Husserl's emphasis). By contrast, Husserl describes both aesthetic consciousness and the phenomenological attitude as disinterested. Danielle Lories observes that Husserl's description of aesthetic consciousness 'leans on' Kant's *Critique of Judgment*, translating it into phenomenological terms.[43] For Lories, Husserl takes Kant's idea of disinterestedness – in a similar way to Heidegger (in his Nietzsche lectures) – in a positive sense as *favour*. Husserl, however, clearly distinguishes between the aim of aesthetics – as the seeking of disinterested pleasure in appearances – and the aim of phenomenology – as a concern with the constitution of objects towards the founding of philosophical knowledge. Aesthetics and phenomenological research would appear to be parallel disciplines in Husserl's view. But whereas the phenomenological attitude, for Husserl, is directed towards the variations of appearance with the aim of synthesizing these into a unity, aesthetic consciousness is directed 'toward what appears in its respective "manner of appearing" (*Erscheinungsweise*)',[44] it 'aims at the object only "for the sake of the appearance"'.[45] By this Husserl means that while the phenomenologist directs attention *through* the appearance *to* the object, the aesthetic contemplator merely directs attention to appearance itself.

Husserl clearly differentiates between objective position taking and aesthetic position taking. However, is not the concept of form, in some way, as Derrida suggests, fundamentally aesthetic? Although Husserl's characterization of aesthetic consciousness is undeniably complex, he seems to overlook one of Kant's most important observations. For Kant, judgements of taste are not affective or subjective but quasi-objective. For example, I can say that I do not like the taste of a certain dish, but this does not mean that I would insist that others should not like it as well. On the other hand, if I judge something to be beautiful then I am essentially of the opinion that others must find it beautiful as well. By relating aesthetic consciousness to feeling rather than taste, Husserl is able to reclaim the concept of form for the methodical procedure of supposedly aesthetically neutral phenomenological seeing. Although Husserl is certainly aware of the problem of aesthetic value judgements acting as position-takings, he does not see the need to bracket them out in the eidetic reduction. This is because although both the aesthetic judgement and the eidetic reduction ultimately have their sights on form, Husserl views aesthetic contemplation and phenomenological investigation as distinct activities. There would seem to be no effective means, in this procedure, of ensuring that aesthetic taste, as a value judgement – that would impose an *ought* – would be absolutely put out of play in the eidetic reduction.

Where phenomenological research crosses over with creative practice, the problem of aesthetic presuppositions becomes more pronounced. This is the problem that troubles Schaeffer's reduced listening. Although Schaeffer's ultimate goals may be musical, he stresses the importance of avoiding aesthetic position taking: 'If music is a unique bridge between nature and culture, let us avoid the double stumbling block of aestheticism and scientism, and trust in our hearing, which is an "inner sight".'[46] It is my contention that, in the context of phenomenological sonic research – however much its aims may be musical rather than epistemological – taste, functioning in terms of the 'suitable object', constitutes a position taking that would upset its ambitions to be a presupposition-free methodology. Sonic research constitutes a species of phenomenology, in as much as it is concerned with the material aspect of sound as it is given to consciousness, but it does so according to a *telos* of musical aesthetics. It is an approach that aims to be scientifically objective, but is it guided by values that are, if not subjective, at least grounded by the quasi-objective criterion of taste? My argument is that this particular way of thinking, derived from Schaeffer's theories – which has tended to dominate the discourse of 'sound theory' in recent years – radically misconstrues the nature of sound and listening. This approach, which rigidly insists on the independent status of the sound object, as sound-in-itself, ultimately objectifies the aural event into an ideal unity and isolates sound from its world, and thus carries out a suppression of context.

I hope to have demonstrated that the charge of essentialism, which Kim-Cohen has extended to Husserl and Schaeffer, is well founded. However, unlike Kim-Cohen, I do not wish to simply abandon Husserlian approaches to sonic art. Rather, in a double movement, I call for a shift from first phenomenology to the hermeneutical-existential phenomenology of Heidegger, along with a grammatological radicalization of Husserl's and Heidegger's thought in Derridean deconstruction. I would argue for a direction exemplified by Cage's radical abstention from taste and learned habits – that lets phenomena be. I see this project as one which works with some of Husserl's greatest discoveries – discoveries which Husserl never followed through. These include the idea that the present is not simple but a widened phenomenon that shades off in retentions and protentions; the idea that the constitution of phenomena includes elements that are not present; the idea of experiential horizons; and the idea that nothing can be given without pre-delineations. These ideas I will take up in much more detail in Chapter 6.

Although Schaeffer's project of sonic research is a quite remarkable application of Husserl's methodologies into the field of sound and music, it remains a phenomenology of aesthetic experience. However, Schaeffer frames the study as an investigation into the essence of music; thus it would be unfair to note its failure as an investigation into the phenomenon of sound, or of listening. Schaeffer never claimed that it was. What is required is an investigation into sound that is without aesthetic bias and remains open-ended in its structure. This is what I claim Cage prepares the ground for. This open phenomenology of the sonic world would be enabled by the chance operation or some other procedural *epochē* which suspends subjective presuppositions. Chapter 3 will look at the possibilities that Cage's (and post-Cagean) theories and practice present as an alternative to the Schaefferian and aesthetic paradigms. Cage's utilization of non-intentionality and indeterminate operations – in order to bypass taste and memory, and let sounds be themselves – constitutes an aesthetic abstention that plays the part of a rather different kind of phenomenological *epochē*: one that opens the way to what Ihde calls the 'second phenomenology' of Heidegger.

# 3

# Chance as *epochē*

## John Cage and non-intentionality

In the twenty-first century, the term 'experimental art' is often used to describe 'innovatory' practices that engage with new technologies and collaborate with scientific research in order to approach real-world problems. However, in the early 1950s, John Cage offered a much more simple definition which, for himself and many others, became the guiding axiom of any experimental art practice: to initiate 'an action the outcome of which is not foreseen'.[1] Although this description of an experimental practice may seem a long way from the teleological, goal-driven, collaborations between art practice-based research and science, technology, engineering and mathematics (STEM), these two conceptions of experimental art have one thing in common: they are both concerned with exploring and revealing pre-existing complex relationships (social and physical) and processes much more than they are with creating new objects. While Cage's work remained bound up in a largely musical-poetic aesthetic paradigm, the process-driven work that emerged in his wake began to branch out into an uncovering of complex reality. First of all, through the use of the chance operation one avoids the falling back into ingrained habits. It suspends the immediacy of spontaneous action and free improvisation. Further, the phenomena that are 'let' to emerge are not reduced to formal idealities, as they tend to be in the Schaefferian reduction to pure musicality consisting of culturally universal, per-cultural or a-cultural objects.

It could be argued that all art involves experimentation to some extent. Artists test materials and techniques; however, the experimental action defined by Cage and others is not one in which trial and error operates. Chance is not deployed in order to fortuitously arrive at a pleasing aesthetic outcome, with the option to try again if that outcome is not met. The 'trying things out' that is part of traditional art practice falls short of this conception of experimental art which, instead – at a certain point in the making of a work – aims at the bypassing of intentional decision making. In other words, experimental art consists of the deployment of rigorous contingency systems as opposed to merely following capricious subjective arbitrariness or controlling instrumentality. Moreover, I would suggest that the chance operation – as it functions in the work of Cage and Duchamp, belongs to what could perhaps be called an existential phenomenological *epochē*, or quasi-phenomenological reduction. My contention is that work that rigidly enforces a process or rule, that suspends the intentions of the artist, performs a reduction that brackets not only aesthetic judgements but also any instrumental, goal-directed decisions, and allows something else to happen.

In Cage's work in particular, the concern is with the material background of existing sound in the world. This is why his *epochē* might be called existential rather than transcendental. The chance operation – in line with Cage's interpretation of the writings of Meister Eckhart – performs a 'detachment' (*Abgeschiedenheit*) that rids oneself of likes and dislikes. It is concerned with worldly actuality rather than any ideal essence. In Heideggerian terms, it is a movement of revealing (*Hervorbringen*) and letting (*Lassen*). Non-intentionality, I suggest, is one way in which the production of art steers a path beyond both the emotional expressivity of lived-experience and the instrumentality of representational thinking.

Such a reduction has more in common with Heidegger's notion of letting than Husserl's transcendental methodologies. Yet I would still describe the deliberate suspension of intention, at heart, as a quasi-phenomenological reduction in the broadest sense in that it reconfigures attention away from a certain 'natural attitude' and towards the things (*Sache*) themselves. As Bret W. Davis observes, phenomenology 'has perhaps always been in its best moments an attempt to think without either actively or passively imposing one's own biases of interpretation, that is, an attempt to think non-willingly in order to let things show themselves'.[2] In other words, in order to encounter things as other than we think they are, or other than how we think they should be, requires an abstention from all presuppositions to do with our likes and dislikes. Focusing on the methodologies of John Cage, this chapter examines the chance operation and other non-intentional, process-based procedures in art, according to their function of performing a certain phenomenological reduction. In order to arrive at the unforeseen, Cage believed that the composer must arrive at a method that 'bypasses taste and memory'. Composing by traditional means involving aesthetic judgements of taste, where expressive intuition and projective envisioning (or internal sonic imagining), involves the creation of sounds, structures and melodies that have, in a sense, been 'foreseen' or 'fore-heard', and have a relation to what one has heard before (memory). In adopting strategies involving systems of chance and contingency, the experimental methodology aims at overcoming the subjectivized notions of genius and self-expression that has dominated modernist art and music.

## Chance and change

Cage's rejection of taste and memory stems from a basic distrust of the dominant notion of expression in art and music. First, Cage sees the function of (his) music as being the initiator of change – change in the receptive understanding of both composer and audience and, consequently, change in regard to the possibilities of what music can be. With self-expression, Cage argues, we simply repeat what we already know according to habit. With the self-expressive determinations of the ego, the composer and listener are not open to change, and music remains within the bounds of the usual and the accepted. Second, the imposition of feelings blocks the way to the listening of sounds as sounds. Cage draws out the implications of Daisetz Teitaro Suzuki's Zen Buddhist doctrine of non-obstruction and interpenetration, as he explains to Daniel Charles:

> Emotions, like all tastes and memory, are too closely linked to the self, to the ego. The emotions show that we are touched within ourselves, and tastes evidence our way of being touched on the outside. We have made the ego into a wall and the wall doesn't even have a door through which interior and exterior could communicate! Suzuki taught me to destroy that wall. What is important is to insert the individual into the current, the flux of everything that happens. And to do that the wall has to be demolished; tastes memory, and emotions have to be weakened; all the ramparts have to be razed. You can feel an emotion; just don't think that it's so important. . . . Take it in a way that you can then let it drop![3]

But this does not mean that one cannot experience music and art emotionally. As Cage continues, 'I give the impression that I am against feelings. But what I am against is the imposition of feelings.'[4] Cage develops Suzuki's doctrine of non-obstruction as a way to avoid imposing his feelings upon his audience and, hence, develops it into his stricture of non-intentionality which, as he says, governs not only his music but also his life. Music then, in Cage's terms, functions to facilitate the audition of sounds as sounds rather than as a vehicle which would serve to convey the composer's inner emotional affects to others. This position was also taken by the younger composers associated with Cage such as Christian Wolff:

> One finds a concern for a kind of objectivity, almost anonymity – sound come into its own. The 'music' is a resultant existing simply in the sounds we hear, given no impulse by expressions of self or personality.[5]

The work generated by way of the chance operation, Cage suggests, resembles 'not the work of a person, but something that might have happened, even if the person weren't there'.[6] Further, the acceptance of chance, for Cage, paves the way to an approach to the sonic universe and to existence itself that is not governed by human, anthropocentric preconceptions.

Cage's operations generally consisted of submitting the variable elements of musical composition – pitch, duration, amplitude and timbre – to a series of decisions or numerical data arrived at by means of an aleatory system. Cage began writing his musical compositions with the aid of a chart system, utilized by some of the European composers such as Pierre Boulez, known as the 'Magic Square', but around 1949 he settled on the *I Ching* (the *Book of Changes*) which involves a binary system of determinations based on the number 64, to be arrived at by the tossing of a coin. Other aleatory systems involved the utilization of observations of slight imperfections in a sheet of paper, superimposing transparent sheets of celluloid imprinted with lines and points, translocating points on star maps and, later, Cage procured lists of random numbers from Bell Laboratories before obtaining his own computer to generate the numbers. Cage's first composition composed according to chance operations, employing the *I Ching*, was *Music of Changes* (1951), shortly followed by *Imaginary Landscape No. 4* (1951). Despite the unfortunate metaphor of 'asking questions' that Cage uses to describe the process in quite a number of interviews, Cage never employed the *I Ching* as an oracle. Even though 'asking questions rather than making choices' might sound like Cage wishes to avoid the labour of solving difficult compositional problems – which is a charge his detractors make – the process was used exclusively as a mechanical means to bracket out decisions of taste, and bring about a shift in perspective. Cage's compositions were constructed with the utmost rigour.

## Indeterminacy

However, as Cage soon discovered, a score that is created by means of chance operations alone remains a fixed score. In its virtual state the score remains the same and allows only minor variations to occur between successive performances. In order to extend openness to the aleatory beyond the fixed score and open up the performance itself to further unforeseen possibilities, Cage developed a means of composing in which the composition remains indeterminate of its performance. Such compositions may also be created by means of chance operations, but they extend the aleatory mechanisms into the sphere of performance and, to a certain extent, into improvisation on the part of the performers. This indeterminacy, however, is not without its problems. Although intention on the part of the composer is radically suspended, a certain voluntarism on the part of the performer is brought back into the work. In other words, the performer, in attempting to improvise during the process, in the worst case, relies on what they already know (according to taste and memory) and, perhaps, in the best scenario, they might indulge in a form of automatism. Abandoning the interpretation of certain events in the score to the caprice of the performer allows the performer to respond in a subjective way to the other sounds that they hear. Cage often complained that his performers were prone to backsliding into aesthetic improvisation. Yet one must sympathize with the performers, since it would appear that improvisational non-intentionality, free from taste and memory, unassisted by the imposition of an 'irrelevant process', would present great difficulties for anyone, let alone trained professionals set in their ways. Cage was well aware of this problem as indicated in an interview with Bill Schoemaker in 1984:

> What I would like to find is an improvisation that is not descriptive of the performer, but is descriptive of what happens, and which is characterized by absence of intention. It is at the point of spontaneity that the performer is

most apt to have recourse to his memory. He is not apt to make a discovery spontaneously.[7]

The composition of music according to chance operations is a rigorous activity. It is 'the highest discipline', according to Cage, because it suspends all aesthetic judgement, but, as Cage argues, it is the composer rather than the work that is subjected to discipline.[8] Indeterminacy, on the other hand, would seem to be troubled by the lack of abstention from subjective values of taste. As Cage says, 'Chance operations are a discipline, and improvisation is rarely a discipline. . . . Improvisation is generally playing what you know, and what you like, and what you feel.'[9] Cage came up with various strategies to circumvent taste and memory in performance, such as letting the performers get in each other's way; giving them instruments to play that they have little or no control over; dividing time in order to reduce repetitions; and creating technical layers of complexity. But none of these strategies seem to be equal to the rigour of chance procedures. In short, non-intentionality and indeterminate improvisation, however constricted, seem to be concepts, in Cage's work, that remain opposed to each other. This is perhaps the result of a tension that existed between, on the one hand, Cage's wish to not force his emotions on an audience and, on the other hand, his politically anarchic desire to not dictate to his performers. To effectively maintain the abstention of taste would require the score to treat the performers as mere machines (as a kind of mechanical indeterminacy), yet Cage's preference was to give his performers a certain humanistic freedom, even at the cost of letting subjective decisions into the work. Cage's reference to spontaneity in the above-mentioned quote illustrates this problem. On the one hand, the chance operation suspends authorial spontaneity. On the other hand, indeterminacy presupposes spontaneity, a way of acting in the moment that must be, however, free from the performer's memory and habits. Cage never resolves this antinomy.

## Silence and non-intention

Perhaps the most well-known, and most notorious, work of Cage's is the so-called silent piece *4′ 33″*. This piece, which was first performed on 29 August 1952, at Woodstock, N.Y. by David Tudor, consists of three sections of silence respectively 33″, 2′ 40″ and 1′ 20″ in duration. David Tudor indicated the beginning of each part by closing the piano keyboard lid, and the end of each part by opening it. The initial idea for the piece came to Cage several years earlier in 1947 around the time of a lecture at Vassar College in which he said that he wished to 'compose a piece of uninterrupted silence and sell it to Muzak Co. . . . It will be 3 or 4-1/2 minutes long – those being the standard lengths of "canned" music and the title will be *Silent Prayer*.'[10] But it was not until after viewing Robert Rauschenberg's white paintings – which Cage describes as 'airports for the lights, shadows and particles',[11] and as 'mirrors of the air', and 'an airport for shadows and dust'[12] – that, as he says, he finally had the courage to write the work.

Near the end of his life, Cage still regarded *4′ 33″* as his most important work. He does not say explicitly why this is so, but it would be possible to say that *4′ 33″* brings together many of Cage's ideas in the one piece. Cage, inspired by Webern, had been using silence in his compositions since the 1940s. Silence, as such, was considered, along with sound, as another musical material.[13] But after studying Zen Buddhism with Suzuki, Cage began to think of silence as the negation of music. *4′ 33″* could also be considered as a limit case or boundary work, an absolute minimalism that cannot be surpassed – the most extreme point of 'not music'. The white paintings of Rauschenberg, which indicated to Cage that modern music was lagging behind painting, could be considered in much the same way. Another way Cage theorized *4′ 33″* was a piece of pure duration – empty time to be filled. This is more in keeping with Cage's consideration of *4′ 33″* as an empty frame, a blank slate which serves to open up listening to the ambient sounds of the immediate environment of the performance. This way of thinking springs not only from what Cage saw as the function of Rauschenberg's white paintings – to act as blank surfaces to catch the play of contingent traces – but also from Cage's mature conception of silence, that is, after he spent some time in the anechoic chamber at Harvard University in 1951, and realized that absolute silence is impossibility since the listening body always generates sound. The earlier conception of silence as the negative spaces in a composition had given way to a new way of thinking in which silence functioned as transparency or letting. Finally, since anything could happen during the empty durational frame of *4′ 33″*, the piece can be considered as indeterminate of its performance.

Despite its simplicity, Cage claims that *4′ 33″* was constructed in a rigorous manner over several days through the building up of many minute pieces of silence according to chance operations which determined the durations. As Cage remarks, 'it seems idiotic, but that's what I did.'[14] Composing, for Cage, is always a discipline that breaks down the composer's prejudices and preconceived ideas in total acceptance. The gradual awakening of the composer's acceptance and awareness of 'sound come into its own', or of 'letting sound be itself', occurs over time, and by way of the working-through of the work. Cage, however, expects this same process of change to occur in his audience, within the duration of the performance. The presentation and framing, of pure duration, as an event or performance is expected to open the audience's ears to the sounds of the world, without assistance or guidance, Zen training, or knowledge of the process of composition. A certain discipline is required, as Cage explains to Daniel Charles: in demanding austerity of the listener 'I am giving him the chance to open himself up!'[15] There are two issues at stake here. First there is the responsibility given to the audience to complete the work. This responsibility requires that the audience member must become, as Cage says, a performer, as much as the composer becomes a listener. But with *4′ 33″* the audience must also become, to some extent the composer, and to be a composer requires a certain discipline. Second, if we accept that works such as *4′ 33″* constitute a revealing of sounds, then how does this revealing happen through the work? Would it not be possible to argue that the same outcome, that is, the unmediated perception of sounds in the world, as sounds in themselves, could be achieved without recourse to the work, albeit with a 'changed' listener?

## Complexity

In her essay 'Chance Operations: Cagean Paradox and Contemporary Science', N. Katherine Hayles, drawing on her work on randomness, chaos and noise in scientific contexts, investigates the idea of chance in terms of three interpretations: intersecting worldliness, temporal asymmetry and informational incompressibility.[16] Hayles understands Cage's methods, quite rightly, as an attempt to open the possibility that would permit us 'to grasp through our intentions a world that always exceeds and outruns those intentions', and 'to subvert the anthropomorphic perspective that constructs continuity from a human viewpoint of control and isolation'.[17] In this way we can think of the chance operation functioning as an abstention that opens the way to a new phenomenological starting point. However, contrary to Husserl's phenomenology, Cage's work is concerned with worldly processes rather than intentional objects. In *Empty Words*, he writes:

> To focus attention, one must ignore all the rest of creation. We have a history of doing precisely that. In changing our minds, therefore, we look for that attitude that is non-exclusive, that can include what we know together with what we do not yet imagine.[18]

Hayles observes that the words 'chance' and 'operation' – since chance is 'in excess of our expectations', and operation derives from *operari* and *opus* – would seem to be at odds. As we have seen, chance operations, in order to function effectively as disruption and displacement, must involve a certain rigour. But the movement of excess and rigour only comes into opposition if the chance operation itself is thought in terms of content or object, with emphasis placed on a goal which aims towards a result which may be said to 'embody' complexity. To make 'chance' or 'randomness' the focus of the inquiry is, I think, to make of the operation more than it is, to give it a certain profundity or to provide it with a *telos* towards complexity. What is at stake, rather, is how chance functions as a radical disconnection from aesthetic voluntarism, and to what extent the multiplicity of processes distance the composer's subjective decision making from the work and allow the work to effectively generate itself.

The difference here might be illustrated in the following way. In an Interview with Cage, Daniel Charles compares the utilization of chance operations to the approach of Xenakis which uses probability formulae to control the direction of statistical tendencies. Cage replies: 'What I hope for is the ability of seeing anything whatsoever arise. . . . If you are in that stage of mutation, you are situated in change and immersed in process. While if you are dealing with a statistic, then you return to the world of objects.'[19] Charles replies: 'Indeterminacy, as you conceive it then could not be *opposed* to what the physicists mean by that word. Your music is not *opposed* to Xenakis's music. It is situated *before* it; it describes its *condition of possibility*.'[20] Because Cage seeks the unforeseen 'anything whatever', the process remains radically disconnected from what it 'lets' emerge. The more irrelevant the process, in Brecht's sense, the more creative subjectivity is distanced, and the more the arbitrary is put out of action. If one of the most essential outcomes of the chance operation is the acceptance of what possibilities exist for it, rather than what we think it should be, then the desire to find complexity, or even a certain resemblance to the operations of nature, in the result would constitute a presupposition. Consequently, the emphasis on what might constitute a more authentically random procedure, where one might wish to value one procedure over another, on perhaps statistical grounds, would seem to constitute a presupposition that would be essentially contrary to Cage's experimental methodology as a way to the unforeseen. The gist of this is that 'chance' and 'operation' mean, in Cage's terms, essentially the same thing: *disconnection*. Chance is not some mystical realm to which appeals are made – however much the mysticism associated with the *I Ching* might suggest this. Nor does chance represent some *a priori* rational mathematical structure underlying the world that can be tapped by the application of theories of probability. Cagean 'chance' is not an idea or an ideal to be encountered in itself. The word, in this context, simply describes an operation that suspends the immediate decision making involved in producing a work of art. Chance is not free play; rather, it is an abstentional operation that allows free play to happen. Finally – and this goes against its historical reception in dada and surrealism – the chance operation is a mere tool. Chance, in itself, bears no interest. What is of interest is its functioning.

## The reception of chance

It is not hard to see how contingency systems allow the artist to bypass aesthetic judgements of taste, but what are the implications of the utilization of such systems in terms of their reception by an audience? Is the experience of listening to an indeterminate piece of music, or a chance-derived artwork, ostensively any different from the experience that one may receive from a work composed by more intentional means? Should the work of art actively work to prevent a subjectivized response, so that the audience might open up to hear sounds as sounds? Cage had indicated in 1965 that his recent work had turned to a concern with processes: 'setting a process going which has no necessary beginning, no middle, no end, and no sections.'[21] Here, certainly, process becomes more important than objects, but if process has primacy, then in what way would an audience – which is not engaged in the making of the work – encounter the process at work? This of course was a criticism made of Cage's methods by the 'minimalist' composer, Steve Reich, in 'Music as a Gradual Process' (1968). Although Cage accepts the results of processes, Reich argues that these processes cannot be heard in the music itself, thus: 'The compositional processes and the sounding music have no audible connection.'[22] Cage responds to this criticism in an interview in 1983 arguing that it is not necessary for the audience to understand, and thus participate, in the process because, he says, 'I'm on the side of keeping things mysterious. . . . If I understand something, I have no further use for it.'[23] Cage somewhat ingenuously dodges the question. On the one hand, there is no doubt that the audience does not share the same access to the process as the composer. However, as far as Cage is concerned, although he does not explicitly say so, the processes he utilizes would be of no interest to an audience; they bear no relation to the sounds produced; the processes, in Brecht's words, are 'irrelevant'. On the other hand, Cage's thinking on this issue participates in a rather standard modernist conception of art as something ineffable, where it is supposed that if a work of art is understood, it loses its power to be a work of art and is, consequently, of no further use. In this way, Cage's conception of art is miles apart from Duchamp's credo of bringing art back into the service of the mind. But this then seems to contradict Cage's distinction between objects and processes. If the work is not an object (a final outcome of a process) but an unfolding process, should – or to what extent should – the process be encountered as part of the work (which is not to say that it must be fully understood in all its causal relations)?

This problem of the illegibility of the aleatory procedure in the work occupied a number of young choreographers involved in the Judson Dance Theater in New York in the early 1960s. The rationale of Elaine Summers's *Instant Chance* (performed in the first Judson programme, *A Concert of Dance*, 6 July 1962) was to make explicit the chance methodologies employed in the choreography. To this end Summers had the dancers throw large coloured and numbered Styrofoam blocks (much like dice) – the outcome of their fall dictating the movement to be made according to a set of predetermined rules. Summers's interest in chance operations (she also constructed a film with Gene Friedman and John Herbert McDowell edited according to aleatory procedures) was most certainly ignited by Robert Dunn's class in choreography – at Merce Cunningham's studio – which employed the use of chance operations which

Dunn had gleaned from Cage's class at the New School of Social Research. (Dunn reportedly used Cage's imperfection overlays method used for *Fontana Mix*.) Summers attended Dunn's class along with McDowell, Simone Forti,[24] Yvonne Rainer, Ruth Emerson and others. The visual artists Robert Rauschenberg and Robert Morris occasionally attended and played significant roles as (non-trained) performers in the Judson Dance Theater.[25]

Simone Forti came to Dunn's class in the autumn of 1960 after spending four years participating in Ann Halprin's Dancer's Workshop which taught the formulation of game-tasks called 'improvisations' (or 'natural activities and tasks') aimed at the breaking of habitual and stereotypical bodily movements rather than as outlets for self-expression. Both Halprin's workshop and Dunn's class aimed to radically break with the traditions of modern dance: its expressionism and reliance on binding movement to literary ideas and musical form. Forti saw chance operations as a starting point generating a fresh point of departure which she then developed along the lines of Haprin's exercises to follow a game-like structure. Emphasizing the importance of the combination of a set of rules and the use of devices or objects, Robert Morris notes that Forti's game-like structures 'effectively blocked the dancer's performing "set" and reduced him to frantically responding to cues – reduced him from performance to action'.[26] *See Saw*, performed at the Reuben Gallery in 1960, involved a long plank teetering on a sawhorse with its ends secured by elastic material. *Slant Board*, which was included in a night of performances programmed by Forti at Yoko Ono's loft in 1961, involved a two and a half metre square board inclined at a forty-five-degree angle against a wall. With the aid of ropes, performers ascended, rested and descended, passing between each other. In Forti's work, objects (which she called constructions) took the form of constraints which had the effect of instilling – against the normative codes of modern dance – ordinary or 'found' movements 'newly invested with dignity'.[27]

Robert Morris observes a trend in art since the Second World War where 'artists have increasingly sought to remove the arbitrary from working by finding a system according to which they could work'.[28] Morris cites Cage's use of chance operations as an example of this thread that has run from Duchamp through to Jasper Johns and Frank Stella and to conceptual art. In opposition to this thread, Morris observes the continuance of another systematizing thread of methodologies that he refers to as bearing towards a phenomenological direction, where the system that orders the work is not derived from a prior and external logical system, but from 'the "tendencies" inherent in a materials/process interaction'.[29] In other words, forms are discovered in the activity of interacting with material properties. In this way of working – epitomized, for Morris, by Pollock's methods – the material, in a certain way, determines the working process and, more importantly for Morris, the process is made manifest in the work. This is exemplified, quite literally, in Morris's 1961 work, *Box with the Sound of Its Own Making*: a 24.8-centimetre cube that plays back, from a tape player concealed within it, the recorded sounds of its own construction. In other words, encountering the process in the work effects the way we read the work. Here we come back to the question: Is it important that the process is seen or heard in the work? The question can be rephrased: Is the process part of the work? Should it be inside or outside?

In the first case, contingency systems such as the chance operation and the found object put in place, in the making process, the most radical abstention from aesthetic position taking. But if no residue remains of the operation, the conditions of the genesis of the work become obscure, and nothing would seem to offer resistance to reading the work, not only in terms of the morphological aspects of audition but, even worse, as a product of the artist's interiority: a product of expression. In the second case, the material/process interaction makes its processes manifest, and thus provides a context for the work, and, as Morris insists, reveals information rather than purely aesthetic form. Yet it must be emphasized that the latter tendency, by inviting spontaneity (particularly in the case of Pollock) and allowing the arbitrary to enter the making process at any point, falls short of the more rigorous aesthetic abstention of the chance operation. Are the non-volitional activities of contingency systems and the revealing of process in materials/process works mutually exclusive? Can we conceive of a radically disconnecting system that, at the same time, reveals itself as such?

I would suggest that works such as Reich's early process pieces combine both radical aesthetic abstention and manifestation of process. Reich argues for perceptible processes that can be heard in the music as it is performed, in fact 'pieces of music that are, literally, processes'.[30] Such (gradual) processes include 'pulling back a swing, releasing it, and observing it gradually come to rest'.[31] In the same year that 'Music as a Gradual Process' was written, Reich composed a process piece entitled *Pendulum Music: For Microphones, Amplifiers and*

*Speakers*, which consists of three or more microphones suspended from their cables directly above speakers. The microphones are pulled back by the performers and then let go in unison, allowing them to swing over the speakers, thus creating pulsed feedback according to changing phase relations. The piece ends shortly after the microphones come to rest. We are able to *hear* the process in such events, Reich insists, because they occur gradually and thus invite 'sustained attention'.[32] But, at the same time, according to Reich, the sound that one hears moves away from intentions, and what is distinctive of such processes is that 'they determine all the note-to-note details and the over all form simultaneously. One can't improvise in a musical process – the concepts are mutually exclusive.'[33]

## Processes and systems

Developing out of an interest in cybernetics and information theory, and his first experiments with 'weather boxes' in 1963, Hans Haacke began using real-time systems in 1965. These systems capture temporal processes and operate independently of human control or perception. Haacke's real-time systems, like Duchamp's readymades, are to a large extent pre-existing and, in a sense, found more than made. However, unlike the readymade, and more like Cage's indeterminacy, they do not result in static, fixed, objects but are amenable to change. Haacke's real-time systems fall into two types. His earlier works involve processes which evolve by themselves independently of any human interaction of either artist or spectator. (Haacke prefers the term 'witness'.) They are essentially contingency systems which operate beyond the control of any human agency, where the look of the work is accepted as the look of a system in action, without aesthetic interference on behalf of the artist. For *Condensation Cube* (1963/1965), Haacke constructed a rectangular clear plastic container containing just enough distilled water to create condensation in distinct ways according to environmental changes. His real-time systems are physically real open systems, and responding to changes in their environment, they employ physically interdependent processes that fluctuate according to cycles and feedback loops. In these works, there is no attempt to solve formal problems. They deal with actualities or 'real stuff – on its own terms'.[34]

Expanding upon these physical systems in the late 1960s, Haacke's second type of system – his real-time social systems – involves spectator participation as one of the interactive elements. In *Gallery-Goers' Birthplace and Residence Profile, Part 1* (1969), visitors were asked to indicate with a red pin, on maps of the five boroughs of New York City, their birthplace, and with a blue pin, their place of permanent residence. Haacke took photographs of each location and arranged them on the gallery wall in accordance with each location's distance from Fifth Avenue, along with other statistical information. Similarly, in this work no formal consideration comes into play in the arrangement of the photographic material. All compositional decisions are determined by topographical information provided by the gallery-goers. Yet, such process works are far from apolitical, as they reveal sociopolitical realities of the art world.

Opening up questions of public space and individual property ownership, Haacke's *Shapolsky et al. Manhattan Real Estate Holdings, a Real-Time Social System as of May 1, 1971* (1971) displays one family's concentrated ownership of tenement buildings in the slum districts of Manhattan (Harlem and the Lower East Side). Taken from public records, Haacke assembled intricate diagrams of cross ownership spanning some seventy different corporations all with a connection to the Shapolsky family. Accompanying these in a large-scale installation are maps and 142 objectively shot and closely framed, black-and-white photographs of the tenement buildings, each with a text detailing the address, current owner, the name on the contract of sale, previous owner, the price, mortgage details and assessed land value. The work, in this form, was rejected in 1971 by the director of the Guggenheim Museum, Thomas Messer, who objected to its potential to attract a libel action, despite all of the information being publicly available. What is not often acknowledged is that in these real-time social systems the work is never simply 'inside' the exhibition. The system proceeds with or without the institution, gathering up reviewers, protesters and, most importantly, Messer himself, as unwitting participants and essential components of the system as it evolves.

Haacke's early pieces resemble Reich's processes, and one can see a direct connection between these early process pieces and the later real-time social systems that are often exclusively considered under the art-historical term of 'institutional critique'. In many ways, Haacke's process works carry out the prescriptions of Sol LeWitt which were published in his 'Paragraphs on Conceptual art' and 'Sentences on Conceptual Art' in the late 1960s. On the one hand, LeWitt's ideas encapsulate the strong rationalistic ideas of conceptual art, for example, in 'Paragraphs' he emphasizes the importance of the idea or the concept preceding the work. After the concept has been formulated by the artist, it is then simply a matter of implementing it without changes, and in such a way 'the idea becomes a machine that makes the art'.[35] On the other hand, LeWitt's 'Paragraphs' and 'Sentences' resemble the non-intentional methodologies of Cage, Higgins and Brecht, where he insists that 'The artist's will is secondary to the process he initiates from idea to completion. His willfulness may only be ego.'[36]

Within these few short pages a number of extremely interesting ideas are developed. However, the full impact of LeWitt's paragraphs and sentences never really surfaces in his own work which remains largely confined to formal geometric seriality. I would suggest that LeWitt's ideas, beyond his own practice, offer us an insightful way to come to grips with the 'real-time' systems and 'real-time social systems' of Haacke, Dan Graham and Martha Rosler during the 1960s and 1970s, and in typological systems of Marcel Broodthaers, John Baldessari, Ed Ruscha, Bas Jan Ader, Bernd and Hilla Becher and others.

Turning to language in a series of self-descriptive, self-referential, grid-like textual constructions that waver between proposal for a work and the work itself, Adrian Piper's work in the late 1960s – such as *Sixteen Permutations on the Planar Analysis of a Square* (1968), *Concrete Infinity 6" Square* (1968), *Concrete Space-Time Infinity 8" Square* (1968), *Block Area Enlargement Series* (1969) and *Here and Now* (artist's book) (1968) – was greatly influenced by LeWitt's process-oriented minimalism. Commenting on these pieces in 1968, Piper explains: 'I am presently interested in the construction of finite systems, that is, systems that serve to contain an idea within certain formal limits and to exhaust the possibilities of the idea set by those limits.'[37] The adoption of these reduced and systematic strategies functioned, for Piper, not only as a means of transcending her own subjective limits and obtaining enhanced critical objectivity but also as the starting point, by way of her key concept, 'the indexical present', for an extension into social and political interventions in response to racism and xenophobia.

The irrelevant process, according to Brecht, is the most effective way of avoiding bias – that is, in phenomenological terms, of avoiding presuppositions

– and thus arriving at the unforeseen. With the irrelevant process, a certain abstraction or codification occurs between the material and the process. Outcomes are mapped to the process by a number of abstract relations. However, because this tends to efface any visible or audible relation between the material and the process, one cannot read the process from the outcome. The irrelevant process suspends aesthetic judgement, and puts aesthetic presuppositions out of play, but obfuscates the process by which it does so. What Morris calls the 'phenomenological' method, on the other hand, shows its processes, but in allowing the arbitrary to enter, it would not seem to involve, in the same way, the restraint that is brought about by the abstentional *epochē* of the irrelevant process. However, the process-based models proposed by Reich, LeWitt and Haacke would seem to strike a balance between these two methodologies.

## Toposonics

Cage and Schaeffer would appear to occupy opposite positions in what is called in sound and music studies the 'contextual debate'. Brandon LaBelle notes how the suppression of a sound's reference or context marks the difference between *musique concrète* and Cage's musical practices where, for Cage, 'Materiality and context form the basis for an exploded musical object'.[38] For LaBelle, Cage democratically opens up musical listening to reveal 'the material presence of the musical moment'.[39] Citing Cage's silent piece, 4' 33", LaBelle writes:

> Context insists because Cage's musical object relies upon it, addressing the very space and time of its experience in all its actuality; further, listening is predicated on the formation of and belief in democratic organization, for each sound is perceived equal to another, as opposed to Schaeffer who proposes that 'sound phenomena are instinctively perceived by the ear with greater or lesser importance as in an aristocratic hierarchy, and not with the equalities of a democracy'.[40]

One might surmise that for Schaeffer, sounds are objects, while Cage thinks of them in terms of processes. But this is perhaps too much of a simplification. Rather, Schaeffer thinks of the sound object as an eidetic unity that forms the raw material for music, and as such, is already on the way to being further reduced to a repeatable ideal musical object. By contrast, Cage emphasizes the actuality of unique, singular, unrepeated, unrepeatable sound. However, I would not agree with LaBelle that this means that Cage's sounds always retain their contextual and spatial relationships. Rather, I would suggest that such contextual practices are to be found in the work of later sound art practices that occur in the wake of Cage's work. Moreover, I would argue that the shift from Cage's modernist musical paradigm to the post-aesthetic field of sound art entails not only a shift of emphasis from temporality to spatiality – in a modernist sculptural sense – but, further, a shift to a notion of situatedness and relation to *place*.

Although Cage's work remains within a modernist tendency which is essentially atopic and devoid of contextual meanings, his work has opened up the space for other artists to engage in relations to world and place. Sound artist Bill Fontana works with found sound sculptures, or ready-made sound installations, that generate automatic self-performance in real time. Fontana then transmits the found environmental sound (often rendered as a multichannel perspective by way of multiple microphones) to another public location where it is reproduced in accordance with a duplicated spatial arrangement (speaker positions match microphone positions). Fontana's work, in this way, produces a decontextualizing and recontextualizing of ambient sounds. Sounds are split from their source by the 'schizophonic'[41] effect of recording/broadcast technology, and replaced in a different environment – sometimes a similar place – often separated by a substantial distance. The schizophonic effect is doubly reinforced by the audition of the de-contextualized sound repositioned in a new setting.

Fontana's works, such as *Oscillating Steel Grids along the Brooklyn Bridge* (World Trade Center and Brooklyn Museum, New York, 1983), present such an acoustic paradox. This work consists of a real-time relocation of the sound of traffic crossing the Brooklyn Bridge. The bridge produces a particular humming sound due to a crossing vehicle's tyres coming into contact with the studded steel grid which comprises the road surface. This sound, which would be quite familiar to many New Yorkers, was relocated in real time, by way of equalized broadcast-quality telephone lines, to the locale of the World Trade Centre. Fontana describes the effect of this work:

> In this architectural context, the familiar humming of the Brooklyn Bridge became an acoustic paradox. The kinesthetic sense of this humming coming

from somewhere about the plaza, from 'somewhere up in the struts' as the *Village Voice* described it, was an important formal element of the sound sculpture. The physical and spatial relationships of the humming sound to the architectural scale of the World Trade Centre towers altered the acoustic scale of the humming. This alteration of scale gave the humming sound of the Brooklyn Bridge a new spectrum of possible acoustic meanings.[42]

Fontana's 'acoustic overlays' alter the acoustic meaning of the environmental sound by raising the question of its meanings when translocated to another site. These pieces, according to Fontana, play with the acoustic memory of a site, replacing old sonic identities with new identities appropriated from elsewhere.[43] In a similar way, Maryanne Amacher's *City Links* (1967–81) – an ongoing series of sound installations – relocates and gathers together live transmissions (over dedicated telephone lines) of diverse sonic environments, creating long-duration, interwoven synchronicities of sound and place.

Amacher's and Fontana's transpositioned sounds coincide with everydayness. Instead of listening with a detached ear, or an inward reflection on consciousness in blind acousmatic audition, the listening experience is opened up to its relation to a dwelling-in-place, in a living situation. At the same time, both projects exceed the naive simplicity of Cage's approach where the frame of music – as in *4' 33"*, piano, pianist and hall – sets a zero point of reception. I would suggest that the work of Fontana and Amacher carries out, in Heidegger's terms, a non-intentional *letting* – in its appropriation of found sound – followed by an *estrangement* that renders the situation uncanny. This disjunction brings the auditory horizonal field into the focus of a new modality that forces a reconfiguration of the sound's relation to everyday space and place. In phenomenological terms, a horizon is the field in which any experiential encounter is explicated. The horizon's borders shade off at the boundaries between what belongs to a particular experience and what remains external to it. In one sense, in terms of Heidegger's early thought in *Being and Time*, what these works demonstrate is that – in contradistinction to the Cartesian model consisting of a 'searchlight' of consciousness, where subjects encounter objects which stand over against us – we are always already installed in the midst of things in our being-in-the-world. In another sense, in terms of Heidegger's later thought – where he begins to think of space in terms of place (*Ort*) and gathering (*Versammlung*), and as event (*Ereignis*) – these works could be said to open up a form of dwelling in accordance with the topological motif which Heidegger calls 'that which regions' (*Gegnet*).[44] Along with the letting of *Gelassenheit* which allows things to rest in themselves, *Gegnet* points to a way of thinking other than the transcendental-horizonal representation of the subject–object relation in which the will of the subject determines, to a great extent, what is seen and what is heard. In similar terms to Cage's letting sounds be, the translocational sound works of Fontana and Amacher simply let sounds happen. However, unlike Cage's works, translocation insistently makes the marginal background of auditory horizons thematic. The out-of-context sound field opens up attention to context and brings about a questioning of the relation of sound to place.[45]

## Relational sound

Schaeffer's sonic research, by admitting aesthetic judgements into the most basic level of categorization of the sound object, would seem to betray its own requirements for a presupposition-free phenomenological starting point. Cage's approach, on the other hand, by imposing a radical abstention that suspends judgements of taste in the compositional process, would seem to bring us closer to sounds, as they are let to be. His work opens up a space which, exceeding the inherent aestheticism of Schaeffer's system, allows sounds to be auditioned on their own terms, freed from imposed cultural-aesthetic determinations. However, Cage's sounds, however democratic their reception, ultimately float in an ether of aesthetic contemplation without any concern for situation, context, place or meaning. Although Cage renders sound as a-cultural (in a similar way to Schaeffer) as sound in or as itself, his sounds are let to rest in themselves free from, on the one hand, the constructs of a representational thinking that includes both calculation and mastery (and the domination of anthropocentric structures of power) and, on the other hand, the imposition of subjectivist values of taste and expression. However, although Cage's 'letting sounds be' can be seen to resemble Heidegger's *Gelassenheit* (releasement), there is one important difference: when it comes to sound, Cage's letting seems less open to thinking.

Cage's musicalization of all sounds certainly re-aestheticizes them. However, the acceptance of letting them be and rest in themselves points us to non-subjective possibilities. Cage, more than any other artist, has explored the *epochē* of non-intention. But Cage's project only presents us with the first step. In 'Several Silences', an essay on Cage, Jean François Lyotard suggests that sounds, in a psychoanalytic sense, are bound, and as such a sound has 'value not for its sonority but for the network of its actual and possible relations'.[46] Rather than casting non-intentionality as a quasi-mystical observance, which would seek to demolish artistic agency in the name of some ego-less, quietism, my aim is to inquire into its value as a starting point which has its place in a way of thinking which would seek to displace the subjectivism of Western metaphysics. The remainder of this study will carry out this investigation. In Chapter 4 I will examine how non-intention, in a certain way, functions in Heidegger's twisting free from aesthetics which is simultaneously a twisting free from the domain of the will.

# 4

# Twisting free from aesthetics and the will

When one speaks about chance operations, or aleatory procedures in the creation of the work of art, one is often confronted with an objection that often belongs to one of two distinct arguments. Both of these arguments emerge from what I believe have become sedimented and ossified conceptions of the work of art. The remnants of these conceptions can still be seen to operate in contemporary art theory but, in their undiluted form, are much more prominent in non-specialist, popular, conceptions of art. One argument, which has its roots in eighteenth- and nineteenth-century romanticism, and for quite some time has tended to be in decline, would contend that the suspension of volition, on the artist's part, would block the transmission of the artist's aesthetic idea, and disallow the transference of the artist's feelings into the work and through to the spectator (who would presumably respond with the same feeling). This argument, which belongs to what we might describe as the 'aesthetic attitude', occurs less frequently in the visual arts in the twenty-first century. It is, however, much more prevalent in the field of music. Another argument, which would be the counterargument to the first position, would seek to put into question the validity of the chance work of art, as art, because, failing to communicate an intentional statement, the work would be seen to be politically impotent and possibly even politically questionable. This argument, which we might call 'representationalist', belongs to a conception of art where the work of art is seen to be the vehicle for the transparent communication of more or less cultural–political ideas and ideological standpoints. Seen from this perspective, the function of such works is to provide social commentary. What is common to both of these conceptions is that the artist's intention, as either a vague, ineffable, emotion, on the one hand, or as an ideological idea communicated with the efficacy of a proposition, on the other, is seen as indispensable to any understanding of the work of art. As Krzysztof Ziarek points out, the domination of these sedimented positions results in the denial of an autonomous force specific to art, and an 'intolerance to art's otherness'.[1] Drawing on Heidegger, Ziarek calls for a third approach where 'art's "otherness" lies in its ability to unfold a mode of relationality that changes the very terms on which we encounter art'.[2]

These standard arguments mobilized against the use of chance in art are deprived of their substance if we engage in a radically different conception of art. Such a different conception, that some have called 'post-aesthetic',[3] springs from Martin Heidegger's thinking on art: in particular the 1936 essay 'The Origin of the Work of Art'.[4] Heidegger certainly does not advocate the use of aleatory procedures in the creation of works of art, but he does stress a 'letting' which involves an unfolding in the experience of the artwork in order for truth to happen in the work. Although Heidegger does not explicitly outline the role of the artist in the creation of the work, he does indicate that work of art transcends the work of the artist, and that in 'great art', 'the artist remains inconsequential as compared with the work, almost like a passageway that destroys itself in the creative process for the work to emerge' (GA 5 26, BW 166). Rather than the artist being the origin of the work of art, Heidegger begins the 1936 essay by proposing that 'art is the origin of both artist and work' (GA 5 1, BW 143).

In his 1956 addendum to 'The Origin of the Work of Art', Heidegger notes an ambiguity in the lecture when it comes to a 'fixing in place of truth' which implies a willing and that would seem to block the advent of truth and, on the other hand, a 'letting-happen' that would clear the way to the advent of truth, and would constitute a non-willing. This later observation is indicative of Heidegger's mature critique of the will – his twisting free from the domain of the will in order to establish the possibilities of a non-willing thinking beyond activity and passivity. The ambiguity that he notes in the lecture is the product of Heidegger's transitional thinking of the will where the idea of the 'most proper' will – a conception of the will in between the self-assertion of the early 1930s and the non-willing of the 1940s – still remains in place. Between the 1936 version of 'The Origin of the Work of Art' and the later of the Nietzsche lectures (1939–40) Heidegger gradually extracts himself from the philosophy of the will, and this has implications for how we might think non-intentionality in art.

## *Destruktion*

Heidegger's 'Origin' lectures are motivated by the necessity to think the concept of art differently, outside the history of aesthetics. In order to establish a conception of art in which truth happens in an opening up instigated by the work of art, Heidegger attempts to think art beyond the matter–form opposition that has, since Plato, determined the thinking of the creative production of the work of art; and to think it beyond the subject–object opposition that belongs to the modern philosophy of consciousness. Put simply, Heidegger thinks the work of art as both a letting be of the truth happening (event) in the work, as a work, and as a knowing that happens as a willing. But such a simple summary is inadequate because Heidegger thinks 'truth', 'knowing' and 'willing' in completely different ways than they are traditionally thought in Western philosophy. That is to say, Heidegger's meditation on the work of art is intimately bound up with what he calls his *Destruktion* of the history of Western ontology.[5]

Far from constituting a destructive shattering of the tradition, *Destruktion* functions for Heidegger as a loosening up of the solidified concepts and philosophemes of the tradition that have obstructed and concealed its own history. The translation of philosophical terminology is neither transparent nor innocent; it always marks a process of transplantation into a different system of thinking that always involves an essential alteration in meaning. Moreover, *Destruktion* is not a critique of the past but, rather, a shaking up of present-day self-evidence and the prevailing conceptions of the tradition. What is important is the implication that there are alternative possibilities for thinking – that is, that our modern subjective–objective way of thinking towards things might not constitute the *only* way of thinking.

In the epilogue of 'The Origin of the Work of Art', written a little later than the 1936 essay,[6] Heidegger, citing a number of transitions, sums up the history of aesthetics as it corresponds to the history of the decline of the essence of truth (*alētheia*) in ancient ontology: beginning with the matter–form pair and culminating in the nineteenth-century perceptual-aesthetic notion of 'lived-experience' (*Erlebnis*) (GA 5 69, BW 206). This history, which carries the original essence of truth and art away from what Heidegger views as the primordial Greek understanding of emerging (*physis*) and unconcealment (*alētheia*), is elaborated with some modifications and additions, in Heidegger's lecture course on Nietzsche ('The Will to Power as Art'), in the section 'Six Basic Developments in the History of Aesthetics'.[7] To summarize, the six stages are as follows: (i) the primordial Greek essence of 'great art' and great philosophy, (ii) the imposition of the matter–form opposition beginning with Plato, (iii) the domination of the subject–object distinction of the modern period (Descartes), (iv) the absolute aesthetics of Hegel, (v) the 'collective artwork' (*Gesamtkunstwerk*) of Wagner and the privileging of 'lived-experience' (*Erlebnis*) and, finally, (vi) art as applied 'physiology': aesthetics experienced bodily in Nietzsche. These two summaries present the problematics of what Heidegger regards as the history of aesthetics as it corresponds to the history of the decline of the essence of truth, or – since they amount to the same thing – the forgetting of being. However, the current phase or epoch of this history – where we are now – for Heidegger is the fifth development, the privileging of lived-experience. The sixth development, Nietzsche's aesthetics of the will to power of art, represents simultaneously (at least provisionally in Heidegger's thinking) the completion of metaphysics and the potential twisting free of it. Nietzsche's thought is seen as being transitional in the overcoming of metaphysics.

## Truth as unconcealment

In contradistinction to the aesthetic view of art, Heidegger argues that the work of art opens up a space in which the happening of truth occurs. We usually think of truth (*Wahrheit*) in terms of veracity or verification, or the idea that something conforms to an adequate representation of something actual, in terms of *adaequatio intellectus et rei* (agreement of intellect and thing). In the 'Origin' lectures, Heidegger proposes, truth happens (*geschehen*) in the work by way of a disclosure – or revealing – as 'unconcealment' (*Unverborgenheit*). It is with this word that Heidegger translates the Greek term *alētheia* – which is usually translated simply as truth (*Wahrheit*). Heidegger conceives of a model of truth where the matter (*Sache*) – the entity under discussion – must come to meet us 'in its specific Being' (*GA 24* 306, *BPP* 215). We do not perform the uncovering. Rather, we are installed within unconcealment, and are attendant to it. As Heidegger says, we are placed in a clearing (*Lichtung*) in the 'midst of beings (*Inmitten des Seienden*)' (*GA 5* 39–40, *BW* 177–8). Clearing is a happening, not a permanent condition. As such, it is constantly pervaded by concealment (*Verbergung*).

This concealment takes two forms according to Heidegger. As he says in the 'Origin' lectures, first beings 'refuse themselves (*Seiendes versagt sich*)' (GA 5 40, BW 178), in the sense of hiding and, second, they are disguised, or obstructed in a way that Heidegger describes as 'dissembling' (*Verstellen*). This does not mean that truth is essentially falsity. Rather, falsity as 'being-false (*pseudesthai*)' as deceiving, as covering up (*verdecken*), belongs to the double concealment which is the event in which unconcealment as clearing happens. Truth is in a certain sense bound up with 'un-truth', since the opposition between clearing and concealment is characterized by 'original strife' (*ursprünglichen Streites*). The work of art performs this strife as a disturbance that keeps open the clearing and resists withdrawal into concealment. The open centre, or region, Heidegger says, belongs to the conflict of world and earth. Truth happens as the strife of unconcealment in the work-being of the work, which sets up a world and sets forth the earth. The *work* of the work of art is thus one of the ways in which, for Heidegger, truth as unconcealment happens. However, this unconcealment is threatened, not only by modern representational thinking but also by the subjective mode of 'lived-experience' (*Erlebnis*).

## *Erlebnis*

In the 'Origin' lectures and in the first series of lectures on Nietzsche – 'The Will to Power as Art' – the critique of the will is confined to Heidegger's critique of the subjective will which is characterized, on the one hand, by the voluntarist self-assertion of modern representational thinking and technics and, on the other hand, the not-willing resignation of *Erlebnis*. Both together form the domain of the will. In German there are two words that can be translated into English as 'experience' – *Erlebnis* and *Erfahrung*. *Erlebnis* is sometimes translated as 'experience' but more often as 'lived-experience'. *Erlebnis* represents, in Heidegger's work of the 1930s, an immediate and private experience. It is a subjective experience that is both unmediated and vague, but which is at the same time deeply felt. It thus epitomizes the intense personal emotional aesthetic experience that came to be so highly valued by the romantics. The word *Erlebnis* contains within it the root *Leben*, meaning life. However, the term has a varied history in Heidegger's writing. It is used in the early phenomenological lectures to describe a pre-theoretical starting point and, later, in *Being and Time*, to expose a questionable starting point for the determination of *Dasein* and, finally, in the 1930s, the word emerges as a description of the penultimate stage of metaphysical aesthetics as the countermovement to rationalism, and the compliment to representational and calculative thinking.

In *Truth and Method*, Hans-Georg Gadamer throws some light on the term. According to Gadamer, in the history of aesthetics, in the wake of Kant, taste is devalued in relation to genius which becomes dominant with romanticism. Moral interest in the beauty of nature is pushed back in favour of man's self-encounter in works of art, and genius becomes, by the nineteenth century, a universal concept. According to Gadamer, this shift was the product of nineteenth-century irrationalism as a countermovement to Enlightenment reason, and 'Kant's doctrine of the "heightening of the feeling of life" (*Lebensgefühl*) in aesthetic pleasure helped the idea of "genius" to develop into a comprehensive concept of life (*Leben*).'[8] *Erlebnis* (a noun) is a secondary formation of the verb *erleben*, and, according to Gadamer, becomes common in that form only after the 1870s. Gadamer notes that the word emerges through biographical literature, where our understanding of a work of art is conditioned by our understanding of the life of its creator. Thus, its use as a standardized term is relatively recent. It is in Wilhelm Dilthey's biography of Schleiermacher that the word comes into a more general use and is then finally popularized in Dilthey's *Das Erlebnis und die Dichtung* (Poetry and Experience) in 1905.[9]

## *Erlebnis* in early Heidegger

The word *Erlebnis* has a complex history in Heidegger's thought, finding its way into his thinking from a number of sources: from the life-philosophy of Bergson, James and Dilthey, the phenomenological neo-Kantianism of Emil Lask and, lastly, the phenomenology of Husserl. Although Heidegger borrows much from Dilthey's concept of 'life', and the historical analysis of man, in conceiving his formulation of Dasein in *Being and Time*, it is clear that Heidegger had by that time distanced himself from the notion of *Erlebnis* in response to the criticisms of Dilthey's project supplied by Dilthey's friend Count Yorck von Wartenburg. The concept of life appears in various forms in Heidegger's habilation work (1916), but it is in the lecture series held in the 'war-emergency semester' of 1919 (*Kriegsnotsemester*, henceforth *KNS*), 'The Idea of Philosophy and the Problem of Worldview', at Freiburg, where Heidegger, as Husserl's newly appointed assistant, begins to examine the concept of *Erlebnis*. In his defence of phenomenological research, against the criticisms of neo-Kantianism – in particular that of Paul Natorp – Heidegger, in response to both world view philosophy and transcendental critical philosophy, attempts to develop, after Lask, the idea of a pre-theoretical 'primal something' (*Ur-etwas*) unfolding out of lived-experience. Heidegger is critical of the neo-Kantian critical–teleological method employed by Rickert and Windelband which, he contends, undermines itself by first positing – in the form of a fundamental guiding axiom – what it ultimately seeks to find. In contradistinction to the neo-Kantians, Heidegger and Husserl seek a new beginning point in what is immediately given in the experience of life itself. However, it soon becomes clear that the inherited concept of lived-experience is not to be uncritically handled by Heidegger. In the KNS we first get a hint of Heidegger's dissatisfaction with the term when he writes: 'The term "lived experience" (*Erlebnis*) is today so faded and worn thin that, if it were not so fitting, it would be best to leave it aside (*GA 56/57* 66, *TDP* 55). What Heidegger's reservations imply is that he is less that happy with the word's Cartesian (subjective) and psychological (objective) overtones. Thus, Heidegger wishes to wrench the term free from the idea of an experience that is essentially *inner* and reflexive, and at the same time to consider it non-objectively, that is, not as a temporally delimited psychical process.

In the summer semester lecture series of 1920, *Phenomenology of Intuition and Expression: Theory of Philosophical Concept Formation*, Heidegger is further dismissive of the aesthetic tendency towards an ideal of harmony in Dilthey's effective complex of life, informed by the triad of lived-experience, expression and understanding (*Erlebnis, Ausdruck and Verstehen*): 'Lived-experience leads to expression, the latter to understanding, and understanding back to lived experience; in this way it comes full circle.'[10] Dilthey's life complex, Heidegger claims, becomes fixed and personal because it is ultimately determined by a humanistic idealism, and what Heidegger calls the aesthetic consideration of history.[11] Although Heidegger utilizes the concept of *Erlebnis* in his early Freiburg lectures, he attempts to think it in a way that seeks to be more original than the subject–object opposition. He thinks *Erlebnis* in terms of the environmental experience of the environing world (*Umwelt*) as life in and for itself. Gradually this conception of life becomes 'factic life' in the early 1920s, and eventually transforms into the concernful and circumspective being-in-the-world of concrete Dasein in the lead up to *Being and Time*.

Although Heidegger's inquiry into fundamental ontology finds a certain amount of inspiration in Dilthey's work, he argues that life (and all derivative 'personalistic' movements), including even phenomenology itself, fails to put into question 'life' itself as a mode of being. This indicates, for Heidegger, that the basic question of Dasein's being has been deflected towards an anthropology by both the Greek (*zōon logon echon*)[12] and Christian (theological being) conceptions of 'man'. The question regarding the kind of entities that we ourselves are, Heidegger insists, cannot be answered in such an indeterminate way as 'life . . . plus something else' (*SZ* 50, *BT* 75). In *Being and Time*, *Erlebnis* is seen as an indeterminate starting point for the questioning of the being of Dasein. Rather than something undetermined or tacitly assumed, one's own Dasein is something encountered environmentally when it '*looks away* from "Experiences" (*Erlebnissen*) and the "centre of its actions", or does not yet "see" them at all. Dasein finds "itself" proximally in *what* it does, uses, expects, avoids – in those things environmentally ready-to-hand with which it is proximally *concerned*' (*SZ* 119, *BT* 155, Heidegger's emphasis). In such a way, Dasein is thrown into the 'there' and brought before itself in a state-of-mind, or *how one finds oneself* (*Befindlichkeit*). This does not in any way resemble the reflexivity of consciousness in the Cartesian tradition, rather, Heidegger contends: 'only because the "there" has already been disclosed in a state-of-mind can immanent reflection come across "experiences" (*Erlebnisse*) at all' (*SZ* 136, *BT* 175).

## The death of art

In the early Heidegger, *Erlebnis* names what is regarded as a general description for a pre-theoretical phenomenological starting point. However, in the work leading up to *Being and Time* this concept is rethought in non-Cartesian, non-anthropological directions as states-of-mind (*Befindlichkeit*,

*Stimmung*) understanding and care (*Sorge*). In the 1930s, however, the word begins to be used in a quite different context, and it is deployed exclusively as a term of derision. No longer questioned ontologically – and with Heidegger's emerging interest in the work of art and Hölderlin's poetry – the term *Erlebnis* is now regarded as central to subjectivist aesthetics. Perhaps the clearest definition of the later sense comes from Heidegger's 1934 lecture, *Hölderlin's Hymns 'Germania' and 'The Rhine'*, where Heidegger characterizes a certain vulgar idea of poetry as 'an expression of lived experiences' whether they be the experiences of an individual, or collectively as a 'mass' or cultural soul, or a particular race – the soul of a people. In Heidegger's writing, *Erlebnis* is certainly associated with late nineteenth-century aesthetics and neo-Kantianism, but also with the cultural philosophy of National Socialism and its 'mania' for lived-experiences. Thus, he associates the concept of *Erlebnis* as an expression of a cultural soul with authors like Spengler and Nazi ideologues such as Rosenberg, and the expression of a race with National Socialist figures like Kolbenheyer who states, 'Poetry is a biologically necessary function of the people' (*GA 39 27, HH 27*).[13]

As the mid-1930s progress, Heidegger begins to conceive of *Erlebnis* as the specific aesthetic reception of art that prevents the work of art from functioning as an event in which truth happens. Both in the epilogue to 'The Origin of the Work of Art' and in the Nietzsche lectures of 1936, Heidegger associates the aesthetic experience of art, experienced as *Erlebnis*, with Hegel's famous pronouncement of the death of art. It is in his *Aesthetics* and *Lectures on Aesthetics* that Hegel announces the decline of the era of great art, beginning at the end of the later Middle Ages. Hegel's decline, where art no longer counts for us as the highest vocation, but something past, is what Heidegger has in mind when he writes, in the epilogue of 'The Origin of the Work of Art':

> Lived Experience (*das Erlebnis*) is the source that is standard not only for art appreciation and enjoyment but also for artistic creation (*Kunstschaffen*). Everything is an experience (*Erlebnis*). Yet perhaps lived experience (*Erlebnis*) is the element in which art dies. The dying occurs so slowly that it takes a few centuries. (*GA 5 66, BW 204*)

Corresponding to this decline of art's power to reveal truth is the increasing dominance, in modernity, of the aesthetic experience of art. With its newly granted autonomous status art loses its function of revealing and preserving the essence of beings: its 'absolute need (*absolutes Bedürfnis*)' (*GA 6.1* 82, *N I* 84). In contrast to what Heidegger describes as the 'necessity' of living questioning at the beginning of philosophy, mere contemplation of the beautiful induces relaxation and pleasure and, as Heidegger provocatively comments, 'art then belongs in the domain of the pastry chef' (*GA 40* 101, *IM* 140).

## Aesthetic experience

Despite Hegel's announcement, Heidegger notes, in the Nietzsche lectures of 1936, that art continues as the nineteenth-century cult of *Erlebnis*, 'the "lived experience" as such becomes decisive' (*GA 6.1* 85, *N I* 86) and 'the world is examined and evaluated on the basis of its capacity to produce the aesthetic state' (*GA 6.1* 90, *N I* 90). Heidegger is careful to make a distinction between Nietzsche's view of art and the commonplace view of aesthetics. From Heidegger's point of view, the aesthetic consideration of art is a meditation which observes the state of feeling aroused by the beautiful, where the work of art is reduced to the bearer of the beautiful and hence the provoker of the aesthetic state of feeling. Heidegger words it in the form of a tautology: 'aesthetics is consideration of man's state of feeling in its relation to the beautiful; it is consideration of the beautiful to the extent that it stands in relation to man's state of feeling' (*GA 6.1* 75–6, *N I* 78) and, consequently, 'man's state of feeling' remains 'the point of departure and the goal of the meditation' (*GA 6.1* 76, *N I* 78). The work of art then becomes an object that is only accessible in terms of the states of feeling, that is, of *Erlebnis*. The knowledge associated with aesthetics is then limited to knowledge of human behaviour in relation to the states of sensation and feeling. With the nineteenth-century cult of *Erlebnis*, art's epistemological functioning is reduced in favour of its capacity to transfer the sensibilities and feelings of the artist. It is not surprising that Heidegger – in keeping close to the subject of Nietzsche's writings – provides as his example the experience of the musical *Gesamtkunstwerkes* of Richard Wagner which he describes as being characterized by 'the domination of the pure state of feeling – the tumult (*Brunst*) and delirium (*Raserie*) of the senses (*Sinne*)' (*GA 6.1* 85, *N I* 86). Art becomes an 'absolute need' but the 'absolute is experienced as total dissolution into sheer feeling (*reine Gefühl*)' (*GA 6.1* 86, *N I* 87). *Erlebnis* then, for Heidegger, is the experience in which art's 'absolute need', of spirit

(*Geist*) in the Hegelian sense, becomes circumvented, or degraded, by feeling and emotion conveyed by way of aesthetic apprehension.

## Machination

In the late 1930s Heidegger becomes increasingly critical of representational thinking, instrumental reason, objectification of beings and the calculative drive of modern technics, but he is also consistently critical of any humanist, anthropomorphic appeal to 'life' as a countermovement to rationality. In the lecture series of 1937–8, Basic Questions of Philosophy: Selected 'Problems' of 'Logic', Heidegger argues that *Erlebnis* not only is a superficial reaction to reason but actually stems from the self-certainty of the Cartesian subject's representational thinking: 'lived experience is only a base descendant of the Cartesian *cogito ergo sum*' (*GA 45* 149, *BQP* 129). Heidegger thus begins to regard *Erlebnis* as intimately connected to the *Machenschaft* of representational thinking. The word *Machenschaft*, in Heidegger's usage, does not mean machination in the sense of plotting and contriving, but rather it is the way in which beings are apprehended in terms of something made, according to a productionist metaphysics, but also the word alludes to power (*Macht*). These two poles – *Machenschaft* and *Erlebnis* – however, do not stand in opposition but, in a certain way, belong to each other; they name 'the two poles between which the ordinary conception of truth – correctness – oscillates' (*GA 45* 148–9, *BQP* 128–9). Lived-experience is described as the mode of contemporary experience where the question of truth is without need or necessity. Heidegger says that at the end of Western thought, where we now stand, lived-experience prevents us from questioning the most obvious, 'what everybody always knows' when it is said, for example, that 'the stone *is*, the sky *is* overcast'. And, consequently, 'Being is something forgotten' (*GA 45* 184, *BQP* 159, Heidegger's emphasis).

Heidegger thus speaks of the necessity for the 'overcoming of metaphysics', in conjunction with the 'overcoming of aesthetics'. However, 'overcoming' (*Überwindung*) needs to be thought, not as conquest, victory, replacing or usurping. Heidegger wishes us to hear, as Gianni Vattimo emphasizes, a certain sense of *Verwindung*, as torsion, twisting free and, at the same time, as incorporating what is left behind. Conversely, overcoming in the sense of replacing is what characterizes, for Heidegger, the object of Nietzsche's thinking of the will to power. Nietzsche's thinking promises to be the countermovement to Hegel's absolute knowledge as spirit of the will. Instead, Heidegger argues, it belongs to it and completes it. In the essay 'Overcoming Metaphysics', Heidegger contends that the will to power prepares the way for what he calls the final stage of the will's development in the completion of metaphysics as 'will to will' (*Wille zum Willen*). According to Heidegger's reading of Nietzsche, truth and art (conceived as values) both come under the dominance of the will to power, where truth is thought as stability, and art is thought as 'lack of mindfulness' (*Besinnungslosigkeit*) and *Erlebnis*. In Heidegger's thinking – under the heading of technics – planning, calculative thinking and stability come together with Nietzsche's idea of the creator-genius, who produces art as a stimulator of lived-experiences which, in turn, guarantees the business of art and culture. In 'Overcoming Metaphysics', Heidegger claims that:

> The will to will (*Wille zum Willen*) presupposes as the condition of its possibility the guarantee of stability (truth) and the possibility of exaggerating drives (art). Accordingly, the will to will arranges even beings as Being. In the will to will, technology (guarantee of stability) and the unconditional lack of reflection *Erlebnis* first come to dominance. (*GA* 7 83, *EP* 99)

Together, modern technics and *Erlebnis* obstruct mindfulness (*Besinnung*) and the thinking of the history of being. *Erlebnis* is here related to a certain reception of Nietzsche's thought in the nineteenth century, characterized by the 'Wagnerian cult', which interpreted his work in an aesthetic direction. Instead of being careful and mindful, Heidegger observes, this thinking loses itself in superficiality, ahistoricality, opaqueness and the 'chaos of life' (*GA* 7 77, *EP* 94).

By 1940 Heidegger sees Nietzsche's conception of art as a configuration of the will to power as remaining thoroughly within subjectivity, where subjectivity now incorporates not just the subjective will but the will as will to power. The question of being stands outside the subject–object correlation, and that means standing outside of the domain of the will. Although Nietzsche opposes Cartesian subjectivity, Heidegger contends that, for Nietzsche, man is still subject and his 'interpretation of being as a whole as will to power is rooted in the . . . subjectivity of drives and affects and at the same time is essentially co-determined through the projection of beingness as representedness'.[14] Will to power *is* will to will and the metaphysics of subjectivity attains its peak.

## Wonder and estrangement

From the time of the earliest iterations of his 1935–6 essay, 'The Origin of the Work of Art', and his lecture course, *Introduction to Metaphysics* (1935), Heidegger had begun to utilize a different sense of the Greek word *technē* than he had in the period of fundamental ontology, where it was restricted to its narrow sense in Platonic-Aristotelian philosophy – that is, as the know-how of making and producing equipment and handicrafts. *Technē*, in the late 1930s, becomes more like *physis*, the powerful upsurge that is the emergent-abiding sway (*das aufgehend-verweilende Walten*) of beings, but it is *other* than it. The counter violence of *technē* against *physis* is characterized, as Heidegger shows – in *Introduction to Metaphysics* – in Sophocles' poem, *Antigone*, by *deinon*, the uncanny (*Unheimlich*) and violent (*Gewalt*) (*GA 40* 121–2, *IM* 169–70), by which man 'holds sway' (*walten*) over *physis*. However, by 1936 – in the final published version of 'The Origin of the Work of Art', and in the first series of Nietzsche lectures – Heidegger no longer characterizes *technē* in terms of primordial violence, and much of the voluntarist emphasis of the earlier versions and *Introduction to Metaphysics* has disappeared. Although *technē* is still described in terms of a self-emerging eruption, Heidegger stresses that this eruption, a going forward (*Vorgehen*) in the midst of *physis*, 'is no kind of attack: it lets what is already coming into presence arrive' (*GA 6.1* 80, *N I* 82).

In the lecture course of 1937–8 Heidegger takes a slightly different turn and reinscribes *technē* as the basic attitude towards what the Greeks called *thaumazein*, translated by Heidegger as wonder (*Er-staunen*), the basic disposition (*Grundstimmung*) of philosophical questioning. Wonder is not to be understood as a quest for the marvellous or the exceptional. Rather, in wonder, the most usual, the everyday, becomes most unusual; like *deinon*: strange. Wonder cannot escape this condition by penetrating the unusualness by way of explanation, as that would render it as something that is not: assimilating the other to the same. Instead, for Heidegger, wonder dwells in between the most usual and the unusual. In this between, 'wonder (*das*

*Er-staunen*) – understood transitively – brings forth the showing of what is most usual in its unusualness (*Gewöhnlichsten in seiner Ungewöhnlichkeit*)' (*GA* 45 168, *BQP* 145). We can begin to see that *technē*, considered in the broad pre-Socratic sense, refers to a kind of knowledge that cannot be reduced to calculation, explanation or circumscription. This is the knowledge that guides artistic creation, but it is also the knowledge that *is* artistic creation, that constitutes the work of art. Such a knowledge differs from rationality in that it constitutes a sustained questioning that knows no closure.

Creating the work of art is not, as we have seen, a production – in the sense of fabrication tools and equipment, or handicrafts. But this does not mean that making art is simply a more profound or noble activity. For Heidegger, artistic production is entirely other. It is not thought in terms of the fabrication of a representation present in the mind of the artist: an eidetic image or idea, but rather as instituting the very conditions for things that already exist to disclose themselves. Creation (*schaffen*) is not thought in the way that modern subjectivism interprets it as the wilful activity of genius, but as the drawing up as of water from a spring (*schöpfen*). The artist thus opens up a world by letting something be. But this work of opening up, even as it involves acceptance, is far from passive. Rather than being spontaneous or intuitive, the process of creating involves thinking which issues from wonder. The work of art inaugurates a disturbance in which there occurs a suspension of habitual relations to the world. That is, the work instigates the condition, or rather the attunement of wonder, in which thinking (*Denken*) happens in terms of the 'preservation of the wondrous (*Bewahrung des Er-staunlichen*)' which maintains *physis* in unconcealment. In the same sense, in the 'Origin' lectures, Heidegger claims that the 'thrust' of the work of art – the very fact that a work of art *is* a work of art – transports us out of the realm of the commonplace and into the extraordinary. As Heidegger writes:

> The more solitary the work, fixed in the figure (Gestalt), stands on its own and the more cleanly it seems to cut all ties to human beings, the more simply does the thrust (*Stoß*) come into the open (*Offene*) that such a work is, and the more essentially is the extraordinary (*Ungeheure*) thrust to the surface (*aufgestoßen*) and what is long-familiar (*bislang geheure*) thrust down (*umgestoßen*). But this multiple thrusting (*vielfältige Stoßen*) is nothing violent, for the more purely the work is itself transported into the openness (*Offenheit*) of beings – an openness opened by itself – the more

simply does it transport us out of the realm of the ordinary (*Gewöhnlichen*). (*GA* 5 54, *BW* 191)

The word *Stoß* is usually translated as 'thrust' (as it is by both Julian Young and Albert Hofstadter).[15] However, the word can be translated into English in a number of different ways as 'stroke', 'jolt', 'kick', 'knock', 'push', 'shove' and so on. *Stoß* is thought in the sense of a physical shock. We might render *Stoß* as 'jolt',[16] and thus hear Heidegger to say that 'The setting-into-work' of truth [that the work of art instigates] jolts up the extraordinary (*Un-geheure*) and at the same time jolts down the ordinary (*Geheure*) (*GA* 5 63, *BW* 200, translation modified). What produces the *Stoß* is not any particular form or content but the bare fact that the work of art as a work *is*: the 'that it is (*Daß*) of [its] createdness', which is normally used up in usefulness (in equipment), and usually sinks back into inconspicuousness (*GA* 5 53, *BW* 190). However, the extraordinary that is jolted up is not a special modality of consciousness, or an escape from boredom, in a distracted turn to spectacle. Rather, it is a disposition or attunement in which the usual is found to be extraordinary. It is in this attunement, and in the preservation of this attunement, that thinking happens. Moreover, this thinking requires 'dwelling'. Thus, in the 'Origin' lectures, Heidegger tells us that 'Preserving (*Bewahrung*) the work, as knowing, is a sober indwelling (*Inständigkeit*) in the extraordinariness (*Ungeheuren*) of the truth that is happening in the work' (*GA* 5 55, *BW* 192, translation modified).

## Knowing, willing, letting

Because the work of art transports us into the Open and out of the realm of the ordinary, Knowing, as well as doing, prizing and looking are thought in other than usual terms. They are, in their normative forms, Heidegger says, 'restrained' (*GA* 5 54, *BW* 191). This restraint (*Verhaltenheit*) allows the work to be what it is. Further, the restraint of the normative concept of knowing opens the space for another mode of knowing. This knowing, which is not the mere accumulation of facts or information, is initially described by Heidegger in the following terms: 'He who truly knows beings knows what he wills to do in the midst of them (*was er inmitten des Seienden will*).' The willing mentioned here should, as Heidegger insists, be thought in terms of the notion of resoluteness (*Entschlossenheit*) formulated in *Being and Time*.

The willing referred to in 1936 is certainly not the will of self-assertion that characterizes the Rectorial Address of 1933. Rather, Heidegger's notion of will has the character of grasping the essence of beings – being itself. Such a grasping of being is, for Heidegger, 'to remain knowingly exposed to its sudden advance, its presencing' (*GA 6.1* 56, *N I* 59). This notion of will is distinct from determinate agency. It is rather a mode of being that 'lets' the truth of beings come forth, in a way that is neither simply active nor passive, or, as Heidegger will remark in his later work, 'beyond the distinction between activity and passivity' (*GA 13* 41, *DOT* 61). Knowledge occurs through the work of art as a willing that, as preservation, Heidegger insists, 'does not deprive the work of its independence, does not drag it into the sphere of mere lived experience (*Erlebnis*), and does not degrade it to the role of a stimulator of such experience (*Erlebniserregers*)' (*GA 5* 55, *BW* 193). Rather than reducing the experience of the work of art to a private experience, preserving grounds being within the historical sending of the happening of truth, and enables Dasein's ecstatic-temporal entry into unconcealment. Art is thus something that happens in relation to the historical unfolding of being. Willing is, in a sense, for Heidegger, a kind of letting, and letting is conversely a kind of willing, or rather, knowing is a willing that is grounded in questioning, and willing is resoluteness.

## Resoluteness

In *Being and Time*, resoluteness is one of the ways in which the human existent (Dasein) – an entity which understands itself in terms of its own existence – surpasses the unavoidable 'thrownness' into the given situations of the everyday world, and comes into its own, being-one's-self. In the thrownness of the 'they' (*das Man*) Dasein makes no futural choices about itself and what it will be but is simply carried along. In order to escape this situation, it needs to be shown its possible 'ownmost' (*eigentlich*) self through an *existentiell* modification of the they-self. In this way – through the running ahead to, and holding open the possibility of, one's own death – Dasein becomes ownmost, 'authentic' being-one's-self. Here we encounter a problem of translation. *Eigentlich* is usually translated as 'authentic', which sets up an opposition between exceptional and originary purity, and fallen degraded banality, which, as Jean-Luc Nancy argues, is inconsistent with the existential analytic of *Being and Time*. However, as Nancy notes, at the same time, one cannot fail to notice Heidegger's '*existentiell* prejudice' which is manifested as a disdain for the banality of everyday existence and the privileging of the authentic, original and exceptional.[17] In *Being and Time*, resoluteness (*Entschlossenheit*) is conceived by Heidegger as 'a distinctive mode of Dasein's disclosedness (*Erschlossenheit*)' (*SZ* 136, *BT* 175). Heidegger often hyphenates the word 'resoluteness' as *Ent-schlossenheit* in order to emphasize its literal meaning: 'uncoveredness'. The decision (*Entscheidung*) of resoluteness, which is just as much an open letting as it is a decisive action, calls for the equiprimordial disclosure of the Self along with the 'there' in being-in-the-world, and as unclosedness brings the standing-within of preservation.

In a 1953 parenthetical note to the 1935 lecture series *Introduction to Metaphysics*, Heidegger maintains that 'all willing is grounded in letting' (*GA* 40 23, *IM* 22–3), and directs our attention to the 1930 lecture, 'On the Essence of Truth', where he insists that letting be, as freedom that is ek-sistent, standing outside itself, is not possessed by the human being as a property. Rather, freedom, in a certain way, possesses the human being. But this standing outside of *Existenz* is also a standing inside, as we saw in Heidegger's 'Origin' lectures, 'the out-standing standing-within the essential sunderance (*Auseinander*) of the clearing of beings' (*GA* 5 55, *BW* 192). This points to the indeterminate character of disclosure, as both fixing in place and letting be, which Heidegger observes in the 1956 addendum to 'The Origin of the Work of Art': 'this letting is nothing passive but a doing of the highest degree . . . in the sense of thesis, a "working" and "willing" that in the present essay is characterized as the "existing human being's ecstatic entry into the unconcealment of Being"' (*GA* 5 71, *BW* 208). Thought this way, willing is not goal-oriented striving, nor must letting be thought of as neglect. Rather, both willing and letting are resolute.

## Nietzsche's aesthetics

Heidegger contends that Nietzsche's aesthetics remains within metaphysics. In considering creation and the essence of art solely in terms of the artist,

Nietzsche continues the nineteenth-century aesthetic attitude of *Erlebnis*. As Heidegger reads it, in Nietzsche's conception of art the reception of the work of art follows in the wake of the artist-creator so that the beholder of the work participates in the state of feeling of the creator. Although Nietzsche's conception of the aesthetic state (of *Rausch*) as tumult may differ from the expression of soulful lived-experiences of felt emotions, the model, as Heidegger sees it, is essentially the same: art transmits the emotional states – albeit the physiological feelings – of the artist to the receiver. Against this conception, Heidegger argues that, as in the 'Origin' lectures, inquiry into art should proceed from the work itself and in that way unfold creation in a mode of bringing-forth (*Hervorbringen*) that is adequately distinguishable from the bringing-forth of utensils. The essence of art, for Heidegger, is to be sought in the actual work of art itself which is where truth happens. Because the work is not a 'mere' thing (*bloße Ding*) among others but, rather, something worked, Heidegger finds it necessary to turn to an inquiry into the work's createdness. However, he attempts to think createdness in terms other than the *ens creatum* of Christianity and its derivative notions. Instead, he thinks of the creative process as a 'bringing-forth' (*Hervorbringen*), or an 'eruption' (*Aufbruch*).

Although Nietzsche's conception of art falls into aesthetics – even though it is an extreme aesthetics – a 'masculine' aesthetics – Heidegger finds the resources in Nietzsche's meditation on art to set in motion a self-overcoming of aesthetics. If art as the most transparent form of the will to power has the capacity to function as the countermovement to nihilism, this capacity lies in the non-aesthetic determinations of Rausch (rapture, intoxication) and beauty: where Rausch is the basic mood and beauty is the attunement. Here Heidegger, pushing Nietzsche's terms to the limit, proposes that '*Rausch* as a state of feeling explodes the very subjectivity of the subject. By having a feeling for beauty, the subject has already come out of himself; he is no longer subjective, no longer a subject' (*GA 6.1* 124, *N I* 123).

Heidegger's reading of Nietzsche's self-overcoming of aesthetics proceeds from a seemingly ambiguous position on the role of the will. At one point, Heidegger takes Nietzsche and Schopenhauer to task for their misinterpretation of Kant's requirement of disinterest in the aesthetic judgement of works of art. The disinterest that is essential to the pure aesthetic judgement is commonly thought – and also defined by Schopenhauer – as a form of quietism that suspends all willing in a 'sheer apathetic drift' (*GA 6.1* 108, *N I* 108). In contradistinction, Heidegger interprets disinterest in the judgement of the beautiful by drawing on a word that is used quite sparingly in the *Critique of Judgement*: favour (*Gunst*). As Heidegger interprets it, *freie Gunst* is a free granting and 'letting (*lassen*) the beautiful be what it is' (*GA 6.1* 109, *N I* 109). This letting, however, does not put the will out of commission in the sense of reducing the comportment to the beautiful to a passive 'not-willing'. Rather it purifies the relation between Dasein and world, so that the beautiful essentially determines us in a way in which 'we ascend beyond ourselves' (*GA 6.1* 113, *N I* 113). For Nietzsche, this disclosure of the beautiful occurs in rapture (*Rausch*). Although Nietzsche's rhetoric may at times sound like Wagner's submersion into *Erlebnis*, for Heidegger it is the exact opposite. Nietzsche's mood of rapture (*Rausch*) 'is rather an attunement in the sense of the most supreme and measured determinateness' (*GA 6.1* 113, *N I*, 113). Yet there seems to be a tension between free granting and letting, on the one hand, and wilful determinateness, on the other hand. How does Heidegger accommodate this contradiction?

What makes Heidegger's position on the will in the years 1936 to 1940 quite confusing is that in 'The Will to Power as Art' the ecstatic 'most proper will' is described in a positive sense as 'self-willing' and 'will to will', the very terms which are used in a negative sense in his later thinking. Further, the not-willing (*Nichtwollen*) of aesthetic *Erlebnis* must be distinguished from the non-willing (*Nicht-Wollen*) thinking that appears in the mid-1940s, in *Feldweg-Gespräche* (1944/45) and *Gelassenheit* (1944–55). Not-willing is simply the obverse of self-assertion which together forms the domain of the subjective will. Passive resignation and the self-assertive will to mastery over beings belong together. In the later 1930s, however, that which escapes this subjective willing is the authentic willing of the 'most proper will'.

For Heidegger, by way of 'the grand style', Nietzsche grasps the essence of creation in art through a distinction between the classical and the romantic. Whereas the classical is active and flows out of itself, the romantic constitutes a reactive form of creation that stems from the artist's dissatisfaction with himself and the world. It is a counter-will characterized by Heidegger as 'a wanting-to-be-away-from-oneself' (*Von-sich-weg-wollen*) (*GA 6.1* 161, *N I* 136) and is as such a 'not-willing' (*Nichtwollen*) which stands in opposition to the most proper will (what Brett Davis describes as 'ecstatic incorporation'). Heidegger puts it this way: 'Will is open resoluteness (*Entschlossenheit*) toward itself, because willing is willing beyond itself (*über sich hinaus wollen*), it is the strength that is able to bring itself to power' (*GA 6.1* 38, *N I* 41). In such a way a self-overcoming of aesthetics is made possible where aesthetics, 'within itself, is led beyond itself. . . . Such states are what they essentially are when, willing out beyond themselves, they are more than they are. . . . The artistic states are – and that means art is – nothing else than *will to power*' (*GA 6.1* 130, *N I* 129–30, Heidegger's emphasis). The work of art becomes less important for Heidegger after 1940 when a certain pessimism regarding modern art begins to be expressed. Unlike Gadamer, Heidegger was not interested in avant-garde art, with the exception of a few select artists including Paul Klee and the Basque Sculptor Eduardo Chillida.

## Displacing aesthetics

We have seen that in Heidegger's 'Origin' lectures, letting is associated with knowing, and with willing that is in a certain way a kind of letting or non-willing. For Heidegger the preservers of the work of art are equally much a part of the work as the work's creators. While the preserver is what wilfully lets the work endure, such a description should not be limited to the work of curators and museums. I would suggest that Heidegger saw himself as a preserver – particularly in relation to Hölderlin's poetry. The notion of the preserver can thus be taken to include an 'authentic' way of receiving the work that is neither one of thematic interpretation, nor of passive contemplation but, rather, involves, as Heidegger stresses, indwelling or 'standing-within' the openness opened up by the work. In other words, what we find in the notion of preserving is the possibility of a non-aesthetic, and non-conceptual, encounter with the work of art. However, from what we have seen, the possibility of such encounters depends on the work's capacity not only to render what is the most usual – and even its own existence – strange, but also to keep the open space that the work of art breaks open, in a state of lingering openness. This process of estrangement interrupts the willing non-passivity of the receiver, paving the way to a thinking (i.e. a questioning) that is other than willing.

The displacement of aesthetics involves a rethinking of the work of art's createdness as an event that lets phenomena emerge, rather than producing an object according to a preconceived idea or a wilful act. This bringing-forth (*Hervorbringen*) out of concealment is, for Heidegger, named in his reinterpretation of the original senses of the Greek words *technē* and *poiēsis*. It is my contention that Heidegger's notions of primal strife, letting, non-willing thinking and gathering pave the way for a reassessment of the avant-garde strategies of defamiliarization and creative indeterminacy. It is particularly in relation to these two ideas that Heidegger's project for the overcoming of aesthetics finds consonance (beyond his knowledge of modern art) with actual practices (that also remain unaware of his philosophy). I am arguing that, in a certain way, to a certain extent, the contingency theories of John Cage, and some of the post-Cagean and Fluxus artists, open up possibilities for rethinking art in a certain way outside of both aesthetics and instrumental thought (this is not to say that this constitutes the only way). It is well known that Cage derives his notions of indeterminacy, interpenetration, change and the like from Eastern philosophy: Zen Buddhism in particular, and from the mystical tradition of Meister Eckhart – to whom Heidegger's notion of non-willing thinking is indebted. Chapter 5 will examine these connections. I am certainly not the first to observe a correlation between Cage's notions of indeterminacy and the thinking of late Heidegger. Gerald Bruns links Cage's chance operations to Heidegger's notion of *Gelassenheit*.[18]

Far from comprising the surrendering of will to a higher power, these strategies of chance and indeterminacy, or systems and constraints, become the practical carrying out of *Gelassenheit*. In other words, the chance operation in its rigorous form of artistic practice may be seen to be one answer to Heidegger's riddle in *Country Path Conversations*: how does one will non-willing? As Davis points out, although *Nicht-Wollen* may be translated as either 'not-willing' or 'non-willing', the neither active nor passive middle-voiced sense of non-willing, rather than the passive surrender of will, is what comes to light in Heidegger's later work. The chance operation in artistic practices is unthinkable without this idea of the artist's resolute intention to make, name and preserve the work of art *as* art. As the artist Robert Morris points out, in an essay published in 1970, this non-willing, where 'the artist has stepped aside for more of the world to enter the art', not only restricts the deployment of the arbitrary in the working process but involves a certain commitment, which involves 'going through with something'.[19] Moreover, the avant-garde practice of putting creative, or even conceptual, decision making a step removed from the will of the artist – by letting phenomena be – allows an encounter with these phenomena that avoids the distortion of aesthetic and conceptual presuppositions. In this sense, such a practice could be said to perform a fundamental phenomenological operation, albeit one in which the central focus is towards a radical otherness rather than the ideality of truth and meaning.

Can certain sound and media art practices instigate the presuppositionless conditions for a knowing that happens as a preservation of the wondrous in the most usual? Can they be conceived of as inaugurating the disposition (*Stimmung*) which, as Heidegger says, 'transports us into this or that basic relation to beings as such', or 'More precisely . . . transports (*Ver-setzende*) us in such a way that it co-founds the time-space (*Zeit-Raum*) of the transporting (*Versetzung*) itself' (*GA 24* 154, *BQP* 134). 'To "listen to" *Stimmung*', as Michel Haar observes, 'it is necessary not only to eschew the definitions given by the rational faculty of the understanding but to take one's distance from the egocentric *interiority* of feeling and its *intentionality*.'[20] What would this listening be?

# 5

# Purposive purposelessness

Chance figures in Cage's work as a way of substituting self-alteration for self-expression. Art then becomes not the process of closing oneself off from the world, in order to express something inner out into the world, but a process of opening the self up to the world to accept the contingent. This, I would contend, is the basis of Cage's philosophy. In this chapter I will examine some of the philosophical currents that inform Cage's doctrine of openness to the world. The aspiration of Cage's work is asking questions that lead to a new way of knowing life and the world (our relation to our immediate environment) through sound. Cage often refers to the 'happening' of this knowing simply as *change*. In an interview with C. H. Waddington, in 1972, Cage clarifies his position.

> So I want to give up the traditional view that art is a means of self-expression for the view that art is a means of self-alteration, and what it alters is *mind*, and mind is in the world and is a social fact. . . . We will change *beautifully* if we *accept* uncertainties of change; and this should affect any planning. This is a *value*.[1]

Cage's idea of change originates not only from the tradition of Zen Buddhism but also from the thought of Meister Eckhart, and in particular Eckhart's statement quoted by Cage: 'we are made perfect by what happens to us rather than what we do.'[2] A state of 'unselfconsciousness', unknowing or 'ignorance' is what is required, according to Eckhart, to initiate the change that brings us to perfection. But this unknowing does not come from a lack of knowledge; rather, it emerges through the overcoming of self-will (*Eigenwille*) which, for Eckhart, presents an obstacle to God's revealing of true being. The unselfconsciousness that Eckhart proposes, and the empty 'no mind' (*wu-nien*) of Zen, for Cage, are one and the same. Cage maintains that the composer and listener must remain, in the words of Eckhart, 'innocent and free to receive anew with each Now-moment a heavenly gift.'[3] In Eckhart's terms, the word 'free' (*ledic* in Middle High German, *ledig* in modern German), as Brett Davis points out, means both empty and free from worldly attachments.[4] But this emptiness does not mean adopting a simply passive attitude or doing nothing. We still act, but rather than acting according to our own will, all action issues out of what Eckhart calls the 'ground'.

The sources of Cage's thinking, for the most part, can be traced to Eastern philosophy, from Kegan Zen Buddhism, through access to the courses of Daisetz Teitaro Suzuki, but also from Sri Ramakrishna, Daoism and the work of the Indian art historian Ananda K, Coomaraswamy. There is no indication that Cage had ever read Heidegger,[5] but he was quite familiar with Eckhart's vernacular writings, first introduced to him through Coomaraswamy's *The Transformation of Nature in Art*, and later through Suzuki's lectures. However, it is known that Cage had encountered the two-volume English translation of Franz Pfeiffer's 1857 collection of Eckhart's sermons by C. de B. Evans (first published in 1924) before he began his study with Suzuki at Columbia University in New York in the early 1950s. The Evans translation is the same translation that Coomaraswamy references, and is one of two translations that Suzuki references in *Mysticism, Christian and Buddhist*.[6]

Eckhart's work receives a warm reception in Heidegger's work, at first in the early work (his 1915 *Habilitationsschrift*), but more significantly after the turn (*Kehre*) where the idea of releasement (*Gelassenheit*) is gleaned directly from Eckhart. Heidegger also engages in a dialogue with Zen Buddhism, and there are indications that his thought was significantly influenced by Daoism. Thus, in this chapter I do not intend to merely point to parallels between Eckhart and Cage but more so between Eckhart and Heidegger as well as Heidegger and Cage simply because I think it is much easier to come to grips with Cage's philosophy from the atheistic perspective of Heidegger rather than the theistic perspective of Eckhart. Heidegger's later thought offers a non-theological appropriation of Eckhart's sermons, and at least on the surface, Cage's Zen-influenced interpretation of Eckhart, I would contend, is much closer to the thought of Heidegger which reinscribes Eckhart's 'God' and 'soul' in terms of being and Dasein.

## Detachment

Daniel Charles describes his series of interviews with Cage in 1970 as a 'multiple and unique gloss of Chuang-tze',[7] and an attempt disclose Cage's Daoism. Charles frames many of his questions from a philosophical as much as a musical perspective, and as much as he seeks to bring out Cage's Daoism, he also formulates his questions in alignment with the thought of Eckhart, Heidegger and Zen Buddhism. In the course of inquiring into Cage's chance operations Charles puts the following question to Cage:

> Your teaching – if you accept that term – then, could be defined as a pedagogy of non-intention? A detachment with respect to will?

Cage responds:

> A progressive detachment, yes, and one which would not fall back into any attachment. A detachment that would not repeat anything.[8]

In referring to 'detachment', it is certain that both Cage and Charles have in mind the sense of this word from Eckhart's treatise *On Detachment*. Detachment translates *Abgeschiedenheit*,[9] which, in Eckhart's terms, signifies the soul's separation from worldly things. In Eckhart's language, the soul withdraws from any interest in creatures, in favour of a purer relation to God: ultimately a breakthrough to the Godhead. In terms of this breakthrough, detachment involves a letting go (*Ablassen*) of self-will. Self-will is let go in the process of a releasement to God's will. The terms 'detachment' (*Abgeschiedenheit*) and 'releasement' (*Gelassenheit*) are almost synonymous in Eckhart's thought. One could say that releasement includes detachment, or that detachment is the first stage of releasement.

At this point, let me make an important distinction. For Cage, the chance operation is the *epochē* that comes into play in the process of the creation of the work of art. It is, as I have suggested, in phenomenological terms, a *temporary* suspension of the will as a means of bracketing the natural attitude.[10] Detachment, on the other hand, relates to change and self-alteration. It involves the ongoing practice of aleatory procedures as a means of breaking free from the domain of the will, as Cage says earlier 'a progressive detachment'. Unlike the *epochē*, detachment is not temporary: it would not fall back into any attachment. In a similar way to any Zen practice this activity must certainly be a slow process. It is a process that gradually cultivates acceptance of chance and randomness, and simultaneously instils a way of living that lets things (and sounds) be, beyond the domain of the will. The chance operation is an abstention, a bracketing, that leads to the first negative moment of *Gelassenheit*, the giving up of likes and dislikes, a loosening and acceptance leading to the second moment of letting sounds be, in a turn towards being. Cage's practice of non-intention is first a detachment but also a releasement or letting be (*Gelassenheit*) from self-will – the 'likes and dislikes' as Cage often puts it – of the composer. It is worth noting that *Abgeschiedenheit* is sometimes translated as 'disinterest'. Detachment, as Eckhart puts it, 'is minded to be master of itself, loving none and hating none, having neither likeness nor unlikeness, neither this nor that, to any creature. . . . It leaves things unmolested.'[11] In Cage's terms, however, it is not the soul that is detached but the mind.

Heidegger's interpretation of detachment similarly differs somewhat from Eckhart's meaning. Whereas, for Eckhart, it is the cutting off of the soul's affection from creatures, and a withdrawal from worldly things. For Heidegger, as John D. Caputo observes, the first moment of *Gelassenheit* is characterized by Dasein's detachment from beings in order to 'let' being be, and proceeds in a manner of willing not to will.[12] Detachment preserves the ontological difference between being and beings reversing the modern priority of a concern with beings. The second moment of *Gelassenheit* consists of a turn towards being where every vestige of the will is let go. Similarly, for Davis, Eckhartian *Gelassenheit* involves in its first moment a detachment from all created things, whereas Heidegger's appropriation of it involves in its second moment a releasement towards things.[13] How then can *Gelassenheit* be both a withdrawal from beings and movement towards things? Because what Heidegger means by a detachment *from* 'beings' signifies, in the language of *Being and Time*, to break out of a mode of existence caught up in the everyday deficiency of 'the they' (*das Man*); and the releasement *to* things means, in the language of the later Heidegger, a disposition towards the thing which gathers the fourfold (*das Geviert*) of earth and sky, divinities and mortals, in such a way as to provide a site for it.

Detachment and releasement for Eckhart involve an emptying of the soul of any trace of 'self-love' (*Eigenliebe*) and 'self-will' (*Eigenwille*). For Eckhart, our will must become God's will. Heidegger refrains from deploying releasement in what he sees as essentially moral and ethical terms – though one might say there is a broader ethical dimension to *Gelassenheit* (in as much as it raises the possibility of non-anthropocentric ecology). Rather, it is in relation to thinking (*Denken*) that self-will, or any will, for that matter, is to be overcome. To think outside of the domain of the will is to think in a mode of thought not governed by the representational thinking (*Vorstellung*) of modern subjectivism, in which, as Heidegger contends, being and all beings are reduced to objects for human subjects. Heidegger thus conceives non-representational thinking in terms of *Gelassenheit* which does not belong to the determining and entrapping domain of the will – as a willing to know that seeks explanation, or wants to actualize – and, at the same time, is neither mere passive acceptance, nor the submission to a divine will.[14] *Gelassenheit*, lying beyond the distinction between activity and passivity, is both a middle-voiced active letting, or wilful acceptance of the Open, and an openly composed steadfastness – a receiving that gradually leads to determining – that Heidegger calls 'in-dwelling', or 'standing within' (*Inständigkeit*) (*GA 13* 64, *DOT* 81).

It is important to stress that for Eckhart, Heidegger and Cage, detachment in no way constitutes a withdrawal from the everyday world of activity. It is not a reclusion from the world into silent contemplation. Rather, detachment involves activity. This is illustrated in Eckhart's interpretation of the Mary and Martha story where he clearly values Martha's busy activity over Mary's passive kneeling at the feet of Christ. For Heidegger, detachment is an affirmation of worldly existence although it involves – in terms of his early writings – a distancing from the being caught up in things of *daß Man* – and in terms of his later thought – a twisting free from representational thinking and the *Gestell* of modern technology. In both cases detachment constitutes a movement towards a more authentic or originary existence, but it certainly does not renounce everyday life. In the late Heidegger, detachment moves towards what he calls mindfulness (*Besinnung*). For Heidegger *Gelassenheit* requires waiting. For Cage it involves working – 'working for works sake' as Eckhart says – working 'without why'. Cage speaks about an 'active passivity', a seemingly paradoxical phrase which resembles 'purposeful purposelessness'. According to Mathew Mendez, it is active for two reasons: 'first, because adopting a passive stance entails a conscious decision, passivity always already being action and, second, because complicated schemes are required to maintain the stance.'[15] Active passivity involves a will to work non-willingly, a decision to engage in processes (not created objects) without a 'why' in view.

The most cited exposition of the term *Gelassenheit* appears in Heidegger's 1944–5 text *Gelassenheit* which takes the form of a triadic conversation between a scientist, a scholar and a teacher/guide. Here it is introduced into the conversation in the form of a critique of Eckhart:

> Teacher: ... the nature of releasement (*Gelassenheit*) is still hidden.
>
> Scholar: Especially so because even releasement can still be thought of as within the domain of the will, as is the case with old masters such as Meister Eckhart.
>
> Teacher: From whom, all the same, much can be learned.
>
> Scholar: Certainly; but what we have called releasement evidently does not mean casting off sinful selfishness and letting self-will go in favor of the divine will. (*G* 36, *GA 13* 41–2, *DOT* 61–2, *CPC* 70)[16]

Eckhart's *Gelassenheit* seems, for Heidegger, to still belong to the domain of the will for two reasons. First, Eckhart's concept is interpreted by Heidegger in a limited sense as a willing not to will. Second, it is criticized as a relinquishment of self-will to God's will, thus handing the will over to a divine will.

## Without why

In *Der Satz vom Grund* (*The Principle of Reason*), Heidegger juxtaposes Leibniz's principle that 'nothing is without reason' (*nihil est sine ratione*), against a phrase from the poet Angelus Silesius, from the poem 'Ohne warum', from the collection *The Cherubic Wanderer: Sensual Description of the Four Final Things*:

> The rose is without why: it blooms because it blooms,
>
> It pays no attention to itself, asks not whether it is seen.[17]

It is not Heidegger's intention to overthrow reason by appealing to mysticism. Rather, Heidegger wishes to subtly undermine or displace Leibniz's principle and put its ultimate authority into question. He does this by superimposing the counterexample, 'the rose is without why', onto what he renders as a reduced version of the strict form of the principle: 'nothing is without why.' Heidegger construes from the poem that 'man, in the most concealed grounds of his essence, first truly is when he is like the rose – without why' (*SG* 72–3, *PR* 38). We should, in other words, live without why, without seeking reasons. As many commentators have pointed out, the phrase 'without why' originates in Eckhart and, of course, Heidegger is well aware of this, and this informs his interpretation of the poem. In one instance Eckhart writes:

> The just man . . . wants nothing and seeks nothing; for he has no *why* for which he does anything, just as god acts without why and has no why (*ohn Warum wirkt kein Warum kennt*).[18]

In his very early compositions Cage adhered to what he then believed to be the traditional Western conception of music as a 'communication' of the composer's emotions, or intention to convey certain emotions, to the audience – the idea of self-expression. It was Cage's perception in hindsight that he failed in this task. Going through a period of depression and self-searching, Cage decided that he must find another purpose for composing music other than communication. By the 1950s he had come to the conclusion that finding a purpose was not important. In '45' for a Speaker' Cage writes, 'The highest purpose is to have no purpose at all,' which, for Cage, 'puts one in accord with nature and her manner of operation'.[19] In his maxim of 'purposeful purposelessness', Cage affirms a radical practice of living without why.

The phrase 'nature and her manner of operation' in the above-mentioned quote is usually quoted by Cage in the form 'art imitates nature in her manner of operation' which, as Cage frequently reveals, is attributed to Coomaraswamy. The phrase, however, does not appear, at least in that form, in *The Transformation of Nature in Art* – the text that Cage often cites – but as 'for the East, as for St Thomas, *ars imitatur naturam in sua operatione*'.[20] The phrase, as Cage scholars have known for some time, is from St Thomas Aquinas's *Summa Theologiae* 1a 117. [21] Cage certainly misinterprets Coomaraswamy's interpretation of the phrase which by all means belongs to a metaphysical aesthetics. Cage does not question Coomaraswamy's interpretation in order to provide an alternative interpretation. He merely misinterprets it. But he – perhaps naively, or perhaps under the guidance of Eckhart and Suzuki – creatively misinterprets it, radicalizing St Thomas's phrase or, perhaps, even restoring it to its original force, in the process.

Coomaraswamy characterizes Asiatic art as 'ideal in the mathematical sense: like Nature (*natura naturans*), not in appearance (viz. that of *ens naturata*), but in operation'.[22] Edward James Crooks argues – in an extensive and detailed account – that, in essence, Cage's interpretation corresponds to the idea of nature as *natura naturata* while Comaraswamy's sense is of *natura naturans*. In Medieval thought these two terms do not represent two opposing views of nature; rather, they correspond to the active (*naturans*) and passive (*naturata*) aspects of the one self-creating being of divine nature. *Natura naturata* corresponds to material nature perceived through the senses. It is regarded as the effect of mathematical structure and is thus closest to the idea of nature in the physical sciences. It names the objective products of nature. It is natured nature, matter that has been already created or moved to completion. In this way it is passive and finite; its meaning corresponds to the raw materials that the engineer utilizes. *Natura naturans*, on the other hand, in one sense, corresponds to the eternal essence of the natural object, the form or idea in contrast to empirical nature. It is infinite and boundless. It is conceptualized matter. Crooks is quite right to argue that Coomaraswamy understands *ars imitatur naturam in sua operatione* in terms of *natura naturans*. He also makes no error when he demonstrates that Cage's interpretation of the phrase is essentially hostile to symbolic forms and eternal ideas and is thus quite contrary to Coomaraswamy's interpretation. However, *natura naturans* has two senses that diverge according to the inherited tradition. *Natura naturans* signifies not only form (the natural object as it is in God) but also the active moving force.[23] This second sense of an actively producing, inexhaustible and infinite world force is much closer to the Greek conception of *physis*, and is much more aligned to the way Cage understands the phrase. *Physis* means for the Greeks the self-emerging coming into presence. The former (Platonic) sense of *natura naturans* as form/idea would regard art not as a copy of a copy but a copy of a form. The latter sense as moving force (which would seem to come from Aristotle) would put it quite differently. *Ars imitatur naturam*, as Jacques Maritain maintains, means that 'Artistic creation does not copy God's creation, but continues it'.[24] In words more in tune with Cage's thinking, artistic creation is analogous to an act of nature. He writes: 'many composers no longer make musical structures. Instead they set processes going. A structure is like a piece of furniture, whereas a process is like the weather.'[25]

As Maritain argues, *ars imitatur naturam*, 'does not mean: "art imitates Nature by reproducing it", but "art imitates Nature *by doing or operating* like Nature, *ars imitatur naturam* in SUA OPERATIONE"'.[26] If the emphasis is put on the active, moving, sense of *sua operatione*, then Cage's interpretation not only corresponds to *natura naturans* but would seem to be an interpretation is much closer to St Thomas than it would be to Coomaraswamy, since the essence of the distinction *naturans/naturata* lies in the difference between activity and passivity more so than with that which separates the ideal and the empirical. Cage often insists that he is interested in dealing with *processes* corresponding to the activity and operations of nature rather than *objects* of passive matter.[27] Coomaraswamy's interpretation presupposes the Aristotelian form and matter distinction. Cage's interpretation, in a curious way, is much closer to Kant's *Critique of Judgment*.

## Cage and Kantian aesthetics

Does Cage's rendering of St Thomas's phrase radically depart from modern aesthetics? One cannot help noticing how the phrase resembles Kant's description of art in the *Critique of Judgement*:

> In a product of art one must be aware that it is art, and not nature; yet the purposiveness in its form must still seem to be as free from all constraint by arbitrary rules *as if* it were a product of nature. On this feeling of freedom in the play of our cognitive powers, which must yet at the same time be purposive, rests that pleasure which is alone universally communicable, though without being grounded on concepts. Nature was beautiful, if at the same time it looked like art; and art can only be called beautiful if we are aware that it is art and yet it looks to us like nature.[28]

In *The Truth in Painting*, and in the essay 'Economimesis', Derrida singles out the analogical structure, the 'as if' (*als ob*) which he says governs the entirety of the third *Critique*. Although Kant explicitly rejects mimesis – the aesthetic judgement of free beauty depends on the spontaneous imagination, in opposition to the (mimetic) reproductive imagination – he implicitly re-establishes, by way of the 'as if', 'an analogical *mimesis* at the point where it appears detached' (*E* 9). Although works of art are not productions of nature, they must, according to Kant, resemble the effects of natural action at the very moment when they are most purely human works. Derrida writes:

> The artist does not imitate things in nature, or, if you will, in *natura naturata*, but the acts of *natura naturans*, the operation of the *physis*. But since an analogy has already made *natura naturans* the art of an author-subject, and, one could even say, of an artist-god, *mimesis* displays the identification of human action with divine action – of one freedom with another. (*E* 9)

This mimesis is not, as Derrida argues, a relation between two products – thing (or form) and its artistic representation – but between two productions – divine action and human action – between two producing subjects. In this 'true' mimesis, according to Derrida, a divine, immaculate, commerce is set up. In Derrida's terms, Cage's imitation of nature would constitute a form of mimesis, not as a copy of a copy or a copy of a form but, by analogy, as an anthropo-theological mimesis that imitates divine acts. Here we are led back to Eckhart and the question of deferred willing. However, since it is 'analogical', the mimesis here echoes not the content but only the structure of *natura naturans*. However, although it might appear that Derrida is criticizing Kant for falling into a mimetic trap – condemning imitation despite his own condemnations of what he regards as kind of 'servile' imitation – what is really at stake in the essay is that in this other mimesis, this 'true' mimesis, the opposition between nature and art is broken down, and it is at such a point that 'perhaps we rediscover the root of pleasure which, before being reserved for art and the beautiful, used to belong to knowledge' (*E* 9).

## Purposeful purposelessness

Although, in Cage's use, the phrase 'purposeful purposelessness' certainly has a Zen Buddhist ring to it, and is obviously used in an Eckhartian sense, it also seems to have a Kantian resonance. The phrase bears a resemblance to one of Kant's aesthetic concepts: his definition of beauty as '*Zweckmässigkeit ohne Zweck*', variously translated as 'purposiveness without end', 'finality without end' or 'purposiveness without purpose'. The phrases, however, are certainly not equivalent. One can clearly see that in Cage's phrase the subject and predicate are grammatically reversed in relation to their places in Kant's phrase. For Kant, the subject is positive: purposiveness. For Cage, the subject is negative: purposelessness. But this does not indicate a simple reversal of meaning.

One could simply dismiss Cage's 'purposeful purposelessness' as a form of mysticism and find it quite a questionable comparison to line it up against what is a crucial part of Kant's concept of reflective judgements, or, indeed, to place Cage's haiku like aphorisms alongside Kant's systematic approach. However, as we have seen in the quote cited earlier in the chapter, 'the highest purpose is to have no purpose', purposelessness is, according to Cage, the very condition for one to be in accord with nature in her manner of operation. Further, Kant's *Critique of Judgment* is not merely a theory of aesthetic pleasure. Its purpose is to uncover a mode of experience which mediates between the understanding and reason. Although it does not constitute a direct challenge to the principle of reason, in its boldest moments, it attempts to account for a transcendental principle of experience where reason might be at a loss, and where the laws of mechanical causality might not suffice to deliver a cognition. Kant describes a mode of experience which is supposedly not dependent upon reason but is neither irrational nor merely the consequence of ignorance in the subject. In an aesthetic judgement, according to Kant, an object of nature is perceived implicitly as something which has, or seems to have, a purposeful order but any representation of an order pertaining to a purpose is suspended in the act of making the judgement. In other words, an aesthetic judgement cannot be guided by any principle or purpose yet results in a cognition which seems to be organized according to laws.

A judgement, for Kant, is the act which mediates between the higher cognitive powers of understanding and reason. Kant divides judgements into two essential types: determining judgements and reflective judgements (of which there are two: aesthetic and teleological). Determining judgements subsume a particular under the concept of a universal. The reflective judgement, on the other hand, must attempt to find the universal by way of the particular and, at the same time, has no cognitive contribution to make about the particular. Its use would seem quite limited in contrast to determining judgements. But since determining judgements might sometimes fail to find a universal, or a lawful unity, in the face of contingent particulars, reflective judgements find their role. But they are required to operate without objective grounds. As Rodolphe Gasché formulates it, the task of the reflective judgement 'is to render intelligible what is particular and contingent by showing it to have a unity that is thinkable by us, although it does not rest on objective rules'.[29] A judgement of the beautiful, of pure, 'free' beauty, detached from empirical and moral concerns, acts with a certain autonomy, and is free from the constraints of the understanding. It provides and follows its own rules which are, however, devoid of concepts. But how can the reflective judgement give itself its own rule without any *a priori* concept? It does so by using as a guide an additional principle which is that of purposiveness. This enables the mind of the observer to make some sense of, or come to a meaningful approach to, contingent phenomena. While a minimal bestowing of meaning, or intelligibility, of phenomena that would lie below or just on the threshold of constituting a thing is secured by the teleological reflective judgement, in the aesthetic reflective judgement the principle of the purposiveness of nature serves as a new kind of *a priori* which guides or orients the judgement in order to conceive of a formal intelligibility in the contingency of the manifold of natural laws and the objects of nature. Although purposiveness is attributed both to the natural thing and to nature itself, it is the subject that assumes this purposiveness. It is never a property of the object.

## Errant beauty

The aesthetic judgement entails a suspension of any theoretical and practical concern directed towards the object. Reason is bracketed or put out of play in disinterested pleasure. In this sense, purposiveness is without an end, that is, without a goal. However, Kant's whole philosophy is teleological and systematic and, as Derrida observes, purposiveness without an end consists 'of an oriented, finalized movement, harmoniously organized *in view* of an end which is never *in view*' (*TP* 87; Derrida's emphasis). The organized totality of an end is never in view, but according to Kant, we simply assume it to be part of the judgement. Kant's prime example of the beautiful thing that is purposeful without purpose is the wild tulip which, in distinction to the cut tulip or the cultivated tulip, has no goal, no purpose, no use, it is purely contingent. The wild tulip, like Silesius's rose, is without why. For the tulip to be beautiful it must be without purpose but only on the condition that it can be seen to be straining, according to Derrida, towards a final end.

As Derrida views it, the Kantian feeling of beauty is produced by the very interruption of purposiveness. In the aesthetic reflective judgement, finality is not absent but cut off. Of the two essential types of beauty described by Kant, the pure and free beauty of the tulip belongs to *Pulchritudo vaga* and is distinguished from adherent beauty, *Pulchritudo adhaerens*, where the object implies a determinable purpose (Kant gives the example of a utensil). In the latter there is no pure beauty and, as Derrida reasons, there is no pure cut, no interruption of purposiveness since a purpose can be supplied by the beholder of the object. The feeling of pure beauty, then, cannot be attributed to a goal, or an absence of a goal, 'it is the without that counts for beauty' (*TP* 88–9), what Derrida calls 'the *sans* of this pure cut'.

For Derrida, the free, vague, beauty, of the tulip, detached from determination – in opposition to 'adherent' beauty – is simply 'errant'. Errancy here is thought in terms of wandering without destination or destiny. It is related to what Derrida calls elsewhere 'destinerrance'. Free beauty is errant and wandering and must deal with singularities:

> The seed wanders (*s'erre*). What is beautiful is dissemination, the pure cut without negativity, a *sans* without negativity and without signification. . . . The *without-goal*, the *without-why* of the tulip is not significant, is not a signifier, not even a signifier of lack. At least insofar as the tulip is beautiful, *this* tulip. As such, a signifier, even a signifier without a signified, can do anything except be beautiful. Starting from a signifier, one can account for everything except beauty (*TP* 95; Derrida's emphasis).

Derrida provisionally points to this radical implication in Kant's thesis. But Kant also classes works of art as free beauties and Derrida asks: How can they appear to us as non-signifying and cut off from their goal? As Kant clearly states, 'A beauty of nature is a beautiful thing; the beauty of art is a beautiful representation of a thing.' In beautiful art 'a concept must be the ground of what the thing is supposed to be' (*CoJ* §48). But Kant does list particular types of art which have no intrinsic meaning: pure forms, such as music without text and without theme. Like the tulip, they seem to be tending towards some end. But this tension is, as Derrida observes, always cut off, interrupted.

For Kant, there can be no objective rule of taste that would determine what is beautiful through concepts. Yet for works of art there are standards, and although Kant is careful to make a clear distinction between perfection and beauty, he insists that in the judgement of beautiful art perfection must be taken into account and must be part of the judgement. In order to do this Kant introduces the concept of the exemplary product of taste. They are not beautiful by means of concepts and they are not to be employed as models to be imitated. One cannot, according to Kant, attain taste through imitation. Even if taste refers to the exemplar, it must be autonomous (must be a faculty of one's own) and spontaneous. The exemplary model, 'the archetype of taste', Kant explains, 'is a mere idea which everyone must produce in himself, and in accordance with which he must judge everything that is an object of taste' (*CoJ* §17). The exemplar is an ideal model. The ideal is the representation of something adequate to the idea. This idea – which everyone must produce in a judgement of taste – is, as Kant says, a concept of reason, 'hence that archetype of taste, which indeed rests on reason's indeterminate idea of a maximum, but cannot be represented through concepts, but only in an individual presentation (*Darstellung*) would better be called the ideal of the beautiful' (*CoJ* §17, 117). Errant beauty, on the other hand, cannot give rise to any ideal or idea.

The beauty of the ideal is fixed by objective purposiveness which, for Kant, presupposes that an end determines the form of the thing (e.g. the human being, the horse, the building, for Kant, all presuppose the concept of an end). Because it is partly intellectualized, and it appeals to reason, ideal beauty will never give rise to a pure judgement of taste. There is here, as Derrida notes, a cleavage between ideal beauty and pure taste. There is an incompatibility between ideal beauty and pure beauty. They are in opposition, and this opposition appears as a consequence of Kant's conception of man as the goal of nature. As one who is equipped with reason, imagination and understanding, man alone is capable of ideal beauty. The beauty of man is adherent beauty because, like the horse or the building, it 'presupposes the concept of an end that determines what the thing should be' (*CoJ* §16).

Because human self-conceiving cannot be purposeless or goalless, the beauty of man cannot be errant; man cannot be endowed with free beauty. Kant, according to Derrida, places man simultaneously in the centre of the field of aesthetics and also dissymmetrically situates man on one side, not between errancy and adherence, but on the side of adherence. Further, for Kant, ideal beauty consists in the expression of the moral, and it is on this condition that it pleases universally. Judgement of the ideal is not entirely disinterested; however, it still allows no satisfaction from sensory charm. As

Kant says, 'it can never be purely aesthetic' and is 'no mere judgment of taste' (*CoJ* §17, 120). As Derrida argues,

> this moral semiotics which ties *presentation* to the expression of an inside, and the beauty of man to his morality, thus forms a system with a fundamental humanism. This humanism justifies, at least surreptitiously, the intervention of pragmatic culture and anthropology in the deduction of judgments of taste. (*TP* 115)

The disseminating and errant wandering of pure, free and vague beauty would seem to escape this moral humanism. But it is still caught up, as Derrida contends, through the anthropocentric analogy (the 'as if') – we cannot absolutely determine the contingent objects of nature so 'we must act *as if* an understanding (not our own) *had been able* to give them a unity' (*TP* 117; Derrida's emphasis). The purposiveness of nature is 'conceived by analogy with human art which gives itself a goal before operating' (*TP* 117). This goal is given by intention. Beauty appears errant and disseminating but it is not. The course towards anthropo-theologism might seem to be lacking, but sense and destination are restored to errancy. In this way, Derrida contends, the economy of mimesis (economimesis) is restored.

## Non-intention and purposelessness

The *a priori* of reflective aesthetic judgement, the purposiveness without purpose of nature, is ultimately made by analogy to artistic production where an end is presupposed. The spectre of an anonymous intentional purposiveness, modelled on the intention of human agency, hovers over the reflective aesthetic judgement. Art provides the model for the purposiveness which we give to natural beauty. Nature shows itself through its beautiful products as art, 'not merely by chance, but as it were intentionally, in accordance with a lawful arrangement and as purposiveness without end' (*CoJ* §42, 181). As Alison Ross observes, it is as if nature is possessed of an intention. As she points out,

> It is the thought of nature as an art that Kant uses in the 'Critique of Aesthetic Judgment' that supports the attribution to nature of the systematicity of an intention in the 'Critique of Teleological Judgment'. Aesthetic reflection depends for the quality of its feeling on nature's contingency. Nonetheless,

it places itself in the service of an obscure art of moral symbolism and of a teleological reflection, which organises this contingency under the idea of an intentional art.[30]

Nature shows itself as art; however, we never, according to Kant, encounter the purpose of purposiveness. We assume the beautiful product of nature as having a purpose (which we don't care to know), as if it were intentionally designed by someone, or something, for us. Instead of encountering the end or purpose of purposiveness in the object, Kant says that 'we naturally seek it in ourselves' (*CoJ* §42, 181). This inward turn to our (man's) own ultimate purpose constitutes our moral vocation. In a moment which Derrida describes as an interiorizing suppliance (*suppliance interiorisante*) in which we both seek and give, Kant is essentially saying that the beautiful object of nature outside of us appears purposive, but as we are unable to determine its purpose, we seek a purpose from within us and provide the object with this purpose (*E* 14). This interiorizing turn prepares the ground for nineteenth-century subjectivist aesthetics.

For Kant, on the one hand, the purposiveness of nature must seem intentional, although no intention is sought in the aesthetic judgement. On the other hand, 'art always has a determinate intention of producing something' (*CoJ* §45), but for art to be regarded as if it were a product of nature, the artist must not work according to conceptual rules. If this determinate intention were focused on the production of determinate objects, then the art object would depend on concepts for our satisfaction. Hence, Kant says, 'the purposiveness in the product of beautiful art, although it is certainly intentional must nevertheless not seem intentional; i.e., beautiful art must be regarded as nature, although of course one is aware of it as art' (*CoJ* §45 185–6).

Rather than through conceptual rules or determinate intentions, nature gives the (non-conceptual) rule to art by way of genius, the natural gift (*Naturgabe*). Even though the author of a work of genius 'does not know himself how the ideas for it came to him' (*CoJ* §46, 187), and the work is produced through a kind of second nature according to unknown rules gifted by nature. Genius presupposes a form of automatism. In this extraordinary reciprocity, the product of art should resemble the product of nature – which appears to have a purpose and be possessed of an intention but does not (although we give it one) – but at the same time we are aware of it as art – which is the product of an intention although it must appear to be non-intentional. Paradoxically, the product of art must appear to have a purpose and must not appear to have a purpose. In an endless exchange between direct causality and analogy, the work of art must appear to have an intention *directly* because the artist intends to make a work of art. It must appear to not have an intention *analogically* because it receives its rules from nature which *analogically* only seems to have an intention because artistic production provides the model for the judgement of beautiful nature.

Kant never says 'divine intention', but this analogical imitation of divine acts constitutes the onto-theological background of Kant's meditation. Whether the production of the work of art is thought in terms of the seemingly non-intentional, automatic, operation of genius, or as the simulation of divine action, some form of intention is ultimately presupposed. The question is, does Cage's purposeful purposelessness escape this circular economy? I would argue that by installing non-intention at a certain stage of the production of the work of art, Cage effectively breaks this econo-mimetic circuit. For Cage, like Kant's artist of genius, there is certainly a *purposeful* intention *to* initiate a work (and to work), but there is an emphatic suspension of any intention *in* the production of the work – even if what is suspended has the markings of the non-intentional automatism of genius, or is remotely directed by the mimesis that would seek to imitate the actions of a divine will. In the chance operation, indeterminacy and aleatory processes, genius is replaced by nature in her manner of operation. However, nature cannot be ascribed a purposiveness, as that would place the chance operation back into the economy of divine mimesis (this would, for example, occur if we thought the operation as an appeal to an oracle). Nature must be considered in terms of Cage's 'purposelessness', as 'without why'. The rose in Silesius's poem is errant: 'it cares not for itself, asks not if it's seen.' The tulip in Kant's third *Critique* is only provisionally errant. Its 'why' is always ultimately determined in terms of a humanist anthropocentrism. Cage's aesthetics of purposeful purposelessness is not governed from a distance by reason, and there is no place for the exemplary, ideal beauty or perfection. The work of purposeful purposelessness (Cage's) that imitates nature in her manner of operation lets beings be, like the rose, without why. But unlike Kant's *Pulchritudo vaga*, there is no end in view that would reconstitute the economy of mimesis.

## Unconstrained favouring

Heidegger rarely discusses the *third Critique*, but he does defend Kant's definition of the beautiful, as the object of disinterested pleasure, against the misinterpretations of Nietzsche and Schopenhauer. In the Nietzsche lectures ('The Will to Power as Art') he argues that 'in order to find something beautiful, we must let (*lassen*) what encounters us, purely as it is in itself, come before us in its own stature and worth' (*GA 6.1* 109, *N I* 109) and, further, 'we must allow (*lassen*) and grant (*gönnen*) it what belongs to it' (*GA 6.1* 109, *N I* 109). Heidegger focuses on Kant's conception of 'unconstrained favouring (*freie Gunst*)' (*GA 6.1* 109, *N I* 109, *CoJ* §5) which is not a form of indifference, not quietistic surrender of the will, but a granting (*Gönnen*) and letting (*Seinlassen*) (*GA 6.1* 109, *N I* 109).[31] Michel Haar points out that *Gunst* 'comes from *gönnen*, "to grant a gift"'.[32] There are two issues of contention here. First, Kant's analytic of the beautiful would seem to belong to the modern aesthetic attitude of *Erlebnis* that would be, according to Heidegger's view of art, in need of displacement. Second, Heidegger ascribes no independent moment in his history of aesthetics to Kant's *Critique of Judgment*. However, as Jacques Taminiaux points out, Heidegger's procedure here is to meditate on the tenuous signs in Kant's text that bring forward the possibility of superseding their metaphysical delimitation. Thus, according to Taminiaux, it is here that the aesthetic attitude 'overcomes itself', revealing 'something that eludes the power of subjectivity and a fortiori the empire of absolute subjectivity'.[33] Kant's notion of 'favour' (*Gunst*),[34] as a 'letting the phenomenon be within itself, for its own sake', suggests to us, according to Taminiaux, that 'deeper than the correlation of subject and object, freedom consists in being open to the very unconcealing of the world, an unconcealing that precedes and exceeds the theoretical, practical, and hedonistic powers of the ego'.[35] But, as we have seen, this would be true only if the beauty of nature is free, vague and errant, without why. Not only must the judgement of the objects of nature be without interest, but also without an end, without any purposiveness straining towards an end, without any inner searching for man's ultimate purpose within, without being grounded on our moral vocation, without man or a concept of ideal beauty. For Heidegger, Kant's philosophy has a decisive role in the modern metaphysics of the will which begins with Descartes and Leibniz, and develops in German idealism in the wake of Kant through Fichte and Schelling, to an extreme in Hegel and completion in Nietzsche. Although the *Critique of Pure Reason* seeks to trace the limits of reason (*Vernunft*), Heidegger contends that Kant's 'a priori conditions for the possibility' conceals Leibniz's principle of sufficient reason, and even when it comes to the third *Critique*, 'reason is the real theme' (*SG* 124, *PR* 71). Reason as the self-sufficient subjectivity of the subject defines everything else in terms of objects, stands or is thrown over and against. Rather than settling for the more technical word '*Objekt*', Heidegger uses the word '*Gegenstand*' which originated in the eighteenth century as the German translation of the Latin *obiectum*, and literally means 'that which stands over against'. Reason plays the role of laying the ground for objects.

> According to Kant it is only by having recourse to reason (*ratio*) that something can be determined as to what it is and how it is a being for the rational creature called 'man'. However, this now means not just that beings *are* only *qua* objects (*Objekt*) and objects only *objects* for a subject in the sense of modern thinking; it now becomes clearer that this *subject*; that is reason, *ratio*, that is, the assembling of the a priori conditions for the possibility of nature and freedom, is the assembling only in rendering sufficient reasons (*Grundes*). (*SG* 126–7, *PR* 73; Heidegg emphasis)

The relation of nature and freedom to reason is defined by the will. Man takes up his place as the centre of beings and in fact wills himself into this placement. In the *Geschick* (history, destiny) of being in modernity, Heidegger says, 'Being reveals itself as objectness (*Gegenständigkeit*) for consciousness, and this at once says: being brings itself to light as will' (*SG* 115, *PR* 65).[36] In modern representational thinking, as Heidegger sees it, being, objectness and will are one, and Kant's thinking plays a decisive role in fleshing this out.

As we have seen from Derrida's reading of Kant's analytic of the beautiful, 'errant' beauty opens up a breach in the closure of metaphysics, but it does so only provisionally, before being subsumed under the humanism of man's moral self-relation. Free beauty and pure judgements of taste are seen as deficient forms in relation to ideal beauty and judgements of taste bound up with presentation of the aesthetic idea. I would contend that for this reason Heidegger does not follow up on the brief remarks regarding Kant's unconstrained favouring. Further, for Heidegger, the beautiful is not assessed in terms of judgements of taste, but rather by way of a more direct and 'essential relation to the object' (*GA 6.1* 110, *N I* 110). The object appears before us as 'pure object', and this coming forth into appearance is what Plato calls *ekphanestaton*. For Heidegger, Eckhart's prescription via Silesius of 'without why' points to a way of twisting free from the representational thinking of Western metaphysics and opening up the possibilities for a non-willing thinking. For Derrida, Kant's 'purposiveness without purpose', which Heidegger reinscribes as a free granting, has the possibility of opening up a breach in modern aesthetics with its insistence of the 'without', 'the *sans* of the pure cut'. Both strategies turn on the 'without why'. Both, curiously, provide the example of a flower: the rose for Silesius and the wild tulip for Kant. Cage's purposeful purposelessness carries out the active passivity of working without why.

6

# Fluxus and the flux

## Fluxus and the flux

The word 'Fluxus' was employed by George Maciunas in 1962 to name a loose affiliation of international avant-garde artists. Maciunas had perhaps been thinking of the flow of the Lithuanian diaspora, as he intended to use the word originally as the title for a magazine for Lithuanians living in New York. The word 'fluxus' is, of course, Latin (from *fluere*), and is translated into English as 'flux' or 'change', and has the sense of 'a continuous succession of changes', as in the Heraclitian flux, where being is compared to the streaming of a river, where one cannot enter into the same stream twice. Fluxus names a group of artists who, more or less, take the flux as their material: as temporal flux, change and contingency. As John Caputo argues, metaphysics has always desired a quick exit from the flux, to which he proposes a countermovement, stemming from the thought of Kierkegaard, Eckhart, Nietzsche, Heidegger and Derrida, that would seek to restore life, being and existence to their original difficulty in 'the great project of hermeneutic trouble-making' that he names 'radical hermeneutics'.[1] Hermeneutic trouble-making is precisely what Fluxus works do, and they do so, most essentially, at the level of 'experience'.

In this chapter I will, to all appearances, reverse the position that I put forward in Chapters 1 and 2. In turning the tables I will, up to certain point, appear to shift from defending Cage's 'letting sounds be' from Schaefferian phenomenological essentialism and aestheticism, to defending Husserlian phenomenology and critiquing Cage's ontological innocence. If the *epochē* of chance is to have any real value for an audience (or participant-users) in letting sounds be, one would expect it to open something up, interrupt the natural attitude or reconfigure the patterns of perception. In short, it must, at its most basic level, enable something to happen. Something must occur at the level of experience. But it must not be simply 'an experience'. Rather, it must constitute an 'event' that allows us to put in question the idea of experience, to initiate the understanding of a new concept of experience.

Cage's unknowing oblivion is, I would argue, the simple inversion or countermovement to metaphysical closure. As pure openness, it constitutes a naive surrender to the flux that not only refuses conceptualization, reflection and mastery over beings but also refuses 'thinking' in the late Heideggerian sense. Cage's *Gelassenheit* imposes a certain silence. As Daniel Charles, in exasperation, responds to Cage, 'We are always led back to this: there is nothing to say'.[2] Cage, by prioritizing the immediate and the new, seeks an easy way *into* the flux, rather than an easy escape out. Although Cage was a significant figure of influence for many of the Fluxus artists, a quite substantial gulf exists between the two approaches. Dick Higgins remarks that Cage, in contradistinction to Fluxus, 'strove towards "nobility"'.[3] Cage's idea of opening his audience up to 'always new' experience, in order to sharpen and develop the powers of observation and audition, surely has its roots in early modernist theory of the Bauhaus, transmitted by artists such as Lázló Moholy-Nagy and Josef Albers.[4] For Higgins, and the Fluxus artists who developed their own use of 'aleatoric structures' from Cage's pedagogy – George Brecht, Jackson Mac Low, Richard Maxfield and himself – what was needed was an antidote to Cage's purity and nobility, in other words 'the great project of hermeneutic trouble-making'.

Philosophy has traditionally sought to escape the flux and insulate itself from the effects of contingency by striving after the ideal and universal, and to recover meaning from out of existence. However, when the work of art brings us into direct and immediate proximity to the things themselves, it would seem to leave us confounded in the flux without meaning, or access to a way of moving forward. Can strategies of art-making utilizing the framing or structuring of experience lead to a non-empirical phenomenological way of knowing? Is a simple experiential reframing enough to unsettle the codes that routinely frame experience? Perhaps it is possible to say that this problematic forms the starting point of Fluxus. Many of the Fluxus artists, under the influence of George Maciunas, were interested in strategies of pedagogy. As Craig Safer argues, 'Fluxus works highlighted socio-poetic interaction and encouraged epistemological experimentation among participant-users'.[5]

There was certainly an interest in getting close to objects and phenomena but in a way that would avoid the participant falling back into private experience. Rather, there seemed to be in Fluxus a concern with the social exchange of experience, where participants would play through the possibilities, through an engagement with open-ended interactive works and collaborative art games. But this means something other than, on the one hand, the total immersion of immediate experience, or, on the other hand, mediate description and representation. If we are to consider works of art that deal primarily with sense perception as a way of directly encountering the flux, what must be avoided, first of all, is a simple unreflective empiricism that Cage's appeal to direct sensory experience – towards the opened ears of a blank mind – would seem to suggest. Thus, I find it necessary to re-examine the implications of Cage's project, and its development in Fluxus, in terms of the more radical possibilities of Husserl's phenomenology: a post-Husserlian phenomenology that begins with Derrida's observation that presence, in Husserl's thinking, is far from simple.

## Fluxus experience

Two distinct areas of practice emerged out of Cage's class: 'Composition as Experimental Music' at the New School of Social Research in New York in the late 1950s. One group of Cage's students, including Allan Kaprow and Al Hansen, began to stage what were called Environments and Happenings along with other artists such as Jim Dine, Claes Oldenburg, Red Grooms and Robert Whitman. Others such as George Brecht, Dick Higgins and Alison Knowles became swept up in what became known as Fluxus. There were, however, significant differences between these two approaches, as Brandon LaBelle observes: 'In bold contrast to Environments and Happenings, Fluxus veers away from spectacular antics.' Fluxus was more concerned with the everyday, the ordinary, the marginal elements that make-up experience.[6]

On the other hand, Hannah Higgins observes that the stark differences between the two practices began to more and more resemble each other as the artists began to develop their individual directions. Fluxus works, as Higgins notes in her extensive study *Fluxus Experience*, offer 'experiential knowledge',[7] 'sensate forms of knowledge'.[8] Experience, for Higgins, is at the heart of Fluxus events, Fluxkits and performances. However, her most striking claim is that Fluxus works 'problematize the Western metaphysics since Plato and Aristotle, which insists on dividing primary experience (the feel or scent of the pom-pom) from secondary experience (mental concepts about it)',[9] or, as Alice Jardine put is, in her essay 'The Demise of Experience', 'the ancient problem of the relationship between what in everyday language we call "experience" of "reality" and what we then decide to call "knowledge" about it.'[10] Higgins makes a quite valid point. Fluxus works problematize the metaphysical distinctions between matter and form, and the sensible and the intelligible, and bring us to a renewed conception of experience. However, the analytical model that Higgins uses to examine Fluxus experience continually falls back on the very separation between primary and secondary experience that she opposes.

Higgins is rightly cautious of the term 'experience', citing Derrida's suggestion in *Of Grammatology* that the term 'experience' should perhaps be put 'under erasure' – that is, allowed to function and remain visible and legible while at the same time being deeply called into question. For Derrida, the term 'experience' is so caught up in the metaphysical privileging of presence that its very use would seem to be unproductive. As Higgins observes, in the light of Derrida's suspicions around the word 'experience', it is difficult in the contemporary art-theoretical climate (of 2002) – where experience might be seen merely as an effect of textuality – to sustain a discourse which values 'Direct perception, primary information, material knowledge, and experience'.[11] If we are to examine the functioning of experience in Fluxus work as generating material for ontological knowledge, we must not fall prey to, as Higgins warns – following Derrida and W. J. T. Mitchell – falling back into empiricism or a naive objectivity. However, Higgins continues on to argue that rather than impose an external grid of discursive interpretation on Fluxus work, 'Fluxus is better understood on its own terms: as producing diverse primary experiences and interactions with reality, plain and simple.'[12] Higgins follows the naturalist realist approach of Hilary Putnam where experience is thought of as presentational rather than representational. However, the division, previously criticized, between raw, naked, experience (sense perception) and discursive interpretations and associations, remains largely in place. Higgins states: 'The Event and the Fluxkit argue ontologically for the value of primary experience over secondary experiences – that is, interpretations or associations.'[13] Higgins is thus forced to consider Fluxus experience in terms that are essentially intrasubjective and introspective. Such a conception of experience, although it is said to deliver tacit or 'ontological knowledge', must remain confined to a private *Erlebnis* because this model cannot account for inter-subjectivity within 'primary' experience itself. One response to this problem might be to rule out experience altogether and consider the functionality of Fluxus works in terms of the supposed dematerialization of the object in conceptual art, where the physical components of the work are said to act as mere props for the idea, and where the idea precedes the work and belongs to the artist as the artist's meaning-intention, as univocal and unalterable by any reception.[14] This would enable the works to be examined on public, inter-subjective terms. However, this conception is absolutely foreign to Fluxus works, and Higgins is quite right to keep the idea of experience in play. Experience, audience interaction, open structures of meaning and equivocality are essential components of the Fluxus work. Works of art, at a most basic level, are experienced *as* works of art due to an institutional framing. Whereas Higgins argues that Fluxus works 'frame art as experience in Putnam's natural realist sense',[15] I would say that at a more fundamental level, before they frame art as experience, Fluxus works frame experience as art.

In short, Higgins gleans from Derrida that the concept of experience, which is too close to the metaphysical idea of presence, requires deconstruction, and such a deconstruction must avoid falling back into empiricism and naive critiques of experience. But in what is far too brief an account of Derrida's displacement of the concept of experience, Higgins comes to no conclusion on the validity or usefulness of a deconstruction of experience in breaking down the division between primary and secondary experience, or in the examination of 'deconstructed' experience in Fluxus works. In regard to this I propose that in the spectator's involvement in the Fluxus work, experience itself is made thematic, and it is to this extent that the work carried out resembles the transcendental reduction. However, to think this work in terms beyond the reduction to transcendental life involves a displacement of the opposition between primary and secondary experience.

What follows in this chapter is an inquiry into a deconstruction of experience in order to show how a deconstructed 'concept' of experience breaks down the division between the so-called primary and secondary experience. We might well ask if Derrida does indeed have a conception of experience. To arrive at a new 'deconstructed' conception of experience, as

Derrida warns, first involves going beyond naive realism. However, such a step beyond empiricism and naive objectivity involves the exhaustion of 'the resources of the concept of experience before attaining and in order to attain, by deconstruction, its ultimate foundation' (*OG* 60). The first stage of this operation involves the coming to grips with a 'transcendentality' that Derrida would in most other cases put into question. By 'transcendentality', in this instance, Derrida is referring both to Husserl's transcendental phenomenology (the conditions of possibility for experience and meaning fulfilment) and to the ultimate development of Saussurean difference in Hjelmslev's glossematics (the conditions of possibility for meaning and signification in general). That is to say, the deconstruction of experience proceeds by way of a 'going through' transcendental phenomenology and by way of a similar 'going through' structural linguistics. The place where the former is carried out is primarily in *Speech and Phenomena*; the place where the latter is carried out is in *Of Grammatology*. By way of these texts, experience is rethought in terms of a certain post-phenomenology and a certain post-structuralism. It is not, as is commonly thought, that the concept of experience is shown to be largely fictional by way of recourse to structural theories of signification.

For Derrida, the deconstruction of experience involves going beyond transcendental criticism in order to avoid foundationalism. However, if this going beyond proceeds in a straightforward critical move, there is a risk that 'the ultra-transcendental text will so closely resemble the pre-critical text as to be indistinguishable from it' (*OG 61*). In other words, if we simply reject the transcendental in order to overcome it in the name of some ultra, or quasi-transcendental – *différance*, the trace, arche-writing – we risk 'falling-short' of transcendental criticism and end up back in naive objectivism. There is, thus, a necessity for traversing the text of Husserlian phenomenology. The deconstruction of experience involves the 'relinquishment of the transcendental' and not its simple 'abandonment'. As Derrida argues, 'the value of the transcendental arche [*archie*] must make its necessity felt before letting itself be erased' (*OG* 61).

If arche-writing is Derrida's reconfiguration of the concept of experience, can we say that the Fluxus work leads us to some kind of identification with this differential encounter with things? Is experience prefaced by discursivity? It is not that the world, or the real, is forever distanced by mediation, and that we can never get to the thing itself. Rather, it is a question of finding or enabling access to the thing. What is consistently insisted in Derrida's early writing is that there is no pre-linguistic stratum accessible to experience that is not already contaminated by a differential structure of signification. This does not push experience into an ineffable black hole. Nor does it mean that only things that can be talked about are real. It means that there can be no constitution of things, events and the world, without a differential structure that includes signification and language. Here we need to go back to Husserl and re-examine phenomenology before prematurely jumping to an all to quick, vulgar deconstructionist discourse that is often the province of art theory (e.g. all is text, discursivity is primary).

There is a common perception that Derrida has conquered phenomenology and dismissed it entirely, and that he has shown that Husserl's philosophy is not only riddled with contradictions but, even worse, is a hopelessly essentialist philosophy of presence. Hence, the tendency of many commentators focusing on the function of experience in the arts (in visual art, sound and cinema) is to give Husserl a wide birth and, if phenomenology is considered at all, to turn to the embodied phenomenology of Merleau-Ponty. One of the aims of this study is to counter that trend. Further, there are resources within Husserl's writing which Derrida mobilizes that, in many cases, tend to be covered over and restricted by Husserl's highly Cartesian language and unsaid metaphysical assumptions. In many cases it sounds as if phenomenology constitutes a direct appeal to perceptions of the given which is how Husserl's 'principle of principles sounds'. This is misleading. For Husserl, experience is never simple direct perception, and although it would seem to privilege the metaphysical notion of presence at its core (Husserl definitely privileges bodily presence in all intuitions), this presence, as Derrida demonstrates, can never be, according to the more radical implications of Husserl's logic, a simple unity.

## Phenomenology

As Dick Higgins observes, 'We can talk about a thing, but we cannot talk a thing, It is always something else.'[16] Higgins's statement points to the problem of description that stalks phenomenology: how to make explicit in words the phenomenological description of an experience that would precede the descriptive discourse without diminishing what is originary about that experience. In a critical appraisal of phenomenological description, Jean-François Lyotard observes: 'in so far as this life-originating world is ante-predicative, all predication, all discourse, undoubtedly *implies* it, yet is *wide* of it, and properly speaking nothing may be said of it.'[17] Once you describe something, according to Lyotard, the sought-for originary is no longer originary. Lyotard's critique echoes the Marburg neo-Kantian philosopher Paul Natorp's insightful objections to Husserl's phenomenology, where he argues that the description of lived-experiences, or merely looking at experiences, essentially stills the stream, de-vivifying what is originary and, further, mediating the concrete immediacy into abstractions.

These problems only come into focus if there can be said to be a sharp distinction between experience and discursivity, presence and absence. At the most basic level of phenomenological analysis, experience is always divided between presence and absence. The perception, or rather the constitution, of an object, in Husserl's model, is not considered to consist of the reception of sense data, then interpretation, and finally meaning fulfilment. Rather, in a synthesis, perspectival aspects of an object are combined with recollections of previously perceived aspects, along with expectations of what the out-of-view aspects of the object (its hidden side) might look like, which, in turn, are based upon the past constitution of similar objects. Perception is, thus, never simple and direct but involves temporality in the form of recollection, retention, protention and anticipation.

## The as-structure of intentionality

In phenomenology every lived-experience is a comportment towards something as something. This is the structure of what Husserl calls, after Brentano, 'intentionality', where any given object of perception is seen as the thing that it is: the 'as what' it is, thus, one consequence of intentionality is that there is an as-structure to experience. The young Heidegger, working as Husserl's assistant, articulates this idea in a very interesting way. In the perception of a lectern in a university classroom, one does not see first a collection of intersecting coloured surfaces which might then reveal themselves as a box, and which then, in a further step, might be interpreted and understood as a university lectern and then finally given the vocal label 'lectern'. Instead, he argues, 'I see the lectern in one fell swoop' (*GA 56/57* 71, *TDP* 60). The lectern is encountered as a thing that has meaning for the observer. This meaning occurs, as Husserl says, 'as a whole, "at one blow"' (*LU II* 625, *LI II* 287).

One might object that such perceptions occur only for those who possess a certain cultural familiarity with the use of a lectern in a university classroom. However, Heidegger counters this objection by arguing that a farmer from the Black Forest would interpret the object as a piece of university equipment, and further, even an African native ('Senegal Negro'), with no knowledge of European culture whatsoever, would see the object as 'a bare something that is there' (*GA 56/57* 72, *TDP* 61). The traditional African might, on the one hand, misinterpret the object as something to do with magic, or as a shield to hide behind during a fight or, on the other hand, he might have no idea at all what the object is and be totally perplexed in the face of the object – taking it as a form of what Heidegger calls 'instrumental strangeness'. However, as Heidegger stresses, 'the meaningful character of "instrumental strangeness", and the meaningful character of the "lectern", are in their essence absolutely identical' (*GA 56/57* 72, *TDP* 61).[18] In both instances something meaningful is primarily co-perceived and the perception does not consist of a stepped series of sense data. Meaning is immediately co-given with the object but that does not mean that in phenomenology the object simply gives its meaning.[19]

Each experience is apperceived with a meaning, even if this meaning is incomplete, vague or erroneous. For Husserl we experience the 'sense' (*Sinn*) of the object; however, the sense is not perceived passively as something given but actively apprehended and constituted by consciousness. Although we might perceive a certain perspective, a particular aspect or side of an object in a singular adumbration of the object, we experience the whole object as what it is. In intentionality a particular adumbration is not meaningfully given in isolation. Instead, the perceived thing is intended in its totality. In order for this to be achieved, Husserl posits that the 'fullness' of the object is pre-delineated or pre-traced (*vorgezeichnete*), construed in advance. For example, to see a cube as a cube we do not need to see all of its sides. The sides that we do not see belong to the perception potentially. They belong to a fore-structure of anticipation and recollections (including those which have just passed). This is what Husserl describes as the 'horizons' that accompany every perception. In the pre-delineation (*Vorzeichnung*) that pre-forms perception, our expectations are not imaginative constructions but are formed out of our recollection of past experiences. If we were to walk around the object, the potentialities would become actualized. But the full perception of the object does not depend upon this actualization. Further, it must be stressed that by walking around the object and gaining new perspectives the full intuition of the object does not depend on the accumulation of temporally successive perspectives. In each perspective, at the moment of each adumbration, there is a full perception of the thing – as something. Rather, what occurs in each adumbration is a 'filling in' of what was pre-sketched or outlined by the pre-delineated potentialities. Indeed, some perspectives might never be actualized. They are, as Husserl says, left open, and this 'leaving open' (*Offenlassen*) is what makes up a horizon. Horizons are thus open anticipatory fore-structures that have a certain imperfect indeterminateness about them but have a determinant structure (*Hua I* 83, *CM* 45).[20]

What we anticipate lies within a certain range of possibilities, but a range of possibilities left open. The constitution of the object is made up of elements which are bodily present and directly apprehended by sight (or other senses), along with elements which, although they are not strictly absent from consciousness, may not be visibly present to perception. However, in as much as recollection contributes to the fore-structures of horizons, we could say that non-presence contributes to constitution of perceptual objects, and thus that perception has a pres-absence structure to it. This side of Husserl's thought unsettles the other more Cartesian side, where Husserl appears to be saying that direct intuition of the living present is all that counts. Pre-delineation is built into the structure of intentionality, and in this way, the thing does not give itself in its self-presence. Instead, constitution is made up of an intertwining of the actual and the potential, of the explicit and implicit. The task of the phenomenologist is to '*ask any horizon what "lies in it"*, [and] . . . *explicate* or unfold it, and "*uncover*" the potentialities of conscious life at a particular time' (*Hua I* 82, *CM* 45, Husserl's emphasis).

## Ideality

The investigation taken by phenomenology towards knowledge of intentional objects is more than a concern with the empirical moment of an object present to a (particular) subject's perception, for if the objects are to be known and described, they must exist outside a particular subject's consciousness. At the same time, they must be given to consciousness, and reflection on them must be uncontaminated by philosophical presuppositions. But if the knowledge gained from the underlying forms isolated from experience in the phenomenological reduction is to be knowledge at all, it must be universally valid. The same experience must be able to be repeated without variation by different subjects. In order to constitute an object as something with a relatively unvarying publicly, or inter-subjectively, available meaning there must be, for Husserl, an ideal identity. Since the objects of our knowledge must be *ideal* identities, yet they must be found in experience, Husserl's phenomenology must be able to locate an invariable and infinitely repeatable core of intuitive evidence in perception. In contradistinction to what he regards as a prejudice of British empiricism and German idealism, where non-sensory ideal objects are seen to be imminent and subjective, Husserl argues that although idealities do not exist anywhere in the world and do not 'have being in a *topos ouranios* [a heavenly place] or in a divine mind' (*LUII* 101, *LI I* 230), they have a kind of objectivity and a specific unity. However, although Husserl concedes that the transmission of ideal meanings (such as propositions, axioms, geometrical identities) involves signs – such as in the transferal of abstract geometrical identities from the mind of the proto-geometer through the generations, as exemplified in 'The Origin of Geometry' – he grants no semiotic status to the idealities themselves. Instead, the very ideality of the *eidos*, or essence, for Husserl, is what makes it repeatable and available for use with signs.

In *Logical Investigations*, Husserl divides the concept of the sign into two heterogeneous elements: expression (*Ausdruck*) and indication (*Anzeichen*). For Husserl, only expression carries meaning, while indication – a mode of signification that empirically points to or stands for things – is not inherently meaningful; does not express a 'meaning', or a 'sense'. Expression, on the other hand, consists of the transmission of the inner sense or lived-experience of a speaker, outwards – taking the form of linguistic signs in communicative speech. In inter-subjective communication expression is intertwined with indication but pure expression can be seen to take place independently of indication within the immediacy of a self-present consciousness, in the realm of what Husserl calls 'solitary mental life', where expressions '*no longer serve to indicate anything*', yet they still '*function meaningfully*' (*LU II* 24, *LI I* 183 §1, Husserl's emphasis). Derrida argues that Husserl's distinction between these two elements of signification – a distinction that serves to retain the possibility of an ideal self-present meaning – is possible only if expression can effectively take place within the interior monologue of solitary mental life, without any contamination from indicative signification. In interior monologue, Husserl argues, there is no communication, and no work for indicative signs to do, they are without purpose (*zwecklos*) because our mental experience is always immediately present to us in solitary mental life. In the silent monologue that we carry on with ourselves, Husserl says, 'one merely conceives of (*man stellt sich vor*) oneself as speaking and communicating' (*LU II* 36, *LI I* 191 §8, *SP* 49). One represents oneself – or literally places oneself before oneself – in the form of an imaginary representation.

However, in Derrida's view, even if the representations we 'pretend' to make to ourselves are imaginary, representation has still taken place. On the one hand, Husserl applies the distinctions between primary and secondary experience – or between reality and representation – and between effective communication and represented communication, where representation is simply added on, or is an accidental by-product. On the other hand, for Husserl, in effective communication words or signs must operate in a structure that involves repetition, because a sign used once would not be a sign. A sign must be recognizable as essentially the same throughout all of its empirical variations and must be able to be repeated. *Vorstellung* – pure representation where one presents idealities (even words) to oneself in thought – which, for Husserl, is anterior to signification, and does not involve signification – is implied by any act of signification. It would, against Husserl's intention, depend on the possibility of repetition and representation, rather than real presence. Thus, the distinctions between primary and secondary experience, reality and representation, imaginary and effective communication, simple presence and repetition begin to break down. Each can be seen to be involved in the other. This brings Derrida to suggest that 'The presence-of-the-present is derived from repetition and not the reverse' (*SP* 52), and this means that it is possible to say that repetition becomes constitutive for experience of all idealities. However, the self-proximity of lived-experience to itself, and the non-necessity of any signitive operation in solitary mental life, is further justified in Husserl's texts, Derrida observes, by the temporal notion of the present as point or *stigme* which tends to govern all of the *Logical Investigations*. The subject does not need to communicate to itself because, Husserl argues, such mental acts are 'experienced at that very moment (*im selben Augenblick*)' (*LU II*, 36–7, *LI I* 191 §8), in the twinkling of an eye.

## Temporality and experience

Based on a series of lectures given between 1904 and 1910 – *The Phenomenology of Internal Time-Consciousness* – Husserl attempts to account for perceptions of objects which are temporally extended in a relatively brief span of time.[21] Husserl shows that intentionality of temporal objects is stretched and extended rather than knife-edged, and that would seem to radically complicate the view of consciousness immediately present to itself in the instant of the *Augenblick*. For an example, Husserl utilizes the idea of the possibility of the perception of a melody. How is it, he asks, that we perceive a melody as a melody and not as a series of discreet tones bearing no relation to each other? If we were to consider the perception of temporal phenomena purely in terms of a series of discreet points in time, then the melody would not be comprehensible to us. Solutions to this problem such as Meinong's theory of a separate overlapping act that would bring the tones in a final synthesis, or Brentano's recourse to recollective memory, were unacceptable to Husserl. Rather, he proposes that as each note is heard, it is heard in the present, and as next note is heard – in the now – the first note is 'shoved back'. But as the note is shoved back it is retained – or retentionally modified as 'just having been'. This retaining of each note, after it occurs, Husserl calls 'retention'. The future notes that are immediately yet to come are, in much the same way, anticipated. This Husserl calls 'protention'. Perception of the temporal object is then a complex of each primal impression along with its retentions and protentions in a tripled intentionality, but this collection in consciousness of impulses of present, past and future events is maintained up to a given limit – not a hard limit but a gradual attenuation where each point retentionally, or protentionally, adumbrates or shades off.[22]

Derrida wants to play one side of Husserl's arguments against the another: Husserl's insistence of the extended triple intentionality of temporal objects in protentions and retentions, and its implications of a fractured present, against Husserl's continual reliance on the idea of the instantaneous now point. Despite the sophistication of Husserl's model, the spread of gradual attenuation on either side of the present, Derrida observes, is still thought in terms of the 'self-identity of the now as point' (*SP* 61) even though the flow of time – and the structure of lived-experience – is not divisible into discreet moments. This traditional notion of the now is necessary for Husserl because, in maintaining the centrality of the primal impression, it establishes the possibility of objectivity and ideality for the subjective experience of time. However, as Derrida remarks, the concepts of retention and protention tend to undo the primacy of the self-presence of the now. If the primal impression of the now point is what is perceived, and only what is perceived, then the surrounding retentions and protentions must be non-perceptions – non-actualities – and thus merely reproductive. Presence would seem to be compounded with non-presence and non-perception since the continuity of the present now and the non-present retention are both admitted to the primordial impression. What is at stake is the privilege of the living present, and the present now, that forms the core of consciousness and the ground of phenomenology. If presence is allowed to be compounded with non-presence, actuality with non-actuality, then, Derrida contends, 'the other' is admitted 'into the self-identity of the *Augenblick*' (*SP*, 65); thus the idea that signs are 'useless', in the self-relation of internal monologue, becomes questionable. Moreover, the seemingly minor contradictions that Derrida gathers from the strata of *The Phenomenology of Internal Time-Consciousness* and *Ideas I* combine to demonstrate that Husserl's phenomenology, far from maintaining the concept of presence as a self-securing ground, in fact 'prohibits our speaking of a simple self-identity of the present' (*SP* 64).

The temporal coincidence of the self-presence of the subject absolutely transparent to itself in self-identity, the fullness of the self-givenness of presence, the existence of a pre-expressive, pre-semiotic stratum of sense presupposing an ideality independent of signs, and the privilege of living speech as in absolute proximity to the logos are all put into question in the deconstruction of experience. What does this mean for experience? The classical metaphysical idea of language, where thought is seen to be the natural and direct signification of things, and speech is then regarded as the privileged signification of thought, and writing is finally seen to be the secondary and derived signification of speech, essentially governs Husserl's theory of meaning where expression is added to and grants access to a pre-expressive stratum of sense, and indication is, in turn, added to expression. What this indicates for Derrida is that there is a deficiency in experience that is in need of supplementation. The word 'supplement' is here meant in its two senses: as addition and as substitute, or 'in the place of' (*für etwas*), which is what signs do. Experience, as we saw earlier, is, for Husserl, pre-delineated and is a process ultimately involving both presence and absence. However, in reducing the sign, and excluding it in the transcendental reduction, Husserl remains trapped within the metaphysical model of primary and secondary experience. Because there is no *Augenblick*, where the subject is transparent to itself but, rather, the spacing and retentional traces of *différance*, which 'both fissures and retards presence' (*SP* 88), experience is radically rethought in terms of the reversal: immediately given meaning in full presence does not consist of a cluster of idealities available for repetition, but rather repetition provides the conditions of possibility of presence. What is original is not pre-predicative, pre-expressive experience but *différance*, the trace, arche-writing, which are, at the same time, non-originary. What constitutes things is not subjective consciousness but the play of differences, without origin or centre that weaves meaning and the world together in a web or fabric (*textum*). Meaning is not found in the immediacy of perception – which is what Derrida means when he says towards the end of the essay 'Speech and Phenomena', 'there never was any "perception"' (*SP* 103) – but is produced by the play of differences. *Différance*, rather than being something that happens to the transcendental subject, produces it in the first place (*SP* 82). Because signs cannot be excluded from solitary mental life and the sphere of ownness, the transcendental reduction is, in a certain way, shown to be impossible. But it was necessary to go through the reduction in order to locate the retentional trace and *différance*. This ultra-transcendental experience of arche-writing cannot be reduced to the form of presence.

## Fluxus event scores

Fluxus works explicate marginal life. They provoke and play with constitutional activity. My point in criticizing Hannah Higgins has not been in order to provide a better explanation of experience as such but to gain a new perspective in order to approach Fluxus works: one that is not sensualist, nor strictly conceptualist. Husserl's phenomenology provides this. At the same time, we must always remain vigilant against falling back into the idea of presence as the ultimate guarantor of ideality and meaning. Further, the beholding of the artwork, the perception of the artwork, involves a mode of intentionality. The art spectator hardly perceives the work of art as something else – for instance a piece of equipment – but always according to an as-structure of experience (art as art). For Husserl, constitution of the object is not arrived at in a moment of pure and immediate presence; rather, the object is constituted by an anticipatory movement of building up expectations. The most effective Fluxus works are not simply raw reality, bits of reality assembled together, in order for a participant to have an experience – although there are certainly some Fluxus works that fall into this category. While still dealing with the most ordinary elements of everyday life, they bring about a rupture in the constitutive activity of the viewer, redirecting attention to the unfolding of the layers of constitution. Further, not all of these layers of constitutive activity are read directly off the here and now of the immediate presence of the work. The experience of these works occurs as a subtle blending of potential and actual, implicit and explicit. In any experience, constitution is pervaded by certain fore-structures which lead to pre-understanding. In the Fluxus work, very often the pre-understanding that conditions constitution is in some way put into question.

Consisting of short lists of instructions, minimally paired down to very economic language, that explicitly or implicitly call for actions to take place, a proliferation of 'event' scores appeared within the Fluxus milieu between 1959 and 1962. These word-works fluctuate between an expanded musical score, set of instructions, proposal and poem. The three most prolific producers of event scores, La Monte Young, George Brecht and Yoko Ono, were all directly or indirectly influenced by Cage. Further, many commentators have drawn attention to how Cage's score for *4' 33"* functioned as the exemplary precursor of Fluxus event scores.

Young's word scores ranged from simple performance instructions such as *Composition 1960 #10 to Bob Morris* (1960), 'Draw a straight line and follow it', to instructions for performance where a fire is built in front of an audience (*Composition 1960 #2*), or where a butterfly is to be turned loose in an auditorium (*Composition 1960 #5*), to the enigmatic scores: *Piano Piece for David Tudor #3* (1960) 'most of them were very old grasshoppers', and *Composition 1960 #15 to Richard Huelsenbeck* (1960), 'This piece is little whirlpools out in the middle of the ocean.' While some pieces were performed, others were obviously meant as thought experiments, as Zen koans to be pondered.

Ono's first event scores appeared as instructions for the making, contribution to, and destruction of, a series of paintings exhibited at Maciunas's AG gallery in July 1961. These included *Painting to be Stepped On* (1960), 'Leave a piece of canvas or finished painting on the floor or in the street,' and *Smoke Painting* (1961), 'Light canvas or any finished painting with a cigarette at any time for any length of time. See the smoke movement. The painting ends when the whole canvas or painting is gone.' In 1962, at the Sōgetsu Art Centre in Tokyo, Ono took the revolutionary step of exhibiting the instructions without the paintings in a move which pre-empted the dematerialization of the artwork in the conceptual art of the late 1960s. Other notable Fluxus event scores include Alison Knowles's *#2 Proposition* (1962), 'Make a Salad', George Maciunas's *Piano Piece No. 13* (1962), where a performer nails down each key of a piano keyboard, *Piano Piece No. 10* (1962) which calls for a piano to be whitewashed, and Joe Jones's *Duet For Two Brass Instruments* (1964) which involves the inflation/deflation of a rubber glove.

In contrast to Brecht, Ono rejects chance operations, regarding them as constituting a practice of passive quietism – 'Satori by becoming plantlike', where one might 'turn into a reed'.[23] Although Brecht's enthusiasm for chance might be seen to relate much more to his early chance paintings of 1956–7, his scores seem to invite contingency into the here and now of the exhibition space. In many of Ono's scores the influence of Zen is apparent and resembles paradoxical koans where meditational action is to be carried out in the everyday life of the isolated individual, or in the mind of that individual – for example, *Laugh Piece* (1961) 'Keep laughing a week', *Cough Piece* (1961) 'Keep coughing a year.' Many of Brecht's scores, limited to the time and place of the exhibition, tend to encourage social participation and instigate interaction with ordinary, everyday objects (here the model is most certainly the Duchampian readymade). Examples are *Sink* (1962), 'on (or near) a white sink', *Stool* (c. 1962), 'on or near a stool', *Three Broom Events* (c. 1961), 'broom/sweeping/broom sweepings', or *Word Event* (1961) which simply contains the word 'exit'. Ono's scores consist of a finessed blend of simplicity and complexity and often extend into social and gender issues.

Brecht's scores often refer to objects, and usually these objects are the ordinary, familiar objects that might find their way into Husserl's examples of constituted objects: tables, chairs, glasses of water and so on. The event score *Three Chair Events* (1961) specifies a black chair, a yellow chair and a white chair. In the score the 'occurrence' (Brecht's word in the score) associated with each chair is slightly different. The viewer is urged to sit on the black chair, sit on or near the white chair and simply encounter the yellow chair. In a realization of this piece at Martha Jackson Gallery in April 1961, the white chair was placed in the galley under a spotlight with a stack of the printed score nearby, while the black chair was placed in the bathroom and the yellow chair was placed on the footpath outside the gallery. Although we might view the chairs in terms of the idea of found objects, in proximity to Duchamp's readymades, their object status as such does not constitute the focus of the work. Rather, what is made thematic in the work is the space between the textual component (the score) and the object. This spatial and temporal gap is to be filled in with the experience of the spectator.[24]

What the work 'performs' is the unfolding of that experience in terms of the constitution of the object through the combination of adumbrated perceptions, memory and language. Language is not something external to the work (as secondary experience) but functions *explicitly* as a guide and contributor to the constitution of the object in the spectator's experience. Language here functions in a way which in our normal relation to everyday objects is carried out *implicitly*. However, due to the placement of the chairs – one in the gallery space, the others in marginal places in between the gallery and the outside world – the textual work of the constitution of the objects is prone to be interrupted by the perceptual work of constitution, and in the process foregrounds the intertwined role of each. Further, because the chairs cannot be apprehended in the same space, the constitution of all three chairs involves, to some extent, retention and memory. The black and yellow chairs – anticipated by the reading of the score in the presence of white chair – in their apparent absence would have, for the spectator, remained, in Husserl's terms, 'unfulfilled', unless or until the other chairs were discovered and linked – by their colour – back to the work. In this very simple yet open-ended work a number of experiential possibilities are opened up. One of these possibilities is that the black and the yellow chair fall outside the internal horizon of the intentional object – the work of art – falling off into the external horizon of the background environment. In this instance the spectator might perceive the black and yellow chairs not as the chairs referred to in the score – as part of the work – but merely as part of the equipment of the gallery provided for those who may wish to sit in the bathroom (to tie their shoes, for example) or those who may wish to sit outside (to perhaps get some fresh air while resting their legs). In this instance the experiential contextual placement of the chairs overrides the textual symbolic determinations of the instructions in the score. The two chairs are 'hidden', but they are hidden in such a way that they do not break with the context of chairs in ordinary experience – they are not glued upside down on the ceiling, for example. There is the possibility that the contextual, everyday, horizonal aspect of constitution might be too strong for the spectator to identify the chairs as part of the work, perhaps provisionally, or perhaps for the duration of their visit – and they might walk away perplexed. *Three Chair Events*, like many other Fluxus works, in its very simplicity, brings into focus the complexity of the horizon structure of experience. The work demonstrates that constitution does not depend on presence, that presence is not the ultimate fulfilment of meaning and that experience is made up of horizons which may not harmoniously fuse together to create unified and stable sense. This is confirmed by the possible experience of the poor gallery-goer who *cognizes* but may fail to *re-cognize* the black and/or the yellow chairs as the objects referred to in the score. What the event scores perform is a subtle explication of the antecedent conditions of possibility of experience. This experience, as the work well demonstrates, is always already contextured by language and signification. The spectator of Fluxus works does not bathe in a river of sensations. Nor do they merely grasp intellectually, in a detached and distant way, the conceptual intention or idea of the artist.

## Fusion of horizons

Brecht's event scores are essentially open-ended structures of experiential horizons. They are also open to failure where the horizons may not fuse. Dick Higgins, in his essay 'Fluxus: Theory and Reception', accounts for the reception of avant-garde and Fluxus works, not, as they often are, in terms of shock, but as a hermeneutical shifting and fusion of horizons. Higgins utilizes Hans-Georg Gadamer's notion of the 'fusion of horizons' (*Horizonverschmelzung*) in which a unity of meaning is achieved by bringing together the world of the work with the world of the interpreter.[25] For Gadamer, we have an affinity to a tradition. Since our consciousness is shaped by the effective history (*Wirkungsgeschiche*) of our tradition, it also determines the sort of questions we can ask (about alien texts and traditions). We are bound to see things from a certain perspective or vantage point that has its limits. We cannot question beyond this horizon since we are grounded by it. However, our horizons, far from constituting finite limits, are able to shift. We are able to move beyond our horizon, and understand texts, traditions and cultures other than our own by moving and changing and thus enlarging our horizon.

For Higgins the work (in its performance, in its presentation) establishes a 'horizon of experience'. The recipient comes to the work with their own horizon of experience, and in the act of performance/presentation and spectatorship/audition, the recipient incorporates the work's horizon and there occurs – if interpretation results in understanding – a fusion of the horizons. After the event of spectatorship/audition the horizons cease to be actively fused. But the recipient's horizon – if the work has been successful – will have changed and have been permanently enlarged. The recipient instinctively matches horizons, compares expectations and participates in the process. The more actively recipients engage in the process, the more likely they are able to enjoy it. Yet it would seem that what the spectator encounters in the Fluxus event is not some alien or remotely ancient tradition – even though the modality of the Fluxus work radically departs from our aesthetic tradition – but opens onto the most ordinary and familiar aspects of contemporary experience in the Western context. Although Gadamer's notion of a fusion of horizons seeks to reconcile interpretation and experience rendering the strife of the work safe – a criticism made by Caputo in *Radical Hermeneutics* – his thoughtful consideration of the value of avant-garde works points to a more radical conception where the hermeneutic engagement in such works results in a dramatic overturning of previously held positions and an orientation or openness to new experience.[26]

## Contextured experience

The point is that Derrida's analysis demonstrates – *with* Husserl – that there can be no pure immediacy that is not caught up in, or inhabited by, structures of retention and protention. This certainly does not mean that Derrida denies the possibility of presence, consciousness or self-reflection, nor does it mean that nothing is present. Rather it indicates two things: that fulfilment does not absolutely depend on presence and that what is present is unfolded through the significative action of language. What does it mean for the work of art to claim that the differential trace is older than presence? For one thing it means that the claim that a work of art has on us, in our experience of it, cannot be isolated from repetition and language; cannot be removed from the social world to some hermetic and unreachable realm of ineffability. While it can be said that the work of art resists circumscription by language, and is always in excess of signification, this does not mean that the primary experience of the work can be reduced to mute sensuality which casts off discursive interpretation as secondary and derivative; always falling outside the work; always unfulfilling. Moreover, there can be no pure experience in which the work gives itself, no naked encounter with bare actuality – such as in a work like Cage's 4′33″ – that is not already inhabited by language and signs.

We have seen how the work of art that directs us towards bare phenomena – the flux of experience – raises questions regarding access, retention and maintenance. How do we inhabit the work? How do we engage with the flux? My purpose in examining Derrida's 'deconstruction' of phenomenology is to arrive at a way of dealing with what continues to be central to the reception of the work of art: namely experience. Without context and language, the thing – the phenomenon – tends to slip away in contingency. We should not interpret Derrida's comments on perception as spelling the end of experience, or of the dissolution of experience into language. The work of art, like anything else, is experienced, but the particularly modernist, present-to-the-work, mode of engagement with the work might rather be rethought in terms of repetition. This does not mean that experience and materiality dissolve into language and conceptuality, or that we are held hostage to discursivity; rather, it means that, in terms of the way the work of art is encountered, the idea of immediate experience as absolute and primary should not govern the total act of reception from a position that is beyond discursive questioning. This is, to some extent, the way that Derrida himself responds to a question posed by Terry Smith in Sydney in 1999 which I will summarize in the following way: Does the artistic drive to flee from discourse – in either pure opticality, absolute materiality, or dematerialization – equate to a desire to perceive without knowing, or is art always caught up in a form of writing broadly and differentially conceived as *écriture*? Derrida answers that his thinking has attempted to open a space in which sonic, vocal, tactile or optical impressions come to be interpreted as traces in terms of a reading-writing (*écriture*) that is not, however, hierarchically subjected to logocentric authority of verbal discourse. He further responds by saying: 'Visual art is never totally "pure", never free of traces, which, implicitly or not, inscribe the possibility of phonetic or even verbal discourse in the most visual and the mute aspects of so-called visual art.'[27] The compulsion to the purely sensual – pure opticality, pure hapticality, pure sonority – Derrida claims are prevented from reaching pure fulfilment in full plenitude by their own inherent spatio-temporal 'spacing': 'as an interval of conjunction/disjunction, as interruption, and by reference to another trace.'[28] Thought in this way – which I suggest is the very way that Heidegger conceives of the work of art – the work functions in a space in which the work is neither dominated, assimilated or circumscribed by discourse, nor lifted above discourse in a realm of pure mute presence of non-knowing or, as Smith says, 'at least a kind of knowing that is so transparent that it doesn't require a translation back into the world.'[29] We might say, in short, that works of art are in some way intertwined with theory but are not reducible to theory.

7

# The spark of contingency

## Photography, cinema and temporality

The photographic medium has the power to re-present in a way which is outside of human control and intervention; outside of the representations of an intentional act of consciousness. This is an observation made by a number of theorists including Walter Benjamin, Siegfried Kracauer, André Bazin and Roland Barthes. For Benjamin, certain photographs deliver us over to what he calls the 'optical unconscious'; for Kracauer, photography participates in the redemption of physical reality; for Bazin, photography makes distinct the complex fabric of the real; and, for Barthes, the photograph has the capacity to capture the contingent elements that escape the focusing consciousness of the photographer's intention. In all of these accounts the photographic mediation has a distinctly different relation to the real than have other artistic mediums. What gives itself to the camera is essentially different from what gives itself to the eye of consciousness. In this chapter I will examine the works and theoretical rationales of artist that have used the photographic apparatus – in both still photography and cinema – in such a way as to substitute for conscious direction – of camera, place, mise en scène, lighting, framing and focus – some system or systematic procedure, in order to let the camera be an automatic, mechanical registration device. Further, throughout all of the analysis to follow, special consideration will be given to the relation of the photographic image and the cinematic image to time. However, before proceeding to a consideration of these practices, I will first determine what is at stake in the various theoretical positions listed in this paragraph.

I will begin with what is surely the most contentious of the four accounts: Bazin's theory of the ontological equivalence between the photographic image and its referent. In one of his earliest essays written in 1945, 'The Ontology of the Photographic Image', Bazin argues that the photographic image is possessed of 'the instrumentality of a non-living agent',[1] and that in photography 'for the first time an image of the world is formed automatically without the creative intervention of man'.[2] Bazin observes that the photograph is analogous to the moulding of the death mask and is essentially an automatic process of making impressions. As a preserving registration of life after the subject's death, the photograph performs an act of mummification and, hence, Bazin will say that cinema embalms time, duration and change. Providing the example of the Shroud of Turin, Bazin emphasizes that the photograph participates in a continuous transferal of the reality of the pro-filmic event to its representation.

It would be a vast understatement to say that Bazin's ontological realism has received a fair amount of criticism in film theory. By equating the being of the pro-filmic event with the being of the photographic image, and designating that relation as the essence of cinema and the starting point of all criticism, Bazin exposes his analysis to charges of naive naturalism, where the cinematic apparatus is seen to provide a mirroring of the world in a direct, self-giving, image. This naturalism, which participates in an effacement of the trace and signification, proposes absolute transparency between the referent (and its truth) and its representation. Thus, an artful film is, for Bazin, one which directly hands over its subject matter to the spectator with the maximum of verisimilitude. However, as Bazin admits – at the end of 'The Ontology of the Photographic Image' – cinema must also be thought as a language. Yet, although the essence of cinematic meaning certainly does not consist of a natural transparency between thing represented and its representation, Bazin's observation that the very nature of photographic image gives it the capacity to re-present reality without human subjective intervention still holds. Bazin's mistake was to make this fact the overarching basis of his cinematic criticism.

Bazin radically differentiates photography from other representational or analogical reproductions of reality in the plastic arts such as painting. Whereas painting is 'always in fee to an inescapable subjectivity',[3] photography proceeds from the 'power of an impassive mechanical process'.[4] In a similar way, more than a decade and a half later, in his essay 'The Photographic Message' (1961), Barthes argues that 'there is no drawing, no matter how exact, whose exactitude is not turned into a [subjective] style', and, as such, is, in distinction to the photographic image, a coded message. Much like Bazin, Barthes concedes that the photograph, as a continuous registration of the scene it captures, is analogous to its referent. As an objective mechanical recording rather than a transformation, it constitutes, for Barthes, a denoted, non-codified, message – a message without a code. But, of course, the photograph is capable of signifying something, and it certainly also possesses, as Barthes observes, the power of connotation. Connotative meaning issues from the human intervention of framing, lighting, placing, cropping and so on. Going beyond Bazin, Barthes argues that the very objectivity of the mechanical, non-human, registration of the camera reinforces the myth of photographic naturalism. In other words, connotation, which is often more subtle, rests on the innocence of denotation, and it is through this 'innocenting' work of denotation that ideology works silently through the photograph.

Barthes, however, begins talking about a non-coded message in the photographic image from 1970, in his essay 'The Third Meaning: Research Notes on Some Eisenstein Stills', where the 'obtuse' or 'third' meaning is what is left over and still holds us when we take away the informational meaning and the symbolic meanings. This term develops into the better-known notion of the *punctum* deployed in 1980 in *Camera Lucida*. Neither the obtuse meaning nor the *punctum* can be 'objectively' read off the image. The obtuse meaning does not contradict the obvious meaning, nor does it affect the obvious reading if it is taken away. The same can be said of the relation of the *punctum* to the *studium*. If, indeed, the obtuse meaning and the *punctum* are not identical concepts, what is central to both is that the meaning that arises from the photographic image can never be entirely the product of the photographer or film director's intention. As Barthes puts it, 'a photograph's *punctum* is the accident which pricks me.'[5] It belongs to what Barthes describes as the essentially contingent nature of photography.[6]

We might ask what kind of message is the photographic message? Does it constitute a sign? In the terms of Charles Sanders Peirce, the photograph belongs to class of signs that he designates as indexes. The indexical sign is where meaning is intimately bound to an object in a causal relationship. The index is the trace of an event, an indication of the past presence of something – that something has been, has existed. The photograph as a registration of light is the direct index of the scene which it captures. However, the photograph, as Peirce acknowledges, also has the additional properties of the icon, or iconic sign, due to the fact that, like a drawing or painting, it shows something, as a representation. But, for Peirce, the iconic dimension of the photograph is secondary to its indexical dimension. It is the indexical status of the photographic image that radically separates it from the drawing or the painting, a separation that both Bazin and Barthes rigorously maintain. Echoing Bazin, Mary Ann Doane writes: 'In photography, for the first time, an aesthetic or spatial representation could be made by chance, by accident, without human control.'[7] In terms of its status as a sign, the index is potentially exterior to human subjectivity and meaning, and its work of signification is carried out both 'inside and outside of semiosis'.[8] For Doane, the essential role of chance and contingency is to represent this 'outside'. What is of particular interest to Doane, and to this study, is this relation between indexicality and contingency.

## Voluntary and involuntary memory

Although in *Camera Lucida*, Barthes still commits to a certain realism that insists that the photograph is analogical and is an emanation of a past referent rather than a copy of it, he qualifies this position by stressing that the *noeme* of the photograph has little to do with analogy. There is, however, a 'chafing' in this text – observed by Michael Fried, in his *Why Photography Matters as Art as Never Before* – between what Barthes ascribes to the power of the photograph to grant 'a sentiment as certain as remembrance',[9] – here Barthes is discussing the Winter Garden Photograph, depicting his mother as a child – and his remark that the photograph is 'never in, essence, a memory . . . but it actually blocks memory, quickly becomes counter memory'.[10] What seems to be contrary in Barthes's thoughts on the photograph, as Fried observes, turns on the Proustian distinction between voluntary and involuntary memory.[11] This is summed up quite well, as Fried shows in Proust's preface to *Contre Sainte-Beuve*:

> any deliberate attempt on the part of a subject to imprint a contemporary scene on his or her memory will not only fail to capture its reality, it will actually render the latter irrecuperable in the future by the action of involuntary recall. Put more strongly, only scenes and events that escape the subject's conscious attention in the present are eligible to be recovered

in the future, and thus, according to Proust, to be truly experienced for the first time.¹²

In Barthes's vocabulary, as Fried astutely observes, involuntary memory equates to the *punctum* which, for the spectator, 'depends on its nonexistence for the photographer', while voluntary memory, although Fried merely implies it, equates to *studium* – that which the photographer intends to capture.¹³

Similarly, Benjamin regards photography as having a dual nature. On the one hand, photography is *mémoire volontaire*, which is associated with the decline of aura, since the eye of the camera does not return our gaze. On the other hand, in his 1931 essay, 'A Small History of Photography', Benjamin observes something in old photographs such as Dauthendey's nineteenth-century portrait of himself and his fiancé taken just before the birth of her sixth child, after which she slashed her wrists. He writes:

> No matter how artful the photographer, no matter how carefully posed his subject, the beholder feels an irresistible urge to search such a picture for the tiny spark of contingency, of the Here and Now, with which reality so to speak has seared the subject.¹⁴

Photography allows us, as Benjamin suggests, to discover the 'optical unconscious'.¹⁵ This aspect of photography is certainly not analogous to the *mémoire volontaire*. Rather, it seems to be much more aligned with Proust's *mémoire involontaire*. In the introduction to his *Theory of Film: The Redemption of Material Reality*, Siegfried Kracauer quotes Marcel Proust's description of the ideal photographer in *The Guermantes Way*, as emotionally detached observer, witness and stranger. After a long and detailed consideration in which he raises many objections, and protests that Proust's conception is one-sided as a result of his concern with involuntary memories,¹⁶ Kracauer, some five pages later, says, 'no doubt Proust exaggerates the indeterminacy of photographs'; however, 'Proust is again essentially right, for however selective photographs are they cannot deny the tendency toward the unorganized and diffuse which marks them as records.'¹⁷

We are able to get a sense of Benjamin's 'optical unconscious' from his discussion of involuntary memory in the essay 'On Some Motifs in Baudelaire', where Benjamin observes that Proust puts into question the voluntarism of *mémoire pure* as it functions in Henri Bergson's *Matter and Memory*. Benjamin refers us to Freud's statements on memory and consciousness in *Beyond the*

*Pleasure Principle*, where Freud speculates that consciousness may not be the master of our mental processes but might rather be a singular function of them. Freud proposes that the most powerful and affective fragments of memory, held onto by the subject, are those which never entered consciousness in the first place. The formation of memory, in Freud's view, is largely constituted through psychical systems other than consciousness. For Benjamin, translating Freud's theory into Proust's terms, 'this means that only what has not been experienced explicitly and consciously, what has not happened to the subject as an experience, can become a component of the *mémoire involontaire*.'[18] To align this notion of deferral with the optical unconscious of photography is not to say that the camera is simply unconscious – which, of course, it is, since it has no consciousness. Rather, the camera captures what is not consciously 'intended' – in both its literal and phenomenological sense – by the photographer, and the photograph preserves those contingent details. In this way the optical unconscious specifies a relation between photographer, camera and photograph.

## The hauntology of the photographic image

The photographic image, as an index, maintains an existential bond between meaning and referent, as Barthes says it is 'somehow co-natural with its referent',[19] it is modified, or even, as Doane puts it, 'haunted by its object'.[20] Discussing the photographic medium in a text accompanying the photographs of Marie-François Plissart, *Right of Inspection*, Derrida expresses a fondness for the word 'medium' which, he says, 'speaks to me of spectres, ghosts and phantoms. . . . After the first "apparition", it's all about the return of the departed (*le retour des revenants*). . . . The spectral is the essence of photography.'[21] Here Derrida seems to be hinting that the indexicality of the photographic medium, rather than being questioned in terms of Bazin's ontology of the photographic image, might better be thought as open to what Derrida calls in *Spectres of Marx* a 'hauntology' (*SM* 10). There are two reasons why we might say this. First, the above noted existential bond is taken up by Derrida in reference to Barthes's observation that 'The photograph is literally an emanation of the referent'.[22] As such, the photograph does not suspend reference but 'indefinitely defers a certain type of reality, that of the *perceptible* referent'.[23] The photograph, Derrida says, frames the wholly other in endless reference, over and over again, 'It gives the prerogative to the other, opens the infinite uncertainty of a relation to the completely other, a relation without relation'.[24] Second, for Husserlian phenomenology, constitution occurs with a temporal structure of horizons. What is futural in anticipation and protention is to a large degree an effect of the 'past', of memory and retention, and is in Derrida's terms a repetition. But this phenomenological model is limited to temporal succession and continuity. Retention, according to Husserl's theory of internal time-consciousness – or at least in Derrida's reading of it – can only retain a modified present: a past present. In the response to this unquestioned linearity, Derrida introduces what he calls 'the absolute past'. Following Freud's concept of deferred effect (*Nachträglichkeit*), this is the repressed memory of an event which never entered consciousness in any present moment. It is a past which has never been present to a subject, a *mémoire involontaire*.

As Derrida says in *Speech and Phenomena*, what Husserl ceaselessly emphasizes in speaking of reflection is: the presence of the present is thought of as arising from the bending back of a return, from the movement of repetition, and not from the reverse (*SP* 68), 'a primordial and incessant synthesis that is constantly led back upon itself, back upon its assembled and assembling self by retentional traces and protentional openings' (*SP* 152). But when we consider the role of the unconscious, alterity enters this seamless system and temporal disruption is introduced, dividing the continuity of the temporal flow. In *Specters of Marx*, Derrida reinscribes this model, where the future comes back in advance, as 'hauntology'.[25] The singularity of the 'first time' of an event in repetition is necessarily, as a consequence of its singularity, also the 'last time'. Thought in this way, hauntology would always be before any teleology and eschatology. It is a coming back that repeats over and over (like photographic reference). This parallels what Benjamin says of particular nineteenth-century photographs.

> the beholder feels an irresistible urge to . . . to find the inconspicuous spot where in the immediacy of that long forgotten moment the future subsists so eloquently that we, looking back may rediscover it. For it is another nature that speaks to the camera than to the eye: other in the sense that a space

informed by human consciousness gives way to a space informed by the unconscious.[26]

The contingent details of the picture, which the photographer would not have been conscious of at the moment of its exposure, can be read decades later as points (*puncta*) that wound us. They come to us in as envoys of a past that was never present to any consciousness – only the unconsciousness of the camera eye. It is through photographs such as these, Benjamin proposes, 'that we first discover the existence of this optical unconscious, just as we discover the instinctual unconscious through psychoanalysis'.[27]

In distinction to the cinema, the still photograph, Barthes says, is spectral, since it has a relation with a non-shifting referent and emphatically pronounces the temporal modality of 'that has been'. In the cinema we can say that something has passed, but in the photograph, Barthes contends, something has posed or come under arrest. Barthes explains this difference, in Husserlian terms, proposing that whereas the cinema flows by in the same constitutive style, the photograph breaks the constitutive style. The photograph is not futural due to the nature of its arrest; rather, it 'flows back from presentation to retention'.[28] Unlike the cinema, it is not protentional. Yet, a few pages later Barthes announces a new discovery which reveals the photograph's capacity to depict a particular kind of future. There is a new *punctum* in the photographic image, and it is *time*, or more precisely, the uncanny equivalence between the 'this has been' (what Barthes calls the *noeme* of photography), and the 'this will be'. This equivalence supersedes the earlier 'illogical conjunction' in the photograph made in 1964, in 'The Rhetoric of the Image,' between the 'here now' and the 'here then'.[29] This new *punctum*, which Barthes discovers in Alexander Gardner's photograph of Lewis Payne waiting to be executed in his cell, is born of the realization: 'he is dead, and he is going to die.'[30] Opening up the photographic portrait to a hauntology, Barthes summarizes, 'By giving me the absolute past of the pose (aorist), the photograph tells me death in the future.'[31] This strange temporality of the still image is carried one step further. For Barthes, this *punctum* is the sign of his own inevitable death. This means that what is structural to any photographic portrait, regardless of how distant in time its moment of exposure is separated from the present and, presuming that it persists beyond the finitude of its subject, is the photograph's announcement of the inevitability of the spectator's own death.

## Contingency systems

In the twentieth century, in order to capture the singular and contingent, a number of photographers and filmmakers sought to escape the conscious gaze of the camera operator and let the camera act as an automatic mechanical registration device, in order to allow and enable what Luc Sante calls 'the genius of the medium'. In his book, *Evidence*, Sante documents a collection of photographs of crime scenes taken by New York City Police between 1914 and 1918. The photographs taken by ordinary police officers are shot in an entirely objective way aiming at full coverage. Many are taken with an extreme wide-angle lens high above the victim on an extra-large tripod – the frame extended as wide as possible in order to capture the maximum of forensic detail. We see the legs of the tripod in the shot, often with the shoes of the police officers. This absolutely non-artistic vernacular photography, with its forensic motives, reveals a rich field of ephemeral detail providing a view of the texture of life and the social fabric of the period.

A similar richness of contingent detail is achieved in Ed Ruscha's serial photographic book projects. *Twentyfour Parking Lots* (1967), (actually thirty-one) aerial photographs of empty parking lots taken on a Sunday from a helicopter straightforwardly and non-artistically depict these spaces in their out-of-use state, by way of a typology of the mundane. *Every Building on the Sunset Strip* (1967) consists of a 750 centimetre accordion folded document (images 1 5/8 inch high). The series of images, covering a four-kilometre stretch of the Los Angeles's Sunset Boulevard known as the Strip, was photographed in the harsh light of noon using a motorized 250 Nikon mounted on a moving pickup truck in two sweeps, covering both sides of the street (one side inverted in the document), producing what Ruscha refers to as a 'very democratic view of what this entire thing looks like not highlighting anything that is particularly sociologically interesting or anything. I would give as much attention to a concrete curb as I would a building'.[32]

John Baldessari's *The Back of All the Trucks Passed While Driving from Los Angeles to Santa Barbara, California, Sunday 20 January 1963* (1963) in a similar way documents a series of events according to a rule-based system. The work consists of thirty-two images depicting the backs of various trucks shot from the vehicle travelling behind them, prior to each one being passed, and arranged in a four by eight grid. Several artists have repeated Baldessari's project including Franco Vaccari with his *700 km di esposizione Modena Graz* (1972) which consists of a four by five grid of twenty photographs, and Eric Tabuchi's *Alphabet Truck* (2008) which, taken over a much longer timespan, is limited to shots of the backs of trucks that display one single alphabetic character (usually in a corporate logo). Each of the twenty-six shots, covering the entire English alphabet, is precisely framed so that the back of each truck sits dead centre in the photograph and are all exactly the same size. The words 'every' in Ruscha's title and 'all' in Baldessari's title – and also the later work, *Car Color Series: All Cars Parked on the West Side of Main Street, Between Bay and Bicknel Streets, Santa Monica at 1:15 P.M., September 1, 1976* (1976), a series of seven photographs – rather than signalling a totality, describe the enabling limits of a constraint that disallows any editing or selection of the material. Much like Cage's acceptance of all sounds, these approaches to photography take a 'democratic' attitude. All presuppositions of what a thing looks like are supressed, and in this way the contingent detail of the *mémoire involontaire* asserts itself.

This self-generating seriality is also deployed by Bernd and Hilla Becher whose photographs of industrial structures are likewise exhibited in serial grid arrangement. The Bechers, whose life-long collaboration began in 1959, take a taxonomic or typological approach to documenting ordinary, but slowly disappearing, industrial architecture built in the nineteenth and twentieth centuries. These structures include water towers, cooling towers, blast furnaces, mine lift winding towers and gas reservoirs. Taking these photographs with a large format camera, the Bechers adhere to a strict system of rules where all compositional aspects are decided in advance. The photographs are taken in spring or autumn when there is more chance of a slightly clouded sky generating a diffused light which produces a minimum of shadows. The structures are photographed straight-on from a raised position in order to be free as possible from perspectival distortion, occupying the full frame, equally scaled and centred. There is an effort to eliminate extraneous detail from the photograph such as human figures, foliage and clouds, where practically possible. The images carry no connotation, no historical or social commentary. They are simply denotative, representing the object accurately, honestly and objectively. The photographs are grouped according to the function or, we might say type, of the industrial structures arranged in a grid (most often of nine images, but, sometimes four, six, eight, twelve and as many as twenty-four). In these tableaus one is immediately stuck by the singularity that emerges out of a technological sameness. The 'thingness' of the structures is brought about by the regularity of their functional design in opposition to a certain contingency signalling their difference. What is accidental in each photograph is amplified by its proximity to the others in the series.

Although the Becher's photographs provide a documentation of disappearing industrial architecture, they present their subject in a minimal way which strips away representation and proceeds in a manner which is strictly formal without subjective aestheticism. This same minimalism applies to the serial systematic photographic work of Ruscha and the work of Baldessari discussed earlier. We could also include in this description a number of works from the 1970s such as Jan Dibbets's *Shutterspeed Piece,* Konrad Fischer's *Gallery I* (1971) and *Shadows on the Floor of the Sperone Gallery* (1971), Hans Haacke's *Shapolsky et al. Manhattan Real Estate Holdings: a Real-Time Social System, as of May 1, 1971* (1971), Douglas Huebler's *2/variable piece no. 70* (1971), Eleanor Antin's *Carving: A Traditional Sculpture* (1972), Gerhard Richter's *48 Portraits* (1972–88), Bas Jan Ader's *In Search of the Miraculous (One Night in Los Angeles)* (1973), Charles Ray's *All My Clothes* (1973) and Martha Rosler's *The Bowery in Two Inadequate Descriptive Systems* (1974–5).

## Structural cinema and structural materialist film

Much of the work mentioned in the previous paragraph is characterized by the favouring of what Stephen Heath refers to as images of 'minimal potency'. Heath uses this term to describe the cinema of 'structural/materialist film', where potent signifiers, such as Peter Gidal's example of the image of a pregnant woman, are avoided in favour of banal images which allow 'for the attention to the *film's* process, *its* construction'.[33] Structuralist/materialist film sought to self-reflexively shift attention to the 'experience of the process of film in the viewing situation',[34] and pitted itself against other currents of experimental avant-garde filmmaking of the 1960s and 1970s. For the political vanguard of structural/materialist film, centred around the London Filmmakers Co-op – less so than allied filmmakers on the continent, and the North American filmmakers and artists that fell under the name 'structural film' – the aim of the project was to subvert what they called the cinema of illusion, by which they meant all narrative, mainstream cinema. This study is not the place to evaluate the problems introduced by such a programme. What I will focus on here, in examining structural/materialist film and structural film, is the way in which minimal potency is deployed, and how very often the camera is utilized in a mechanical way that curtails subjective decisions. Along with a reduction in the content of the image, one finds in structural and structural/materialist cinema static, locked-off, shots where action is not followed by the camera, but rather the camera is left to accept whatever comes into frame.

Many structural/materialist films were shot according to a predetermined system. The Austrian filmmaker Kurt Kren organized the shooting of his films around a detailed script or 'score' which was often determined mathematically. Kren's *48 Köpfe aus dem Szondi-Test* (1960) and *Bäume im Herbst* (1960) were shot this way using in-camera editing. A subcategory of the structural/materialist formalist film which came to be known as 'British landscape films' aimed to capture a non-anthropocentric perspective through the use of systematic and mechanical camera operations. Malcolm Le Grice describes this sub-genre as 'films where the event on the screen is essentially to be considered as the direct record of an event which took place in and through the camera, that is, films which largely do not involve any later transformation through editing or reprocessing'.[35] In Chris Welsby's *Wind Vane Film* – of which there are different versions made in 1970 and 1972 – the panning operation of the tripod was controlled by an attached wind vane to allow panning of the camera to be determined by the direction of the wind. In *Windmill II* (1973) and *Windmill III* (1974), a small windmill was placed in front of the camera, its flat mirror blades partially obstructing the landscape beyond. The reflective blades (covered in a mirrored fabric called Melinex) reveal the landscape behind the camera juxtaposing it in a wipe pattern that becomes more confused as the wind speed increases and the blades turn faster. Peter Wollen observes that within the British landscape films, 'A profilmic event, which is a conventional signified ("landscape"), intervenes actively in the process of filming, determining operations on the "specifically cinematic" codes'.[36] The specifically cinematic codes in *Windmill II*, and *III*, can be seen not only in the wipe transition produced by the blades but also in the camera shutter. The rotating windmill effectively operated as a second shutter, and in this way the speed of the wind determined a subtle effect on the depth of image – sharpening fast-moving elements and fragmenting slower movement (human figures that cross the frame) as the wind speed increases.[37]

In the production of the much more ambitious *Seven Days* (1974), Welsby used a piece of astronomical equipment – an equatorial stand – used by astronomers to maintain a stationary relation to the star field that, when aligned with the earth's axis, rotates around its own axis at the speed of the earth's rotation. By the use of this mechanism the camera was always pointing at the sun or its own shadow (the decision to switch between being determined by the amount of cloud cover). One frame was taken every ten seconds during the hours of daylight. As Welsby explains, 'The final shape of the film is consequently a product of the interaction between the predictable mechanistic nature of technology and the chance-like qualities of the natural world.' [38] Also captured over an extended period, Welsby's *River Yar* (1971–2), made with William Raban, was shot through an upstairs window in a water mill on the Isle of Wight. A camera recorded the view of the tidal estuary one frame every minute (day and night) for two separate three-week periods in autumn and spring using identical framing in each setup. The spring and autumn sequences were projected on two adjacent screens. In this work, Welsby sees the natural temporal cycles as the determining agency in the structure of the film. Resembling the English landscape films, *La Région Centrale* (*The Central Region*, 1971) is a three-hour film shot by Michael Snow on a remote mountaintop in North Quebec. Snow utilized a robotic camera arm that allowed shooting in any direction without encountering the mechanism in the frame. The apparatus was pre-programmed for both camera motion and zoom. Le Grice, comparing this film to Welsby's, argues that although Snow's film is procedural, its shape is determined in advance rather than its shape being determined by a system that remains outside of the filmmaker's decision making.

## Time as film's concrete dimension

While the cinematic image shares with the (still) photographic image a genesis that is to some extent mechanical and independent of the conscious volition of a human subject, and while the photographic image has a relation to time as a 'this has been', the cinematic medium has as its primary dimension, or material, temporality itself. It is this realization that brought Le Grice and other members of the London Filmmaker's Co-op to explore the notion of 'duration as a concrete dimension of cinema'. With this focus on duration came a rejection of what they saw as the 'illusory' representation of time in cinema. Narrative film brings together a combination of different temporalities: the time of the action shown, the time of the story and finally the time of the duration of the film itself. Taking a stand against the compressed representation of time, the implied time of the narrative in conventional cinema, Le Grice and Gidal strongly advocate a one-to-one relation between the duration of shooting (or recording) and the duration of projection (or the duration of the film itself) so that represented film time differs in no significant way from the viewing time experienced by the spectator. It is interesting to note that, for Le Grice and Gidal, this equivalence does not necessarily presuppose a continuum of recorded time and does not preclude editing (discontinuity), as long as the splice is foregrounded, functioning to demarcate each shot as a piece of time, rather than montaging different shots in a representation of continuous duration achieved by the 'invisible' cutting of narrative cinema. With duration not necessarily linked to a continuum, the splice, as Gidal argues, in making itself obvious, forms a de-repression of duration.[39]

Gidal recognizes these autonomous shots, which he sees literally as pieces of time, in a number of structural/materialist films including Kurt Kren's *Bäume im Herbst*, a mathematically determined montage of dense bare tree branches and Lucy Panteli's *Across the Field of Vision* (1982), a montage of eight hundred shots of seagulls of varying length, scale, speed of movement and tonality. Like Kren's film, the subject matter does not vary from shot to shot and the viewer is not provided with any orientation or sense of scale, since the shots never include any traces of land or sea within them. A disruption of any stable reference point also occurs in Joyce Wieland's *Sailboat* (1967). Just beneath an indeterminate hazy horizon a small yacht moves across the field of vision coming into frame on the left and moving out of frame on the right. The sequence repeats several times. At first it is difficult to establish if the following shots are the results of reprinting or if they are further takes of the same yacht, or shots of different yachts. It is hard to tell if the camera is static and the yacht is moving, or if the camera is being panned. These ambiguities gradually become resolved throughout the course of the film's two minutes and forty-five seconds as the scale of the yacht is gradually reduced and the constant jerkiness of the camera suggests that some degree of panning is occurring.

Among the North American 'structural' films, Le Grice singles out Michael Snow's *One Second in Montreal* (1969) as a film which utilizes duration as a material. The twenty-six-minute film presents a series of still images of park sites proposed for a monument in Montreal shot in winter under conditions of heavy snow. The duration for which the stills are held steadily increases towards the middle of the film and then progressively decreases towards the end. This pattern of varying duration, for Le Grice, allows a 'qualitative awareness of the relationship of durational experience to the rate of change of presented information',[40] thereby, as Annette Michelson observes, 'forcing upon the spectator the consciousness of time as duration'.[41] Although Michael Snow's *Wavelength* (1967), consisting of a forty-five-minute zoom, would seem to be a prime example of the foregrounding of time as a concrete dimension of film, Le Grice argues that the represented or 'interior' duration of the film is contrived in favour of narrative expectations through invisible editing. Snow is here accused of covering up breaks in the filming in order to establish a clean continuum.[42]

Le Grice, however, applies these same criticisms of *Wavelength* to his own film made in the same year, *Blind White Duration* (1967) in as much as it 'establishes an "implied" duration of quite a different order to the material duration of the film'.[43] *White Field Duration* (1973) made six years later is essentially a response to the problem encountered in *Wavelength*. The later film falls into a category of 'pure cinema' where the content of the film, what the film is about, and even the pro-filmic event, is the material element of film itself. For Peter Wollen, such films constitute a double reduction, first through the exclusion of non-cinematic codes (music, speech, gesture, facial, expression, narrative) and, second, a reduction to the optical, photo-chemical substrate.[44] George Landow's[45] *Film in Which There Appear Sprocket Holes, Edge Lettering, Dirt Particles, etc.* (1965–6) consists of a lab colour test strip (a young woman's face with colour bars) loop printed in exact repetition, where with each reprinting the registration of dust particles subtly increases. In Le Grice's *White Field Duration* for the first section of the film, the only image is a continued scratch on clear celluloid. The second section of the film presents a re-filming of the first section. In both Landow's and Le Grice's films there is an ontological equivocation, as the structural filmmaker Paul Sharits notes, between the registered dust particles and scratches, and the actual dust particles and scratches that build up on the print with each screening, which reminds him of 'Vermeer's multiple mappings of mapping procedures'.[46] For Sharits, this 'equivocality of film's "being" is perhaps cinema's most basic ontological issue'.[47] And, as Peter Wollen observes, it is, as Sharits sees it, the consequence, of cinema's dual nature as recording/registration technology and optical/material process.[48]

An early precursor to Le Grice's *White Field Duration* is Nam June Paik's *Zen for Film* (1964) which consists of clear leader for most of its eight minutes, the other ten seconds taken up by brief single-frame flashes of the words 'FLUX-FILM - 1 - ZEN - FOR - FILM - BY - NAM - JUNE - PAIK'. Like Le Grice's film, it totally excludes any iconic reference. The point of Paik's film, as Craig Dworkin proposes, is time,[49] or as Le Grice and Gidal would say: duration as a concrete dimension. However, Dworkin points to two distinct durations: the duration of the film as it is projected and the duration of the film's, or more precisely, the print's 'life' as it proceeds slowly to its inevitable destruction with each screening. This latter duration is signalled by the build-up of scratches as the film print changes from screening to screening, and in this way, as Dworkin suggests, 'the material of the film inscribes time'.[50]

The exemplary model and essential precursor to the structural/materialist concern for the one-to-one equivalence of shooting time to screening time is the early cinema of Andy Warhol: *Eat* (1963), *Sleep* (1963–4), *Empire* (1964), *Haircut* (1964), *Blowjob* (1964) *Couch* (1964). In these films we find not only a one-to-one durational equivalence but, further, long periods of inactivity or minimal change in the pro-filmic event, and in some – *Eat* (the painter Robert Indiana eating for the forty-five-minute duration of the film), and *Empire* (a locked-off view of the Empire State Building for eight hours and five minutes) – we find a focus on the ordinary or commonplace. In both *Eat* and *Empire* – which, I would argue, represent the most distilled representations of Warhol's early filmmaking – each reel of exposed film is simply joined together in its entirety sequentially so that the fogging on the reel ends and the lab's punch marks can be seen in the finished film.

For Le Grice, Warhol's 'most significant innovation', this one-to-one equivalence of shooting time to screening time (although Warhol in *Empire* extends the screening time with a slower projection speed) presents a 'shallow time' that is 'the equivalent to the abandonment of deep, illusory perspective in painting, in favour of a shallow picture space, directly relatable to the material nature of the actual canvas surface'.[51] The extreme length of these films (which are the precursors to what is called today 'slow cinema') forces a shift in attention from the interior space and time of the film to the time-space of its projection, inducing what Le Grice calls 'a functional boredom'.[52] Warhol has said that he made *Empire* in order 'to see time go by'.[53] This should not be taken as a flippant remark. According to Ronald Tavel (as related to David James), Warhol 'would sit and watch [his own films] for endless hours ... with absolute fascination and he was puzzled why the public wasn't equally fascinated'.[54]

## Boredom and art

Boredom, as Dick Higgins considers it in his essay 'Danger and Boredom', plays an important part in performance and the artwork. If boredom is prolonged, through the work, it eventually delivers us over to a state of intensive euphoria. Boredom, according to Higgins, frames intensity by bringing emphasis to what it interrupts. Higgins recalls one of John Cage's classes at the New School for Social Research in the summer of 1958 where Cage suggested performing one of George Brecht's pieces in total darkness. For Higgins the result was an 'extraordinary intensity that appeared in waves' as the audience wondered if the piece was over or not. Higgins relates that the class was asked to guess how long they had been in the dark. While the actual duration was 9 minutes, guesses ranged from 4 minutes to 25 minutes.

Higgins cites Erik Satie's composition, *Vexations*, a 32-bar piano piece that specifies 840 repetitions. The piece, often played by a team of pianists taking turns, lasts for about eighteen hours.[55] Higgins asks: 'Is it boring? Only at first. After a while the euphoria ... begins to intensify.'[56] John Cage relates the experience of performing *Vexations* to Daniel Charles: 'In the middle of those eighteen hours of performance, our lives changed.'[57] The note at the top of Satie's score reads: 'To play this motive 840 times in succession, it would be right to prepare oneself previously, and in the most dead silence, by earnest immobilities.' As Cage argues, these remarks are to be taken in the spirit of Zen

Buddhism: 'Satie has a concern for inactivity and for repetition far beyond, say, even Andy Warhol, not only in terms of time but in terms of the extent of activity.'[58] Elsewhere, in *Silence*, Cage writes:

> In Zen they say: If something is boring after two minutes, try it for four. If still boring, try it for eight, sixteen, thirty-two, and so on. Eventually one discovers that it's not boring at all but very interesting.[59]

## Profound boredom

Heidegger examines the phenomenon of boredom in *The Fundamental Concepts of Metaphysics*, a lecture series that followed the publication of *Being and Time*. Rather than merely constituting one of many affective states, Heidegger, here, regards the mood of boredom as a fundamental attunement (*Grundstimmung*), in a similar way to his deployment of the mood of anxiety (*Angst*) in *Being and Time*. He had briefly touched on boredom in the 1929 lecture 'What Is Metaphysics?' where he writes: 'Profound boredom, drifting here and there in the abysses of our existence like a muffling fog, removes all things and human beings and oneself with them into a remarkable indifference. This boredom reveals beings as a whole' (*GA 9* 7–8, *BW* 99).

If we stick with it and stay open to and not resist it, boredom as an existential orientation has the capacity to disclose something to us. If awakened, profound boredom provides the opportunity to find out and understand how things stand with us or, in other words, what our Dasein is, our being-there in the midst of things, an opportunity to find ourselves, not in our psychological status or personality, or set of values, but our basic being-there – our attunement to the world. Further, for Heidegger, boredom gives us an understanding of the structure of temporality. As he has indicated in *Being and Time*, Dasein is not merely constituted by time, Dasein essentially is time. It is Heidegger's aim to get a better understanding of this temporality in a way that is not merely mathematical (objective) or personal (subjective); thus he must demonstrate that boredom is infused in temporality, and the more 'profound' boredom becomes, the more it is deeply implicated in this non-objective, non-subjective time. In short, boredom provides one way towards understanding what Heidegger calls originary temporality.

Heidegger elaborates on three forms of boredom. The first, 'being bored by something', where something, someone or some situation bores us. In this form of boredom time drags, becomes long. Indeed, the German word for boredom, *Langeweile*, literally means 'long-while'. In boredom, time is lengthened. In being bored with something we attempt to stave off boredom by engaging in some activity. Whereas in the first form of boredom something external bores us, the second boredom, being bored with something (*sich langweilen bei etwas*), 'arises out of Dasein itself' (*GA 29/30*193, *FCM* 128). It involves time we have put aside that we seem to have taken for ourselves, but in fact, have taken *from* ourselves. Heidegger's example is a casual evening get-together that has no particular necessity, where one simply attends for the sake of it. Here we steal time from ourselves, we waste it. Time becomes a stretched 'now', a standing now of the 'during' of the evening. In this standing now we are cut off from our historical (having-been) and futural (to come) selves. We become boring to ourselves. Finally, the third form of boredom is *profound boredom* where 'it is boring for one' (*es ist einem langweilig*). Heidegger utilizes the German impersonal sentence structure which is like saying in English 'it is raining'. Here the 'it' is more like an intransitive verb than a substantive. In this sense we cannot say that it is boring for you, or for me, but in the more general sense of 'for one'. Moreover, it is not an object that is boring, nor a subject that is boring. What bores *is* not a thing but a sheer event that simply bores.

Unlike the first variety of boredom we are no longer concerned with the passing of time, we don't watch the clock, nor, as in the second form of boredom, is time a standing 'now'. But this does not mean that profound boredom delivers us over to a state of timelessness where we are situated outside the flow of time. Rather, a strange kind of temporality occurs. We become an undifferentiated de-personalized no one. What bores us in profound boredom is not things, not our own person, but time itself, or more strictly, 'temporality in a particular way of its temporalizing' (*GA 29/30* 236, *FCM* 158). But in being bored in such a way we are disclosed to our own Dasein's existential possibilities. In profound boredom we are entranced by the temporal horizon (an unarticulated unity of having-been, present and to come); however, boredom impels (in a rupture) Dasein into the moment of vision (*Augenblick*) in which its possibilities (of doing and acting) are disclosed.

As Heidegger indicates, the moment of vision, the *Augenblick*, is Kierkegaard's term, and translates the Danish *Øieblikket*, 'instant' or, literally, 'glance of the eye'. In 1927, Heidegger criticizes Kierkegaard's conception of time and the instant in terms of what he sees as an erroneous relation between 'the now' immanent to time and eternity. However, Kierkegaard's notion of the instant cannot in any way be equated to the now, presence or the interior self-presence of the subject to itself. As David J. Kangas observes, the instant, which is Kierkegaard's reinscription of Plato's 'the sudden' (*to exaiphnēs*), is an event that grants presence in terms of an infinite beginning. However, between *Being and Time* and the 1929–30 lectures, it seems that Heidegger may have re-assessed Kierkegaard's notion of temporality and the instant. In *The Basic Problems of Phenomenology*, Heidegger attributes the instant to Aristotle and the *kairos*. But in a 1930–1 seminar on Plato's *Parmenides*, Heidegger discusses the instant in terms of *to exaiphnēs*. In boredom one is exposed to temporalization which is what self-consciousness cannot interiorize through recollection or anticipation; thus self-consciousness is shown to be non-identical with itself – 'never finished, and never in possession of itself'.[60]

Kierkegaard has a similar conception of extreme boredom[61] in which, as Kangas observes, representational consciousness is ruptured, and self-consciousness is confronted with 'temporality *as* the nothing interlacing all existence – with time as *Afgrund* (abyss)'[62] and 'being *as a whole*, being as no-thing, is disclosed in its abyssal distinction from beings'.[63] This is essentially what Heidegger is saying in 'What Is Metaphysics': that boredom brings about the experience of the nothing (*Nichts*). Further, Kierkegaard, according to Kangas, takes Eckhart's *Gelassenheit* in the spirit of overcoming the self-will (*Eigenwille*), as overcoming self-possession, as the 'becoming one's own groundlessness, becoming nothing, letting go of one's self-understanding'.[64] In the 1929–30 lecture course, Heidegger is still far from pondering the non-willing thinking of *Gelassenheit*. Yet what is at stake, in the *Augenblick*, for Heidegger, is the self-liberation of Dasein which is achieved by Dasein resolutely disclosing itself to itself.

And this resolute self-disclosure is the moment of vision which is 'nothing other than the *look of resolute disclosedness*' (Blick der Entschlossenheit) (*GA 29/30* 224, *FCM* 149, Heidegger's emphasis). As we saw earlier, *Ent-schlossenheit*, hyphenated and reinterpreted as openness to being, is associated in the later

Heidegger with Eckhart's detachment (*Abgescheidenheit*) and releasement (*Gelassenheit*). Clarifying his methodology in the lectures on boredom we find an early occurrence of the term *Gelassenheit*. If we attempt to drive of boredom, we risk installing a second lived-experience which obscures it. Further, we should approach boredom from a perspective which is free of sedimented theories and artificially prepared attitudes, such as the transcendental reduction. Rather, 'what is required is *releasement* (Gelassenheit) *of our free, everyday perspective*' (GA 29/30 137, FCM 91, Heidegger's emphasis). As Kangas sees it, Kierkegaard formulates the basis of a post-transcendental subject where there is 'ineradicable difference and non-identity at the heart of self-consciousness'.[65] In a similar way, in an analysis of Heidegger's 1930–1 seminar on Plato's Parmenides, Jussi Backman describes Plato's 'instant', not in terms of the temporal 'now' but as that which mediates between presence and absence, in a way analogous to Derrida's notion of *différance*.[66] Derrida, employing his oft-quoted but never referenced phrase, which he attributes to Kierkegaard – 'the instant of the decision is madness'[67] – refers to Heidegger's dismissal of the Aristotelian concept of time determined as the movement of rotation (*kuklophoria*), in which the gift, including sacrifice (the 'gift of death'), would be impossible. For Derrida, a gift is only possible on the condition of a paradoxical instant (*Augenblick*) which constitutes an effraction of the temporal circle; an instant which is not a now, nor a part of time, but rather an 'atemporal temporality'[68] that 'tears time apart'.[69]

As Heidegger indicates, we cannot simply induce boredom. We cannot simply observe boredom, nor should we wish to do so. It must be experienced, and when it comes, it comes out of the blue. The Fluxus artists (and the Fluxus like activities) were very much concerned with investigating such modes of experience, not simply observing them but living them, living through them. Along with Fluxfilms, structural/materialist film and Warhol's cinema, one could also speak of Chantal Ackerman's films – certainly her three-and-a-half hour *Jeanne Dielman, 23 Quai du Commerce, 1080 Bruxelles* (1975), but perhaps more so the non-narrative films *Hotel Monterey* (1972) and *News from Home* (1976), consisting of long durations of locked-off shots where action is simply 'let' into the frame. What these works deliver is not boredom as such, nor the simple experience of boredom, but a reconfiguration of attention that, through repetition, redirects out attention to our own temporality. Not our *sense* of temporality but the temporality that constitutes one as a subject.

If these works grant the spark of contingency, what does that mean? On its own it means nothing – in as much as Alain Badiou and Ray Brassier insist that being means nothing – because the world and reality have no intrinsic meaning.[70] Certainly, reality is mind independent but meaning does not simply drop from the sky. Rather, as I have been arguing, meaning is a constituted effect of an anonymous system of traces, and it is never simply 'out there', nor is it the internal property of an individual subject. One might object by pointing to the oft-accidental discoveries of new phenomena in science. Does not science in this way find truth in unmediated reality? Thomas Kuhn observes that while normal scientific procedure does not explicitly look for novelties or anomalies – in fact it is deeply suspicious of them since they may well indicate a contaminated data set – there are often unforeseen discoveries in which new kinds of phenomena emerge, and they are regularly discovered by accident. Once isolated and verified by normal scientific procedure, they form the basis of a new accepted paradigm and a new structure of scientific expectations. However, Kuhn stresses that the unexpected new phenomenon 'emerges only with difficulty against a background provided by expectation'.[71] Further, the new phenomenon could not occur *without* this background of anticipation.

What this means is that here is never any pure objectivity that directly reads truth off the bare, indifferent, non-relative, non-human reality. As Bruno Latour says, the single scientific image gives us nothing. The idea of unmediated scientific objectivity is mythical. Rather, for Latour, the more we engage in mediation, the closer we get a grasp of reality.[72] What the speculative realism of Brassier and Quentin Meillassoux seems to be saying is that we have no business thinking the outside world in terms that are relative to us.[73] Yet reality has no meaning independent of a relational discourse which constitutes it for us. Without some sort of relation (or 'correlation') between thinking and reality there would be no meaningful access at all to reality. Nothing could be said of it.

So, what does the spark of contingency give us? As we encounter contingency and singularity in these mediations (works of art), we move closer towards the real because the real is infinitely removed from ideality (universals). The more we think the real away from ideality, the closer we get to, in certain sense, its radical otherness which means, conversely, the more distanced we become from any epistemological grasping the real. The real has infinite depth and can never be fully constituted in any absolute way. As Heidegger says, being always withdraws. Letting always occurs against a background of anticipation. In such a way, letting is nothing passive. It is not a form of transparency where the real gives itself in its truth and meaning. But still there is a question of access to the real. Such an access is never direct, never complete, never absolute, but always mediated, indirect and always involving elements of experience which are both present and absent. There can be no access without mediation, no singular access. Rather, access is gained through different modes, configurations and constructions.

8

# Poethics

I want to say something about the ethics of non-intention. That is, I *mean* to say something regarding the meaning, and/or what is meant, in artistic works involving non-intentional procedures. The language that I am employing here, which is our ordinary common-sense language, seems to assure me that I am capable of writing something meaningful in regard to my intentions. This is the sense of the French locution *vouloir-dire* that Jacques Derrida often employs. In English, this is highlighted by the double sense of the verb 'mean' where 'to mean' signifies 'to intend' and also 'to signify'. When I make such statements such as 'I want to say . . .', I find myself in a rather uncomfortable relationship with what I 'wish' to discuss in this chapter, namely the writing of non-intention. This non-intentional writing is perhaps more appropriately associated with John Cage's paradoxical phrase: 'I have nothing to say and I am saying it.' In one sense, we can take this as signifying an attitude of non-expressivity. But, further, it can perhaps be taken in the more radical sense of *possessing* nothing to say, or that what can be said cannot be a possession of one's own. The upshot of this certain non-possession is that what can be said is not *in* the subject but always already out in the network of differential traces. It is through this problematic that I will approach the possibility of an ethics of non-intention which may be an ethics of *Gelassenheit*: a 'po-ethics'.[1] This chapter seeks to argue that the chance operation, rather than constituting a law or principle, functions as a quasi-phenomenological *epochē* that suspends intention and decision in the course of the compositional process. Further, I argue that the non-intentional *epochē* opens up a kind of ethics. Addressing current concerns with ethics, non-intentionality is examined in terms of Derrida's critique of philosophical voluntarism, from his early notions of iterability to the later work on justice. Here I demonstrate that the later work of Derrida's 'ethical turn' – where it concerns the question or 'madness' of decision – extends an inquiry which was already underway in the earlier work.

I turn again to Cage who not only composed music and multimedia works but also generated a considerable amount of literature by means of chance operations, such as his mesostic[2] poems. Like the poet Jackson Mac Low, who adopted chance procedures in 1954 after encountering Cage's *Music of Changes* (1951),[3] Cage constructed a number of texts based on other texts, where aleatory operations are used to 'write-through' the source text. Tyrus Miller suggests that the writing-through of Ezra Pound's *Cantos*, in separate instances by both Cage and Mac Low, functions as an ethico-political gesture that is actively anti-political rather than being simply aesthetic and apolitical.[4]

In one of the Charles Eliot Norton lectures at Harvard (1988–9), a member of the audience puts a question to Cage concerning the experimental methodology of his writing. The participant points to an apparent contradiction between non-intention (taking things as they are) and intention (compositional choice) in Cage's description of the construction one of his aleatorically determined mesostic poems. As the participant points out, when it came to words rather than sounds, Cage seemed to be violating his own compositional rules by censoring the results of chance operations – as Cage had stated in the previous week's lecture: 'I went through and eliminated all the words I didn't like.'[5] In his defence, Cage explains his methods in the following terms: that he is 'hunting' for ideas and in order to uncover them, he must eliminate any other word that might get in the way of these ideas. Although Cage here speaks of musical or non-syntactic qualities (aesthetic qualities), the overriding determination for eliminating certain words would seem, rather, to be a concern with meaning. It would seem that Cage refuses to allow the limitless generation of meaning because such a relinquishing of authorial responsibility might inadvertently misrepresent his views on certain issues: such as his objections to militarism and government. Thus, Cage responds to his interlocutor:

> I don't know what it is that I will find but I'm looking in the mix for them [a series of words] and the only way that I can see them is to take out the ones that don't belong to them. And I use the word 'like'. It's because I'm in the position of writing a text that uses words. It's a different kind of language but it is every now and then highly suggestive, I think. And I want that suggestion to be in a spirit that I agree with.[6]

This exchange raises some interesting questions about an experimental ethics, or the ethics of non-intentionality. In particular we might ask: How does the surrendering of intentional agency come to terms with the call to ethical–political responsibility? Before returning to this issue I will briefly review Cage's project to see what is at stake here. We might say that his project can be best summed up in terms of the idea of 'experimental action', which he describes as 'simply an action the outcome of which is not foreseen'.[7] In order to arrive at the unforeseen, the unexpected or the surprising, Cage employs chance operations such as the use of the *I Ching* where coins are tossed in substitution of making choices (in the writing of the Norton Lectures (I-V) Cage utilized Jim Rosenberg's generative software 'Mesolist'). For Cage, the chance operation forms a constraint that puts out of action taste and memory. In his music composition, the constraint acts as a way of suspending judgements which might exclude certain sounds on aesthetic grounds (taste). Similarly, the constraint functions to prevent the habitual repetition of what the composer has done before or heard before (memory). I wish to argue here that the constraint functions as a form of bracketing, or an *epochē*, in phenomenological terms. In order to be effective, the rigour of the constraint must be observed. All outcomes must be accepted without revision. If one did not accept the final outcomes, and proceeded to consciously and subjectively alter the work, then the whole point of the constraint would be voided. As Cage observes in an interview (with Joan Retallack), 'It's very clearly stated in the *I Ching* that if you don't like the results of chance operations you have no right to use them (laughs).'[8] It is this perceived departure from rigour that concerns the questioner. If Cage abides by the chance operation in music absolutely, then why does he not do so in the production of poetry?

It seems that, as Cage sees it, sounds can be taken as they are, in any contingent arrangement because, rather than being 'suggestive', they merely fall into a non-meaningful, non-symbolic, regime of form, or are, alternatively, incorruptible indices of the real, while words and language, by contrast – possessing suggestion and connotation – carry the risk of ideological determination. Words and representation call for responsibility. In conversation with Joan Retallack he describes his removal of unwanted words as the consequence of a different way of working. He explains that when working with words rather than sounds, he is paying attention to the nature of language, where 'The sound sometimes becomes so powerful that one can put meaning aside. And vice versa.'[9] Words, in the syntactical arrangement of sentence or message, on the other hand, represent for Cage 'training, government, enforcement, and finally the military'.[10] It is not that Cage's ethics need to be put into question. Cage argues for a strong libertarian ethics of individualism and freedom: a normative ethics of principals. However, a very different ethics presents itself in Cage's work, and the shift from the modality of sounds to the modality of words marks the site of contestation between these two kinds of ethics. When it is a matter of sounds, it is an ethics of *Gelassenheit*, where no sound is privileged over another in accordance with taste, likes or dislikes. Further the *epochē* (the chance operation) that enforces this letting contains within it the ethics of a promise that must be kept. When it comes to words, however, Cage seems to be tempted to overrule chance determinations in the name of an ethics of principle.

## *Vouloir-dire*

'I have nothing to say and I am saying it' might, at first, sound like an attitude of semantic irresponsibility or a declaration of emptiness and silence. But, on the contrary, Cage takes responsibility for his words (*I am* saying it), even though these words do not come from an *ego cogito* that would take ownership in the sense of an originary source in absolute proximity to a self that is fully present to the moment of their genesis (I *have* nothing to say). The need for intervention in Cage's chance-determined writing at first seems to confirm the common view that either such texts can have no meaning at all, since there is no intention involved, or that where intention is not present there will always be a risk of meaning betraying its author's principles. When Cage says he has nothing to say, we can understand this in the sense of having nothing to express or, better, of having no need to express something, or to represent, or having no desire to impart anything from himself. Further, this can be read in terms of Meister Eckhart's stricture of dispossession of one's will to possess one's self – to sink into nothing (Cage was an avid reader of Eckhart). But still, he is 'saying it' or, rather, letting it be said.

The artistic, or musical, idea of expression that Cage eschews is synonymous to the linguistic idea of expression. The word suggests the projection of something inner, subjective and personal – an emotion, something envisaged or imagined, an inner hearing, or a mood – to an outside, where it resonates with the empathetic emotions of an audience or receiver. Thus, the common view of language regards speech as the voluntary expression of an inner stratum of pre-linguistic sense that is transported and made transportable by words. What is common to both aesthetic and linguistic conceptions of expression is the model which describes the outward projection of something inside which is always privileged as primary, original and prior to the outside realm of social relations and fulfilled meaning. The root meaning of expression derives from the Latin *exprimere*, consisting of *ex*, meaning 'out', and *primere* which signifies 'to press'. Expression thus means to 'press out'.

This metaphysical model of expression is encapsulated by Derrida's observation in *Speech and Phenomena*: 'Ex-pression is exteriorization. It imparts to a certain outside a sense which is first found in a certain inside' (*SP* 32). Here Derrida examines the motivations behind Husserl's move in the *Logical Investigations* to make a rigorous distinction between 'expression' (*Ausdruck*) and 'indication' (*Anzeichen*), where expression refers to meaningful signs (primarily those of living speech), and indication refers to empirical forms of signification including symbols, marks, indexical traces and gestural/facial expressions. One of the aims of Derrida, in *Speech and Phenomena*, is to work towards the unsettling of what he sees as a 'transcendental' voluntaristic privilege in Husserl's work. It is important at this point to observe that the phenomenological term 'intentionality' – which means, the aiming of consciousness towards something – should not be confused with the ordinary non-phenomenological usage (that I am employing in 'non-intentionality'). But still, phenomenological intentionality remains, for Derrida, 'caught up in the tradition of a voluntaristic metaphysics – that is, perhaps, in metaphysics *as such*' (*SP* 34; Derrida's emphasis). As Derrida puts it, 'for if intentionality never simply meant will, it certainly does seem that in the order of expressive experiences . . . Husserl regards intentional consciousness and voluntary consciousness as synonymous' (*SP* 34). The very idea of consciousness, for Husserl, cannot be disassociated from a spirit (*Geist*), a will or a pure intention. Husserl wishes to exclude from the category of expression anything that escapes this animation of a 'voice' (whether interior and silent, or externalized and sounded). In Derrida's view, what Husserl cannot help reproducing is the traditional metaphysical model that consists of voluntary exteriorization of a pre-expressive substratum of sense that is both pre-linguistic and self-transparent.

Expression is, thus, not only exteriorization but, moreover, voluntary exteriorization. What is expressed is meaning (*Bedeutung*), an ideal object with no real worldly existence. Meaning inhabits and animates the ideality of expression as a 'wanting-to-say'. For Derrida, Husserl confines this operation to the act of speech, even if this act takes place within the isolation of solitary mental life (silently speaking to oneself). In the auto-affectivity of hearing oneself speak (*s' entendre parler*) meaning seems to the subject to be produced from within itself. The meaning – what the speaker wants and means to say – is auditioned in the immediate moment of its production and instantly presented to the consciousness of the speaker which secures it as the intended meaning. In expression, meaning – that which wants to say – goes out of oneself while remaining before oneself – in consciousness, inside oneself as self-present to oneself.

As far as Derrida is concerned there is a privilege given in both phenomenology and linguistics to the plenitude of intentional meaning; of wanting-to-say (*vouloir-dire*) that would exist ideally behind and before every expression and would find its perfect vehicle in living speech. '*Vouloir-dire*' is the locution used by Derrida to translate the verbal form of Husserl's use of the German word *Bedeutung* ('meaning').[11] Although both words would be translated into English as 'meaning' or 'signification', the literal sense is 'wanting-to-say'. What Derrida is locating in Husserl is the metaphysical idea which insists that behind and before any expression there lies something originating and intrinsic to it. The conception of a silent intuitive presence before speech rests on a presupposition that 'prior to signs and outside them . . . something such as consciousness is possible' and moreover, 'even before the distribution of its signs in space and in the world, consciousness can gather itself up in its own presence' (SP 146–7). In the translator's introduction to *Writing and Difference*, Alan Bass points out that Derrida's deployment of *vouloir-dire* refers to the metaphysical concept of voluntarism, the critique of which, he observes, emerges from Heidegger's confrontation with Nietzsche's doctrine of the will. That is, it would seem to form a unique polar opposite to the later Heidegger's notion of a non-willing thinking of *Gelassenheit*. What is at stake is the primacy of a certain fusion of will and consciousness that wants to say and means to say which, for Derrida, constitutes the illusion of voluntary meaning being present to itself. We might say that this critique of the primacy of the will is Derrida's way of continuing Heidegger's thought in a demythologized tone.

## Iterability

In 1971 Derrida published an essay, 'Signature Event Context', in which – in opposition to J. L. Austin's conception of perfectly successfully communicating speech acts that serve as the basis of all communication – he introduces the general condition of 'iterability' in which meaning in each case is cut off from the original intention of the speaker. In 1977, the essay was translated into English and appeared in the journal *Glyph* in which – in its second issue – there appeared a polemic response to Derrida's essay from the American philosopher John R. Searle. In response to Searle's attack, Derrida wrote 'Limited Inc abc . . .', and an afterword, 'Toward an Ethic of Discussion', in answer to questions submitted to him by Gerald Graff (the editor of the book *Limited Inc*[12] which contains all three texts). What is in question, in Derrida's engagement with Austin, and subsequent argument with Searle, is precisely what is at stake in *Speech and Phenomena*: 'the plenitude of intentional meaning (*vouloir-dire*), and all of the other values – of consciousness, presence, and originary intuition – which organize phenomenology' (*LInc* 58). That is, the primacy of intention in the fulfilment of meaning. In order to cast doubt on the possibility of the ethico-political responsibility of non-intentionality, the classical move would be to conceive of a model of communication that would be absolutely uncontaminated by aleatory effects, and this is what, in Derrida's view, Austin and Searle seek to achieve.

For Austin and Searle, successful communication depends upon an intentional force that is transparently delivered and received under the optimal conditions of the localized physical proximity of both parties, and an absolutely constraining context. This pure performative would be the kind of utterance against which all other (impure) utterances could be judged. Derrida complicates this model by arguing that not only are utterances able to be interpreted (and misinterpreted) in conditions where the source of intention is empirically absent but, further, in the pure instances of the performative speech act under optimal conditions, even when all parties are present, there is always some degree of interpretation involved. Meaning is not immediately present to all involved. Derrida seeks to undo the model of the pure exemplary performative by focusing on the elements that Austin wishes to exclude from successful communication, even though Austin himself recognizes them as structural possibilities. Austin excludes the possibility of citation or 'quotability' in the performative utterance – along with instances of non-serious intent, or non-ordinary linguistic exceptions as in the case of poetry – insisting that such 'stage utterances' would be abnormal or parasitic. Derrida's conclusion is that any pure speech act is already contaminated by the very elements that would define an impure speech act. This, he says, is due to the condition that he calls 'iterability' which structures not only the possibility of any linguistic act but also the impossibility of such acts.

In order for something to mean something it must be repeatable. There would be no communicable signification, no recognition, if something presented itself only once. Iterability is this possibility of repetition but, moreover, it is a repetition that alters, that never returns to the same place in the text, never returns an unalterable univocal meaning. In this sense, for Derrida, pure repetition is impossible and iterability is structured by both identity and difference. This is because iterability is already divided or split.[13] Each time a self-contained identity is constituted in a signifying element, it is simultaneously split because this identity can only be maintained in accordance with a differential relation to other elements not present. In this way, there is always a non-present remainder of the differential and iterable mark. This also means that, for Derrida, any utterance or signifying element can not only be taken out of context but also be radically disengaged from an originating intention. Every mark, whether it be spoken or written, has 'the possibility of its functioning being cut off, at a certain point, from its "original" desire-to-say-what-one-means (*vouloir-dire*) and from its participation in a saturable and constraining context' (*LInc* 12). In this way, iterability divides intention, 'preventing it from being fully present to itself in the actuality of its aim, or of its meaning' (*LInc* 57). Each signifying element can further 'be *cited*, put between quotation marks; in so doing it can break with every given context, engendering an infinity of new contexts in a manner which is absolutely illimitable' (*LInc* 12, Derrida's emphasis). Iterability contaminates what it enables to repeat. The consequence of this, as Derrida sees it, is that 'it leaves no choice but to mean to say (to say) something that is (already, always, also) other than what we mean (to say)' (*LInc* 62). In this way accidents in communication are never just accidents but are, rather, structural to all communications. The gist of this is that a speaker's (or writer's) intention can never be unquestionably relied upon as a way of determining the meaning or what is meant by a particular utterance.

It's not that Derrida wants to annihilate intention – to declare it absent from any linguistic exchange – which is how Searle *mis*-understands him – rather, what iterability calls into question is any absolute guarantee that intention may seem to provide for the fulfilment and delimitation of meaning. Iterability does not limit or cause an absolute breakdown of intention or a failure to get things done in the world of social relations. What it limits is intention's undividedness: its self-present securement of its own operation. However, the dividedness or cleft (*Brissure*) of iterability is very far from constituting a negative condition. Derrida employs the botanical term 'dehiscence' which, significantly, relates iterability to another important word for Derrida: 'dissemination'. Dehiscence refers to the propagation or dissemination of pollen by the anther (part of the stamen) by splitting in such a way that the two chambers appear to be one (dehiscence also occurs in fruit and seeds). As Derrida notes in 'The Double Session', it is a kind of 'quasi-tearing' (*Diss* 205). In this way, the dehiscence of iterability 'limits what it makes possible, while rendering its rigor and purity impossible' (*LInc* 59). It has the workings of an 'undecidable contamination' – and Derrida emphasizes the positive sense of this – that is essential for the possibility of production and reproduction. It is both generative and disseminative. If non-intentional writing is generative, in this sense of dehiscence and dissemination, it is not due to an animating intention of an *ego cogito*; it is due to the generative possibilities of the system of language itself; or, better, of the systematic play of differences; the anonymous field of spacings.

## The ethico-teleological values of philosophy

Iterability may seem, at first, like a kind of trivial inversion of the normal way of conceiving semio-linguistic communication, but what is at stake here is an ethical consideration. That is, most importantly, the consideration of iterability leads us to a reconfiguration of the ethical. What is presupposed in the intentional model that Austin and Searle advocate is what Derrida calls the 'univocity of ethico-teleological values in language' (*LInc* 76), where 'every methodological aspect of discourse involves decision . . . the more confident, implicit, buried the metaphysical decision is, the more its order, and calm, reigns over methodological technicity' (*LInc* 93). Those concepts that would seek to govern from the centre, Rodolphe Gasché describes as 'desiderata', which, since Plato, have been ethico-teleological values 'not only of what is but what *ought* to be'.[14] In Derrida's terms, these values, as we have seen, not only animate hierarchical binary distinctions where the negative term is subordinate to the positive but also emphasize a priority in which one concept precedes another in such a way that the metaphysical tradition conceives 'good to be before evil, the positive before the negative, the pure before the impure, the simple before the complex, the essential before the accidental, the imitated before the imitation, etc.' (*LInc* 93). In such a way, a hierarchy of ethico-teleological distinctions is set up in Austin's theory of the speech act: standard/non-standard, pure/parasitic and so on. Moreover, Derrida continues, the methodological strategy of first positing the pure, simple, normal, complete, in order to then think the derivative, the impure, the non-standard and the accidental, conforms entirely to this metaphysical *telos*. By maintaining Austin's opposition between serious or normative forms of discourse and non-standard or parasitic forms, such as poetry, and arguing that only the serious forms are able to fully realize an intention, Searle, in Derrida's view, insists that normative linguistic exchange *ought* to be serious and literal since only such language can be fully intentional, and that language *ought* to tend towards such an ideal: the perfect communicative transferal. This reproduces, according to Derrida, 'the given ethical conditions of a *given* ethics' (*LInc* 122, Derrida's emphasis). There is, as Derrida cautions, nothing pejorative in such an ethics. The prescription of an 'ought' that is normative, and subscribes to an ideal purity, does not produce a 'bad' or 'wrong' ethics. What it does, however, is to exclude or marginalize all other possibilities – possibilities such as Cage's poetics – and disallows the opening of another ethics which may be an *an-ethtics* – not simply an anti-ethics.

Derrida shows us the inherent problems that are built in to a model of ethics centred on intention as a wanting-to-say. But there still remains the question of how, or if, authors of non-intentional works, such as Cage and Mac Low, can be held responsible for what they produce. How can one, in the play, acceptance or letting of language, bypass definitive semanticism without surrendering ethical–political responsibility? In the afterword of *Limited Inc*, in reply to a question from Gerald Graff (the book's editor), Derrida explains how the singularity of the undecidable 'opens the field of decision' (*LInc* 116):

> It calls for a decision in the order of ethical-political responsibility. It is even its necessary condition. A decision can only come into being in a space that exceeds the calculable program that would destroy all responsibility by transforming it into a programmable effect of determinate causes. There can be no moral or political responsibility without this trial and this passage by way of the undecidable. Even if a decision seems to take only a second and not to be preceded by any deliberation, it is structured by this *experience and experiment of the undecidable*. (*LInc* 116, Derrida's emphasis)

This establishes the framework for his later work on law and justice where, in 'Force of Law', Derrida maintains that justice depends upon an *epochē*, a suspension of the law in its generalizable form, in order to open a space for a decision that does not fall into programmable calculability: to provide the conditions for what Stanley Fish calls a 'fresh judgment' (*FL* 961).[15] He argues, 'A decision that didn't go through the ordeal of the undecidable would not be a free decision, it would only be the programmable application or unfolding of a calculable process' (*FL* 963). Elsewhere, in *The Beast and the Sovereign*, Derrida argues that every decision must transcend the order of the programmable in such a way that 'the difference between the deciding decision and the undecided decision itself becomes undecidable'.[16] The law in each singular case must be reinvented, but this re-invention involves both suspending and conserving an existing law. The decision of a judge cannot slavishly conform to the law, as if the judicial system were a calculating machine, but neither should such decisions be arbitrary without respect to the law. What is interesting here is the *epochē* or suspension and how it functions. The *epochē* of chance that Cage utilizes in his production of texts could be said to follow a similar rationale. Judgement is suspended for long enough for the possibility to open up for a 'fresh judgment'. In this way, non-intentional writing opens up a space for an ethico-political decision that is largely unforeseen. If the decision were to be foreseeable, it would be assured of its felicity to its own principles and, thus, be programmable. The final decisions that Cage makes are made possible, and even structured by, the experiment of the chance operation which allows for the unforeseen. In Derrida's judicial case the law is intermittently suspended so that a fresh decision can come into view. In Cage's case the decision is suspended in order that a fresh analysis or reading can be made which then, in a supplementary step, allows a free decision. But in each case, in each ethico-political decision, it is singularity that is prioritized over the generalizing principle.

Such an operation involves, in the most basic terms, re-invention, and the bringing about of something new and different. At this point it must be emphasized that I am not equating iterability – or deconstruction or différance – with Cagean non-intentionality or indeterminacy. Derrida makes it very clear in his answer to Graff that neither undecidability (*LInc* 148) nor différance (*LInc* 149) equates to indeterminacy.[17] The undecidable, as we understand it in the Derridean sense, refers to a highly determined strategy of locating and deploying certain terms as non-concepts (such as *pharamakon*, hymen and *parergon*) which, by oscillating between two possibilities, resist the structure of binary opposition without necessarily forming a third term. It is by way of such strategies that Derrida puts the primacy of the self-presence of meaning-to-say into question in order to discover its force and necessity, and determine – in the act of tracing each exigency back to its deployment in the text of philosophy – its 'intrinsic limit' (*LInc* 93). But at the same time these undecidables are 'pragmatically determined' (*LInc* 148). At many of the decisive moments in each text, meaning is, in a certain way, *found*, and any deconstructive intervention must proceed not by way of the imposition of a will, but by the necessity of what the text demands and according to its syntactical structure:

> The *incision* of deconstruction, which is not a voluntary decision or an absolute beginning, does not take place just anywhere, or in an absolute elsewhere. An incision, precisely, it can be made only according to the lines of force and forces of rupture that are localizable in the discourse to be deconstructed. . . . This analysis is *made* in the general movement of the field, and is never exhausted by the conscious calculation of a 'subject'. (*Pos* 82, Derrida's emphasis)

Deconstruction, thus, always begins wherever we find ourselves in the text (of philosophy). We might say that there is some element of chance in Derrida's work, but such contingency is far removed from Cage's chance operations. However, we could say that if there is certain constraint within Derrida's methodology, it consists of finding the resources for the deconstruction of an author's text(s) within the confines of the author's text(s).

## The subject

Against a normative ethics of a moralist humanism, entailing the necessity for a univocal enunciation of a 'positive' message which, she argues, actually suppresses the ethical function and denies the specificity of art, Julia Kristeva proposes that the textual practices of the avant-garde (Mallarmé, Lautréamont, Joyce, Artaud, Bataille), which posit and dissolve meaning and the unity of the subject, encompass the ethical because such practices involve the dissolution of narrowly subjective narcissistic fixations, and transgress the constituting processes of the symbolic. The ethical, in Kristeva's view, cannot be stated. It can only be practiced in a way that 'pluralizes, pulverizes, "musicates" [truths] ... on the condition that it develop them to the point of laughter'.[18] For Kristeva, avant-garde texts reveal 'the moment of struggle exploding the subject toward heterogeneous materiality' – 'the moment that dissolves all constitutive unity', where the subject is forced to abandon any meta-position.[19] However, as Elizabeth Grosz points out, such a view does not sit easily with feminist politics where the destabilization or dissolving of the subject cannot be seen to contribute in the struggle towards the overcoming of patriarchal oppression. Although all subjects are constituted by language and the symbolic, the female subject is constituted differently than the male. Transgression, Grosz argues, is only an available option for those subjects with a secure and stable place in the symbolic.[20]

Alice Jardine maintains that although what is needed is the elaboration of a new gendered speaking subject, it is not possible to investigate sexual difference and to pursue work on the female subject within the 'epistemological legacy of representation' and the traditional and comfortable conceptions of the speaking subject as neutral, stable, unified, transparent to language, 'master of its discourse, a Man'.[21] Kristeva's call for the transgression of the symbolic tends to valorize intonation, rhythm, rhyme, motility and the musication of language, carving out a space for the maternal and materiality that she calls the 'semiotic Chora' (and in this sense is open to the musical experimentation of Cage, La Monte Young, Kagel and Stockhausen).[22] However, Kristeva is reluctant to embrace chance in the production or reception of texts and is hostile to what she sees as Derrida's 'involuntarism'. But does the apparent involuntarism of citationality amount to a retreat from the problems of theorizing a gendered speaking subject, as Kristeva and Jardine maintain?

In the late 1980s, prior to her engagement with Derrida's 'Signature Event Context', Judith Butler combined the speech act theory of Austin and Searle with a radical phenomenological theory of constitution which argues that the subject is conditioned and constituted by discourse prior to any expression through discourse. In opposition to the presumptions of an essentialist substantial model of identity, the performative action reveals, for Butler, that gender is performatively constituted. In 2010, Butler puts it this way:

> If we say, for instance, that gender is performatively constituted, then we call into question whether there is a stable gender in place and intact prior to the expressions and activities that we understand as gendered expressions and activities. The presumption that gender is a metaphysical substance that precedes its expression is critically upended by the performative theory of gender.[23]

Drawing from Derrida, Butler argues that although identity is constituted by performative acts, the identity and agency produced is largely an illusion that reiterates norms and discursive conventions and at the same time dissimulates or conceals these repetitions. Hence, a subject is never (completely) the author or pure originator of the performative action. For Butler, discourse precedes and enables (and disables) the 'I' who speaks. Rather than there being an 'I' which stands behind and before the performative act, the subject is positioned by social recognition which forms it. Discourse, preceding subject formation, constrains the trajectory of the subject's will.

Drawing on Merleau-Ponty, Butler proposes that the gendered subject comes to be through the 'stylization' of bodily gestures and movements, through the repetition of such acts which constitute one's belief in the self-formation of a unified subject. The performative is, according to Butler, not so much a deliberate and intentional act but, rather, the workings of a citationality which repeats discursive conventions and sexual norms within dominant structures of power. However, like Derrida, Butler insists that the performative is not only open to failure but failure is structural to its functioning, incorporating

Slavoj Žižek's Lacanian view that the symbolic discursive formation of the social field is constituted by the excluded traumatic real, which the symbolic cannot accommodate within its discursive limits, rendering it inconsistent, contingent and unstable.[24] Rather than cause for despair, Butler finds this failure of the complete determination of a stable subject to be promising of new subjectivities. If a gendered subject is constituted through the stylized temporal repetition of acts and gestures, then it can be constituted differently, and because subject formation is never complete but always unfinished and unstable it holds the promise of change – of disrupting and breaking from gender legacies. If the production of the gendered subject is the effect of a concealed citationality, is it conceivable that the dissolution of the (any) subject would be a (necessary) first step towards the formation – through reconfiguration and re-constitution – of new gendered speaking subjects?[25]

## The swerve

In Derrida's response to Graff, he adamantly states that 'I do not believe I have ever spoken of "indeterminacy", whether in regard to "meaning" or anything else' (*LInc* 148). This is, however, not strictly the case. In 1983 (five years before the afterword), in 'Mes chances. Au rendez-vous de quelques stéréophonies épicuriennes' (translated into English as 'My Chances/ *Mes Chances*: A Rendezvous with some Epicurean Stereophonies') Derrida explores indeterminacy in a slightly different context. Asked to speak on the subjects of psychoanalysis and literature, at the Washington School of Psychiatry, Derrida questions the inherent possibilities of indeterminacy that may occur in a lecture which is destined to those addressees (*destinaires*) he does not know, and who belong to a field that is not his own. Drawing on the ideas of the Democritian atomists, Derrida suggests that the lecture may fall upon those to whom it may or may not have been destined, reach its destination by way of 'a chance open to some *parenklisis* or *clinamen*' (*MC* 4). In the cosmology of Lucretius, atoms in the void are constantly falling downwards in parallel paths. The *clinamen* is the slight swerve in motion causing the atoms to collide with each other which leads to the creation of phenomena. The swerve is also related to the genesis of man's free will since it effects the atomic make-up of the mind. In Derrida's use it constitutes the spacing and play of the trace between significance and insignificance, aim and fall, destining and destinerrancy. The *clinamen*, in these terms, is purely contingent.

Drawing on this Epicurean model, Joan Retallack describes Cage's chance operations as a composed *clinamen*,[26] belonging to a poethical attitude: 'A certain poetics of responsibility with the courage of the swerve, the project of the wager.'[27] The swerve, the unpredictable shift in direction, as Retallack proposes, redirects the 'geometry of attention', and has the potential of jolting us out of the default set of predispositions that Pierre Bourdieu calls the 'habitus'.[28] The swerve constitutes 'the collision with contingency that dislodges us from enervated patterns into a charged apprehension of something new'.[29] In contrast to Derrida, the figure of the swerve, in Retallack's sense, is not something arbitrary but the result of an imposed and determined operation or process. For Derrida, on the other hand, there is a certain intertwining between chance and necessity. Drawing from cybernetics and theories of dynamic systems, he observes that the signifying elements of language '*simultaneously* incline toward increasing the reserves of random indetermination *as well as* the capacity for coding and overcoding or, in other words, for control and self-regulation' (*MC* 2; Derrida's emphasis). In this way, the tension between randomness and code both disrupts and regulates 'the restless, unstable interplay of the system'.[30] Derrida falls upon Lucretius's characterization of the falling atoms as being composed not just of matter but of letters or graphic marks (*stoikheion*), where the swerve causes random combinations. A slight deflection in one letter separates two words, *voluntas* (will) and *voluptus* (pleasure), which are intrinsically linked in Lucretius's thought. The substitutability of the one letter in these Latin words has, due to a certain clinamen or destinerrancy in the early editions of Lucretius's poem *De rerum natura*, resulted in an indeterminate reading perhaps skewing Lucretius's notion of freedom towards pleasure, leading Derrida from Lucretius to Freud's pleasure principle.[31]

## Limited/unlimited responsibility

The central question of poethics is, as Retallack puts it: 'How can writing and reading be integral to making sense and *new*sense (sometimes taken for *non*sense) as we enact an ongoing poetics of everyday life?'³² It is to a similar question that Derrida responds:

> I try to *write* (in) the space in which is posed the question of speech and meaning. I try to write the question: (what is) meaning to say (*vouloir dire*)? Therefore it is necessary in such a space, and guided by such a question, that writing literally mean nothing. Not that it is absurd in the way that absurdity has always been in solidarity with metaphysical meaning. It simply tempts itself, tenders itself, attempts to keep itself at the point of exhaustion of meaning. (*Pos* 14; Derrida's emphasis)

A writing that tenders itself at the boundary of the exhaustion of meaning, Derrida emphasizes, is not absurd, nor, would we expect, irrational or aesthetic – either in the sense of formal autonomy, or in the sense of functioning as a signifier for expression (or life) itself (wanting to express without meaning as much as wanting-to-mean). We are reminded of Heidegger's insistence that the irrationality of aesthetic *Erlebnis* would be the completion of representational thinking (*Vorstellung*), and thus 'in solidarity with metaphysical meaning.'

But this play, which involves a risk of meaning, does not escape from ethico-political responsibility. Or, by way of an inversion we might say that it *is* an ethico-political responsibility to keep things in play. On the one hand, as Niall Lucy observes, 'neither "text" nor "writing" can *avoid* being ethical-analytical.'³³ On the other hand, the discourse of philosophy cannot escape, as Lucy argues, the unwanted effects of what it claims to be purely different from, namely, literature and the 'non-serious'. Thus, there can always be other readings or misreadings of any text. An author has responsibility for their text, but since intention is dispersed across various authorial motives, desires, citations, quotations, other authors and so forth, responsibility, as Derrida claims in 'Limited Inc a b c . . .', can only be limited responsibility (*LInc* 75). Or better, intention itself has only a limited responsibility. Language in the aleatoric poetry of the Language Poets, or of Cage, would call to be inflected according to an ethical–political decision that has only limited responsibility, yet the very necessity for keeping meaning in play is an unlimited responsibility.

Poethical texts inscribe the conditions of their own reception. They explicitly prescribe against the idea that there can be one singular univocal reading, and that such a reading could be directly attributed to an authorial intention. Part of the force of works engaging with non-intentionality is their capacity to make explicit the implicit structure of iterability, and thus make legible that the conditions for reading the work do not involve a quest for authorial intentionality. The play of the poetic text cannot escape the pull of ethico-analytic responsibility any more than philosophy can escape the effects of literature and the 'non-serious'. What the structure of iterability shows is that any internality of an 'expressed' meaning is already marked by an externality that consists of a textual spacing of differences and a citational network of referrals to other texts. This is no less true for the work of art. Expression, or the meaning to be expressed, is, as Derrida maintains, 'always already carried outside itself. It already differs (from itself) before any act of expression. And only on this condition can it "signify"' (*Pos* 33). What is given in a work of art is irreducible to an artist's intention. Consequently, the model of intentional expression cannot be a reliable means to accessing what is given in the work of the work of art.

Cage's 'I have nothing to say and I am saying it' is not a statement of intellectual negligence, or of ethico-political irresponsibility. It is certainly not, as Yvonne Rainer maintains, a non-signifying practice, that works to 'eliminate and supress meaning'.[34] Further, Cage's practice does not just indicate a suspension of expression as meaning-to-say but constitutes a putting into question of the primacy of intention as the guarantee of meaning and self-coincidence. In such a way, it opens up a space for different kind of ethics. At this point we might go back and address the substance of the question posed by Cage's interlocutor: Why does Cage take out the words he does not like, rather than rigorously abide by the outcomes of the chance operations? We might answer that ethical decisions come to be made in the space opened up by the suspension of aesthetic decisions – in the space *between* aesthetics and ethics. Derrida's philosophy and the non-intentional artistic works of Cage and Mac Low have one thing in common: they both work towards putting intention in its place; to prevent it from governing all 'meaning' and interpretation; to dislodge it from its position of authority; to disrupt its illusion of immediacy and the efficient expedited express delivery of meaning that we see as the 'postal', or transmission, service of expression.

# Notes

## Introduction

1 Richard Rorty, *Contingency, Irony and Solidarity* (Cambridge: Cambridge University Press, 1989).
2 Jean-Luc Nancy, 'Originary Ethics', in *A Finite Thinking*, ed. Simon Sparks, trans. Duncan Large (Stanford: Stanford University Press, 2003), 176.

## Chapter 1

1 Leonardo, cited in Max Ernst, 'On Frottage' (1936), in *Theories of Modern Art: A Source Book by Artists and Critics*, ed. Herschel B. Chipp (Berkeley: University of California Press, 1968), 428.
2 Aristotle, *Nicomachean Ethics Book Six, English and Greek*, trans. L. H. G. Greenwood (Cambridge: Cambridge University Press, 1909), 96–7.
3 E. H. Gombrich, *Art and Illusion: A Study in the Psychology of Pictorial Presentation*, 3rd edn (London: Phaidon, 1968), 157.
4 Georges Hugnet, 'The Dada Spirit in Painting', in *The Dada Painters and Poets: An Anthology*, 2nd edn, ed. Robert Motherwell (Cambridge: The Belknap Press of Harvard University Press, 1998), 158.
5 Ernst, 'On Frottage', 429.
6 Pierre Reverdy, *Nord-Sud* (1918), quoted in André Breton, 'Manifesto of Surrealism' (1924), in André Breton, *Manifestoes of Surrealism*, trans. Richard Seaver and Helen R. Lane (Ann Arbor: University of Michigan Press, 1972), 20. This idea is echoed by Max Ernst in 'What Is the Mechanism of Collage?' (1936): 'the coupling of two realities, irreconcilable in appearance, upon a plane which apparently does not suit them.' in Chipp, *Theories of Modern Art*, 427.
7 Breton, *Manifestoes of Surrealism*, 36.
8 Avital Ronell, *The Telephone Book: Technology, Schizophrenia, Electric Speech* (Lincoln: University of Nebraska Press, 1989), 99.
9 Robert Motherwell, 'The Significance of Miró' (1959), in *The Writings of Robert Motherwell*, ed. Dore Ashton and Joan Banach (Berkeley: University of California

Press, 2007), 192. See also 'An Interview with David Sylvester' (1962), in the same volume, 210. Breton's definition is: 'SURREALISM, *n*. Psychic automatism in its pure state, by which one proposes to express-verbally, by means of the written word, or in any other manner – the actual functioning of thought. Dictated by thought, in the absence of any control exercised by reason, exempt from any aesthetic or moral concern.' Breton, *Manifestoes of Surrealism*, 26.

10  Sometimes spelled 'Dabrowsky'.
11  John D. Graham, *System and Dialectics of Art* (New York: Delphic Studios, 1937), 19.
12  Motherwell, 'On Jackson Pollock' (1967), in *The Writings of Robert Motherwell*, 225.
13  An example is William Baziotes, Gerome Kamrowski and Jackson Pollock, *Collaborative Painting*, 1940–1, oil and enamel on canvas, 19 1/4 and 9/16 inches. Weinstein Gallery, San Francisco. Accessed 30 January 2019. http://www.weinstein.com/artists/gerome-kamrowski/.
14  Motherwell, 'The Modern Painter's World' (1944), in *The Writings of Robert Motherwell*, 34; Motherwell's emphasis.
15  Ibid.
16  Ibid., 35.
17  David Lomas with Jeremy Stubbs, *Simulating the Marvellous, Psychology – Surrealism – Postmodernism* (Manchester: Manchester University Press, 2013), 251.
18  Ibid., 182.
19  Michael Riffaterre, *Text Production*, trans. Terese Lyons (New York: Columbia University Press, 1983), 238. Cited in Lomas, *Simulating the Marvellous*, 183.
20  Motherwell, 'Parisian Artists in Exile: New York 1939-45' (1977), in *The Writings of Robert Motherwell*, 295.
21  Harold Rosenberg, 'The American Action Painters', *Art News* (December 1952): 22–3, 48–50. Reproduced in *Reading Abstract Expressionism: Context and Critique*, ed. Ellen G. Landau (New Haven: Yale University Press), 191.
22  Thus, he denied her the epithet 'action painter'. Daniel Belgrad, *The Culture of Spontaneity: Improvisation and the Arts in Postwar America* (Chicago: University of Chicago Press, 1998), 118.
23  Ibid., 104.
24  Ibid., 113.
25  William James, *Principles of Psychology*, vol. 1 (1890; New York: Dover, 1950), 105. Cited in Belgrad, *The Culture of Spontaneity*, 113.
26  Catherine Malabou, *The Future of Hegel: Plasticity, Temporality and Dialectic*, trans. Lisabeth During (London: Routledge, 2005), 26.

27 Ibid., 38.
28 George Brecht, *Chance-Imagery*. (ubuclassics, 2004). Accessed 23 November 2019. http://www.ubu.com/historical/gb/brecht_chance.pdf. Originally published as: George Brecht, *Chance-Imagery* (New York: A Great Bear Pamphlet by Something Else Press, 1966).
29 Ibid., 25.
30 William S. Rubin confirms this through reference to a conversation with Arp at Meudon in the spring of 1959. See, *Dada, Surrealism and Their Heritage* (New York: The Museum of Modern Art, 1968), 41 n. 46.
31 Tristan Tzara, 'An Introduction to Dada', in Motherwell, *The Dada Painters and Poets*, 404, see also 'Seven Dada Manifestoes', in the same volume, 92.
32 Hans Richter, *Dada: Art and Anti-art*, trans. David Britt (London: Thames and Hudson, 1997), 60, Richter's capitalization.
33 Marcel Duchamp and Pierre Cabanne, *Dialogues with Marcel Duchamp*, trans. Ron Padgett (London: Thames and Hudson, 1971), 47.
34 Ibid., 48.
35 Ibid.
36 Dick Higgins, *A Dialectic of Centuries: Notes towards a Theory of the New Arts* (New York: Printed Editions, 1978), 30.
37 Brecht, *Chance-Imagery*, 23.
38 John Cage and Daniel Charles, *For the Birds* (Boston: M. Boyars, 1981), 94.
39 Sol LeWitt, 'Paragraphs on Conceptual Art', first published in *Artforum* 5, no. 10 (Summer 1967): 79–83. Reproduced in *Conceptual Art: A Critical Anthology*, ed. Alexander Alberro and Blake Stimson (Cambridge, MA and London: MIT Press, 1999), 13.
40 LeWitt, 'Sentences on Conceptual Art', First published in *0-9* (New York), 1969, and *Art-Language* (England), May 1969. Reproduced in Alberro and Stimson, *Conceptual Art a Critical Anthology*, 107.
41 Raymond Queneau, *Le Voyage en Grèce*, 94, quoted in Jacques Roubaud, 'Mathematics in the Method of Raymond Queneau', in *Oulipo: A Primer of Potential Literature,* ed. and trans. Warren F. Motte Jr. (Lincoln: University of Nebraska Press, 1986), 87.
42 Jacques Roubaud quoted in Motte, (introduction) *Oulipo: A Primer of Potential Literature*, 13.
43 Seth Kim-Cohen, *In the Blink of an Ear: Towards a Non-Cochlear Sonic Art* (New York: Continuum, 2009), 113–15.
44 It could be argued that judgements of taste, being disinterested, constitute a certain *epochē*.

45  Joan Retallack (Talk), 'John Cage's Anarchic Harmony: A Poethical Wager', Chazen Museum of Art, University of Wisconsin-Madison, 22 April 2009. Accessed 23 November 2019. http://media.sas.upenn.edu/pennsound/authors/Retallack/Madison_04-09/Retallack-Joan_Cage-Lecture_Madison_04-22-09.mp3.
46  See Anthony Wilden, *System and Structure: Essays in Communication and Exchange* (London: Tavistock, 1977), 398, on the 'delayed transmission' of Derrida's Différance. See Marcus Boon, *In Praise of Copying* (Cambridge, MA: Harvard University Press, 2010), 157 on Burroughs's 'pre-recordings'.
47  Cage, interview with Irving Sandier, in Richard Kostelanetz, *Conversing with Cage* (New York: Limelight Editions, 1988), 173.
48  Ibid., 169.

# Chapter 2

1  Don Ihde, *Listening and Voice: Phenomenologies of Sound*, 2nd edn (Albany: State University of New York Press, 2007), 17.
2  Ihde does not explicitly say where Merleau-Ponty's phenomenology sits in accordance with this distinction, but it would be reasonable to assume that he considers it to straddle both first and second phenomenology.
3  Kim-Cohen maintains the common view that Derrida simply opposes Husserl. See Kim-Cohen, *In the Blink of an Ear*.
4  Frances Dyson, *Sounding New Media: Immersion and Embodiment in the Arts and Culture* (Berkeley: University of California Press, 2009), 21.
5  Ibid.
6  Ihde, *Listening and Voice*, 6.
7  Frances Dyson, 'Transmitter Bodies: Aurality, Corporeality, Cuts and Signals', *NMA*, no. 8 (1990): 14–19, 14.
8  Ibid., Dyson's emphasis.
9  Ihde, *Listening and Voice*, 13.
10  Andreas Engström and Åsa Stjerna, 'Sound Art or *Klangkunst*? A Reading of the German and English Literature on Sound Art', *Organised Sound* 14, no. 1 (2009): 11–18, 13.
11  Ibid.
12  Kim-Cohen, *In the Blink of an Ear*, xvi–xvii.
13  Ibid., xvii.
14  Ibid.

15 Ibid., xx, Kim-Cohen's emphasis.
16 Ibid., xxi.
17 Christian Metz, 'Aural Objects', trans. Georgia Gurrieri, *Yale French Studies*, no. 60, Cinema/Sound (1980): 24–32.
18 Brian Kane, 'L'objet Sonore Maintenant: Pierre Schaeffer, Sound Objects and the Phenomenological Reduction', *Organised Sound* 12, no. 1 (2007): 15–24, 1.
19 Hans-Georg Gadamer, in his essay of 1963, 'The Phenomenological Movement', remarks that Husserl taught the necessity for 'patient, descriptive, detailed work', and would say, 'Not always the big bills, gentlemen; small change, small change!' *Philosophical Hermeneutics*, trans. David E. Linge (Berkeley: University of California Press, 1976). 132–3.
20 Jacques Taminiaux, *The Metamorphoses of Phenomenological Reduction*, 1st edn (Milwaukee: Marquette University Press, 2004), 7.
21 Ibid., 9.
22 Pierre Schaeffer, 'Acousmatics' excerpt from *Traité des objets musicaux* (Paris: Éditions du Seuil, 1966), in *Audio Culture: Readings in Modern Music*, ed. Christoph Cox and Daniel Warner, trans. Daniel W. Smith (New York: Continuum, 2004), 77.
23 Ibid., 78.
24 Cf. Dyson, *Sounding New Media*, 54, 7.
25 Schaeffer, 'Acousmatics', 78.
26 'Solfège', 'solfeggio' and 'solfa' are more or less equivalent terms referring to the set of syllables: *doh, rey, me, fah, soh, lah* and *ti*, used to represent the notes of the musical scale.
27 *Abschattungen* is regularly translated as 'adumbrations' or profiles, but it also carries the meaning 'shadowing off', or 'gradation in shades'.
28 Schaeffer, 'Acousmatics', 78.
29 Klaus Held, 'Husserl's Phenomenological Method', in *The New Husserl a Critical Reader*, ed. Donn Welton, trans. Lanei Rodemeyer (Bloomington: Indiana University Press, 2003), 17.
30 Edmund Husserl, *Experience and Judgment: Investigations in a Genealogy of Logic*, trans. James S. Churchhill and Karl Ameriks, ed. Ludwig Landgrebe (Evanston: Northwestern University Press, 1973), 343. *Erfahrung und Urteil: Untersuchungen zur Genealogie der Logik*, ed. Ludwig Landgrebe (Prague: Academia, 1939), 414.
31 Ibid., Husserl's emphasis.
32 Schaeffer, *Traité des objets musicaux*, 23, n. 3, cited in Carlos Palombini, 'Schaeffer's Sonic Object: Prolegomena' (1999), 2. http://compmus.ime.usp.br/sbcm/1999/papers/Carlos_Palombini.html, accessed 23 November 2019.

33  Palombini, 'Schaeffer's Sonic Object: Prolegomena', 8.
34  Michel Chion, *Guide to Sound Objects: Pierre Schaeffer and Musical Research*, trans. John Dack and Christine North (1983; Paris: Éditions Buchet, 2009), 102, Chion's emphasis.
35  Ibid., 105.
36  Schaeffer, *Traité des objets musicaux*, 628, cited in Chion, *Guide to Sound Objects*, 105.
37  Chion, *Guide to Sound Objects*, 105.
38  Ibid., 106.
39  What Cage is referring to is Schaeffer's wish to establish an inventory of sounds based on morphology and typology.
40  Cage and Charles, *For the Birds*, 77.
41  In Derrida, *SP* 107–28, also see *SP* 6.
42  Edmund Husserl, 'Husserl's Letter to Hofmannsthal – Phenomenology and Pure Art', trans. Sven-Olov Wallenstein, *Site* 26–7 (2009): 2.
43  Danielle Lories, 'Remarks on Aesthetic Intentionality: Husserl or Kant', *International Journal of Philosophical Studies* 14, no. 1 (2006): 31–49, 38.
44  Husserl, *Phantasy, Image Consciousness, and Memory, 1898-1925*, trans. John B. Brough (Dordrecht: Springer, 2005), 463.
45  Ibid., 464.
46  Schaeffer, *Solfège De L'objet Sonore*, trans. Livia Bellagamba (Paris: Institut National de l'Audiovisuel, 1998), 15.

# Chapter 3

1  John Cage, *Silence: Lectures and Writings* (London: Calder & Boyars, 1968), 69.
2  Davis, *Heidegger and the Will: On the Way to Gelassenheit* (Evanston: Northwestern University Press, 2007), 26.
3  Cage and Charles, *For the Birds*, 56.
4  Ibid., 148.
5  Christian Wolff quoted in Cage, *Silence*, 68. Where Wolff's quote ends and where Cage's writing resumes remains indeterminate in this passage due to lack of concluding quotation marks.
6  Interview with Richard Kostelanetz (1977), in Kostelanetz, *Conversing with Cage*, 52–3.
7  Interview with Bill Shoemaker (1984), in *Conversing with Cage*, 222.
8  Interview with Roy M. Close (1975), ibid., 219.

9   Interview with Stanley Kauffmann (1966), ibid., 223–4.
10  Cage, cited in Brandon W. Joseph, *Random Order: Robert Rauschenberg and the Neo-Avant-Garde* (Cambridge, MA: MIT Press, 2007), 45.
11  Cage, *Silence*, 102.
12  Cage, *I-IV*. Charles Eliot Norton Lectures, 1988–89 (Cambridge, MA: Harvard University Press, 1990), 217. A recording of this session can be heard at: 'Q & A, Part 1', 'John Cage 1912–1992', *UbuWeb*. Accessed 23 November 2019. http://www.ubu.com/sound/cage_norton.html.
13  C.f. Cage, *Silence*, 18; Cage and Charles, *For the Birds*, 39.
14  Cage, *I-IV*, 21. One might question the veracity of this account. Was the approximate length of four and a half minutes (as proposed earlier for *Silent Prayer*) predetermined for this piece?
15  Cage, and Charles, *For the Birds*, 58.
16  N. Katherine Hayles, 'Chance Operations: Cagean Paradox and Contemporary Science', in *John Cage: Composed in America*, ed. Marjorie Perloff and Charles Junkerman (Chicago: University of Chicago Press, 1994), 226–41.
17  Ibid., 227–8.
18  John Cage, *Empty Words: Writings '73-'78*, 1st edn (Middletown and London: Wesleyan University Press and Marion Boyars, 1979), 179.
19  Cage and Charles, *For the Birds*, 147.
20  Ibid. Charles's emphasis.
21  Cage, 'An Interview with John Cage', Michael Kirby and Richard Schechner, *Tulane Drama Review* 10, no. 2 (Winter, 1965): 50–72, 55.
22  Steve Reich, *Writings About Music* (Halifax: The Press of Nova Scotia College of Art and Design, 1974), 10.
23  Interview with Laura Fletcher and Thomas Moore (1983), in *Conversing with Cage*, 208.
24  In the early 1960s she also worked under the names Simone Morris and Simone Whitman.
25  Ruth Emerson continued to use chance operations but not all members of the Dunn's class (participant and wife of Robert Dunn, Judy Dunn, also contributed to the teaching) were enthusiastic about the teaching methods. David Gordon and Valda Setterfield rejected what they saw as the evangelistic adherence to chance procedures, and Yvonne Rainer was dissatisfied with the automatic warrant that chance-based work was given. See Banes, *Democracy's Body: Judson Dance Theater, 1962-1964* (Durham: Duke University Press, 1993), 30.
26  Robert Morris, 'Notes on Dance', *Tulane Drama Review* 10, no. 2 (Winter, 1965): 179–86, 179.

27 Sally Banes, *Greenwich Village 1963 Avant-Garde Performance and the Effervescent Body* (Durham: Duke University Press. 1993), 131. See also, Banes's *Terpsichore in Sneakers: Post-Modern Dance* (Hanover: Wesleyan University Press, 1987), and *Democracy's Body*.

28 Robert Morris, 'Some Notes on the Phenomenology of Making', *Artforum* VIII, no. 8 (April 1970): 62-6. Reproduced in *Continuous Project Altered Daily: Writings of Robert Morris*, New edn (Cambridge, MA: MIT Press, 1995), 75.

29 Ibid., 77.

30 Reich, *Writings About Music*, 9.

31 Ibid.

32 Ibid., 11.

33 Ibid.

34 Hans Haacke, *Hans Haacke: For Real: Works 1959-2006*, ed. Matthias Flèugge and Robert Fleck (Dèusseldorf: Richter, 2006), 257.

35 LeWitt, 'Paragraphs on Conceptual Art', 12.

36 LeWitt, 'Sentences on Conceptual Art', 106.

37 Adrian Piper, 'My Art Education', written in 1968, in *Out of Order, Out of Sight: Selected Writings in Meta-Art, 1968-1992*, vol. 1 (Cambridge, MA: MIT Press, 1996), 5.

38 Brandon LaBelle, *Background Noise: Perspectives on Sound Art* (New York: Continuum International, 2006), 31.

39 Ibid., 32.

40 Ibid., 33. Quote from Schaeffer is from the liner notes to *Pierre Schaeffer: L'Oeuvre Musicale*, p. 72.

41 R. Murray Schafer coined the term 'schizophonia' to describe the dislocation of sounds from their 'origins' or sources imposed by twentieth-century technology: 'The Greek prefix *schizo* means split, separated. Schizophonia refers to the split between an original sound and its electroacoustical transmission or reproduction.' R. Murray Schafer, *The Soundscape: Our Sonic Environment and the Tuning of the World* (Rochester: Destiny Books, 1993), 15.

42 Bill Fontana, 'The Relocation of Ambient Sound: Urban Sound Sculpture', *Leonardo* 20, no. 2 (1987): 45.

43 Bill Fontana, 'Resoundings'. http://resoundings.org/Pages/Resoundings.html.

44 An older (and regional) variant of the word 'region' (*Gegend*) which has the meaning 'free expanse' (*die freie Weite*) GA 13 47, DOT 66.

45 On Heidegger's later thinking of place, see Jeff E, Malpas, *Heidegger's Topology: Being, Place, World* (Cambridge, MA: MIT Press, 2006), and Miguel de Beistegui, *Thinking with Heidegger: Displacements* (Bloomington: Indiana University Press, 2003), 154.

46  Jean François Lyotard, *Driftworks*, trans. Joseph Maier (New York: Semiotext(e), 1984), 92.

# Chapter 4

1. Krzysztof Ziarek, 'Art, Power, and Politics: Heidegger on *Machenschaft* and *Poiēsis*', *Contretemps* 3, no. July (2002): 175–86, 176.
2. Ibid., 176.
3. To my knowledge first coined by Jay Bernstein to describe the philosophic approach to aesthetics deployed by thinkers such as Heidegger, Derrida and Adorno. The term is also used by Ziarek in *The Historicity of Experience: Modernity, the Avant-Garde, and the Event* (Evanston: Northwestern University Press, 2001), and *The Force of Art* (Stanford: Stanford University Press, 2004).
4. '*Der Ursprung des Kunstwerkes*', originated as a lecture at Freiburg, 13 November 1935, repeated in January 1936 in Zürich, then as an expanded three-part lecture on 17 and 24 November and 4 December 1936. All quotations in this chapter are from the modified version published in the Reclam edition of 1960 which was republished in the most recent edition of *Holzwege* in 1978 published as Volume 5 of Heidegger's *Gasamtausgabe*. English translations are from the modified version of Albert Hofstadter's translation in *Poetry, Language Thought* which appears in full in the revised and expanded edition of *Basic Writings*, edited by David Farrell Krell. Both Hofstadter's translation and Krell's modified version of it contain the addendum which was written in 1956 (included in the Reclam edition) but neither contain Heidegger's marginal notes, handwritten in his own copy of the Reclam edition which appear in the *Holzweg*, GA 5.
5. Heidegger's process of *Destruktion* emerges from his early phenomenological work with Husserl. The concept is most widely known from §6 and §44 in *Being and Time*. However, *Destruktion* is first outlined in detail in the 1929 lecture series *Phänomenologie der Anschauung und des Ausdrucks* (*Phenomenology of Intuition and Expression*); and elaborated further in the 1923 lecture series *Einfuerung in die phänomenologische Forschung* (*Introduction to Phenomenological Research*); and in the 1927 course *Die Grundprobleme Der Phänomenologie* (*The Basic Problems of Phenomenology*).
6. Heidegger, in the preface of the *Der Ursprung des Kunstwerkes*, 1960 Reclam edition, writes, 'The Epilogue was, in part, written later [than the Frankfurt lectures].' But the similarity of content in the first series of lectures on Nietzsche, 'Der Wille zur Macht als Kunst' of 1936–7, suggests that much of it was written at around that time.

7 David Farrell Krell suggests that the 'Six Basic Developments in the History of Aesthetics' is what remains of Heidegger's 1935–6 colloquium with Kurt Bauch on 'overcoming aesthetics in the question of art' (*N1 248*).
8 Hans-Georg Gadamer, *Truth and Method*, trans. Joel Weinscheimer and Donald G. Marshall, 2nd rev. edn (London: Continuum, 2006), 52.
9 See Martin Jay, *Songs of Experience Modern American and European Variations on a Universal Theme* (Berkeley: University of California Press, 2005), 222.
10 Heidegger, *Phenomenology of Intuition and Expression: Theory of Philosophical Concept Formation*, trans. Tracy Colony (London: Continuum, 2010), 129. (GA 59) *Phänomenologie Der Anschauung Und Des Ausdrucks* (Frankfurt: Vittorio Klostermann, 1993), 169.
11 Heidegger, *Introduction to Phenomenological Research*, trans. Daniel O. Dahlstrom (Bloomington: Indiana University Press, 2005), 67. (GA 17) *Einführung in die phänomenologische Forschung*, ed. Friedrich-Wilhelm von Herrmann (Frankfurt: Vittorio Klostermann, 1994), 92.
12 *Zōon logon echon* is usually translated as 'rational animal'. Heidegger interprets the phrase to mean: 'that living thing whose Being is essentially determined by the potentiality for discourse' (*SZ* 25, *BT* 47).
13 Heidegger, *Hölderlin's Hymns 'Germania' and 'The Rhine'*, trans. William McNeill and Julia Ireland (Bloomington: Indiana University Press, 2014), 27. [GA 39] *Hölderlins Hymnen "Germanien" und "Der Rhein"* (Frankfurt: Vittorio Klostermann, 1980), 27. In the recently published *Schwarze Hefte* (The Black Notebooks) Heidegger equates lived-experience to boat rides sponsored by the National Socialist Strength through Joy movement. See Martin Heidegger, *Ponderings II–VI: Black Notebooks 1931–1938*, trans. Richard Rojcewicz (Bloomington: Indiana University Press, 2016), 372.
14 Heidegger, *Nietzsche*: vol. IV: *Nihilism*, trans. David Farrell Krell (San Francisco: Harper and Row, 1982), 137. *Nietzsche: Zweiterband* (Frankfurt: Vittorio Klostermann, 1997), 190.
15 Young's translation appears in Martin Heidegger, *Off the Beaten Track*, trans. Julian Young and Kenneth Haynes (Cambridge: Cambridge University Press, 2002). Hofstadter's translation appears in *Poetry, Language, Thought*, trans. Albert Hofstadter (New York: Harper & Row, 1975), and forms the basis of Krell's translation in *Basic Writings from Being and Time (1927) to the Task of Thinking (1964)*, trans. David Farrell Krell, 1st edn (New York: Harper & Row, 1977).
16 Avital Ronell translates *Stoß* as 'jolt', in Ronell, *The Telephone Book*, 63.
17 See Nancy, 'The Decision of Existence', trans. Brian Holmes, in *Birth to Presence* (Stanford: Stanford University Press, 1993), in particular note 45.

18   Gerald L. Bruns, 'Poethics: John Cage and Stanley Cavell at the Crossroads of Ethical Theory', in Perloff and Junkerman, *John Cage: Composed in America*, 215.
19   Morris, 'Some Notes on the Phenomenology of Making', in *Continuous Project Altered Daily*, 87.
20   Michel Haar, *The Song of the Earth: Heidegger and the Grounds of the History of Being*, trans. Reginald Lilly (Bloomington: Indiana University Press, 1993), 41; Haar's emphasis.

# Chapter 5

1   Cage, interview with C. H. Waddington (1972), *Conversing with Cage*, 215–6, Cage's emphasis.
2   Cage, *Silence*, 64.
3   Ibid.
4   Davis, *Heidegger and the Will*, 134.
5   Daniel Charles brings up Heidegger in his fifth interview with Cage. Cage cuts off the question and misinterprets Charles's use of the word 'being' to mean materially persisting objects. This makes it unlikely that he was familiar with Heidegger's work. Cage and Charles, *For the Birds*, 150.
6   Daisetz Teitaro Suzuki, *Mysticism, Christian and Buddhist* (London: Allen and Unwin, 1957).
7   Cage and Charles, *For the Birds*, 9.
8   Ibid., 90.
9   *Abgeschiedenheit* is the modern German word meaning 'seclusion', 'retirement', which translates the Middle High German *abegescheidenheit* (*abegcscbeidcnbcit*) which, in turn, is Eckhart's translation of the Latin abstractus.
10  It is worth noting that in his later writings, Husserl considered the transcendental *epochē* as permanent habitual change of attitude and not a temporary act. See *Hua VI* §40, 153, *The Crisis of European Sciences and Transcendental Phenomenology: An Introduction to Phenomenological Philosophy*, trans. David Carr (Evanston: Northwestern University Press, 1970), § 40, 150.
11  Meister Eckhart, *Meister Eckhart* by Franz Pfeiffer, trans. C. de B. Evans (London: John M. Watkins, 1956), 342. *The Complete Mystical Works of Meister Eckhart*, trans. Maurice O'C. Walshe (New York: The Crossroads Publishing Company, 1979), 367.
12  John D. Caputo, *The Mystical Element in Heidegger's Thought*, Rev. reprint edn (New York: Fordham University Press, 1986), 178.

13  Davis, *Heidegger and the Will*, 137.
14  Davis refers to this traditional theological conception of the surrender of the will to a higher power as 'deferred willing'. In an essay written in 1981, Yvonne Rainer claims that Cage's '*refusal of meaning* is an abandonment, an appeal to a Higher Authority'. Yvonne Rainer, 'Looking Myself in the Mouth', in *John Cage*, ed. Julia Robinson (Cambridge, MA: MIT Press, 2011), 35–48, 47, Rainer's emphasis and capitalization. In opposition to this view I am arguing that Cage's detachment does not constitute deferred willing.
15  Mathew Mendez, '". . . A Power of Sonorous Paradoxes . . .": Passivity, Singularity and Indifference in Jean François Lyotard's Readings of John Cage', *Cultural Politics* 9, no. 2 (2013): 175.
16  This work was first published in abbreviated form in *Gelassenheit* in 1959. This shortened version of the last quarter of the text also appeared in volume 13 of the Heidegger *Gesamtausgabe*: *Aus der Erfahrung des Denkens 1910–1976*, and has been translated into English by John M. Anderson and E. Hans Freund, as 'Conversation on a Country Path about Thinking', in *Discourse on Thinking* (New York: Harper & Row, 1966). The full text was published in GA 77. *Feldweg-Gespräche 1944–45*, in 1995. It has been translated as *Country Path Conversations*, trans. Bret W. Davis (Bloomington: Indiana University Press, 2010).
17  Angelus Silesius, *The Cherubic Wanderer: Sensual Description of the Four Final Things*, cited in Heidegger (*PR* 35).
18  Meister Eckhart, *Deutsche Predigten und Traktate*, ed. and trans. Josef Quint (Munich: Carl Hanser, 1963), 371, *Meister Eckhart*, vol. 1, 118, *The Complete Mystical Works of Meister Eckhart*, 239; Eckhart's emphasis.
19  Cage, *Silence*, 155.
20  Ananda K. Coomaraswamy, *The Transformation of Nature in Art* (New York: Dover Publications, 1934), 15.
21  Douglas Kahn cites David Wayne Patterson, 'Appraising the Catchwords, C. 1942–1959: John Cage's Asian-Derived Rhetoric and the Historical Reference of Black Mountain College' (PhD diss., Columbia University, 1996), 129, in his *Noise, Water, Meat: A History of Sound in the Arts* (Cambridge, MA: MIT Press, 1999), 170. See also, Kyle Gann, *No Such Thing as Silence: John Cage's 4'33"* (New Haven: Yale University Press, 2010), 93. The phrase does appear in Coomaraswamy's essay 'Why Exhibit Works of Art?' (1941) and in *Why Exhibit Works of Art?* (1943) as 'Art is the imitation of Nature in her manner of operation' (38 and 110, respectively). It is likely that Cage came across the phrase from either of these sources since the translation from the Latin conforms exactly to Cage's quotation of the phrase.

22  Coomaraswamy, *The Transformation of Nature in Art*, 11.
23  See R. G. Collingwood, *The Idea of Nature* (Oxford: At the Clarendon Press, 1945), 94, and Wilhelm Windelband, *History of Philosophy: With Especial Reference to Formation and Development of Its Problems and Conceptions*, trans. James H. Tufts (New York: Macmillan, 1914), 336–8.
24  Jacques Maritain, *Art and Scholasticism: With Other Essays*, trans. J. F. Scanlan (London: Sheed & Ward, 1946), 49.
25  Cage, *Empty Words*, 178.
26  Maritain, *Art and Scholasticism*, 157 n. 128, Maritain's emphasis and capitalization.
27  Cage, *Empty Words*, 179.
28  Immanuel Kant, *The Critique of Judgement*, trans. Paul Guyer (Cambridge: Cambridge University Press, 2000), § 45, 185, my emphasis. Hereafter abbreviated in the text as '*CoJ*'.
29  Rodolphe Gasché, *Idea of Form: Rethinking Kant's Aesthetics* (Palo Alto: Stanford University Press, 2003), 16.
30  Alison Ross, *The Aesthetic Paths of Philosophy: Presentation in Kant, Heidegger, Lacoue-Labarthe, and Nancy* (Stanford: Stanford University Press, 2007), 31.
31  Heidegger deploys the word *Gunst* again later in the 1943 'Postscript to "What is Metaphysics?"', where he says that 'originary' thinking, in contradistinction to 'calculative' thinking, 'is the echo of being's favor (*Gunst*), in which a singular event is cleared and lets come to pass (sich ereignen): that beings are' (*GA 9* 105, *PM* 236).
32  Haar, *The Song of the Earth*, 51.
33  Jacques Taminiaux, *Poetics, Speculation, and Judgment: The Shadow of the Work of Art from Kant to Phenomenology*, trans. Michael Gendre (Albany: State University of New York Press, 1993), 70–1.
34  Heidegger's interpretation of *Gunst* in the third *Critique* corresponds to the sense that Meister Eckhart gives it, as 'grace' (*gratia*), a free giving and a thanking.
35  Taminiaux, *Poetics, Speculation, and Judgment*, 71. Taminiaux further points out that the rootedness in nature that Kant detects in the work of art suggests a different order of subjectivity than that of the ego.
36  In deploying his own word '*Gegenständigkeit*', rather than the more usual '*Gegenständlichkeit*', Heidegger seeks to draw our attention to what he regards as the unique mode of presencing that emerges in the modern period. That is, not just what stands over against (*Gegen-stand*) but also what stands opposite

(*Gegenstandig*) and, above all, in the constancy of what persists and endures (*Ständigkeit*). In using this word Heidegger emphasizes that the modern mode of presencing not only has the character of objectification but is also characterized by constant enduring presence.

# Chapter 6

1 John Caputo, *Radical Hermeneutics: Repetition, Deconstruction, and the Hermeneutic Project* (Bloomington: Indiana University Press, 1987), 2.
2 Cage and Charles, *For the Birds*, 151.
3 Dick Higgins, 'Fluxus: Theory and Reception', in *The Fluxus Reader*, ed. Ken Friedman (Chicester: Academy Editions, 1998), 222.
4 Brandon Joseph observes that it was the influence of Moholy Nagy's book, *The New Vision*, rather than Duchamp that brought Cage to an understanding of Robert Rauschenberg's *White Paintings*. Joseph, *Random Order*, 36. Cage would have come into contact with Albers's work directly through Black Mountain College.
5 Craig Safer, 'Fluxus as Laboratory', in Friedman, *The Fluxus Reader*, 136.
6 LaBelle, *Background Noise*, 59.
7 Hannah Higgins, *Fluxus Experience* (Berkeley: University of California Press, 2002), 34. Hannah Higgins is the daughter of two Fluxus artists, Dick Higgins and Alison Knowles. I will use the full names of Hannah Higgins and Dick Higgins where the identity might be confused.
8 Ibid., 37.
9 Ibid., 36.
10 Alice Jardine, *Gynesis: Configurations of Woman and Modernity* (Ithaca: Cornell University Press, 1985), 145.
11 Higgins, *Fluxus Experience*, 58.
12 Ibid., 59.
13 Ibid.
14 The conceptual strategy is employed by Seth Kim-Cohen in *In the Blink of an Ear.*
15 Higgins, *Fluxus Experience*, 49.
16 Higgins, *A Dialectic of Centuries*, 102–3. Cited in Doris, 'Zen Vaudiville: A Medi(T)Ation in the Margins of Fluxus', in Friedman, *The Fluxus Reader*, 94.
17 Jean-François Lyotard, *La phenomenology* (P.U.F), 45, cited in Vincent Descombes, *Modern French Philosophy*, trans. L. Scott-Fox and J. M. Harding (Cambridge: Cambridge University Press, 1980), 61, Lyotard's emphasis.

18  Graham Harman, in his *Tool Being*, critically misquotes the sentence 'the meaningful character of "instrumental strangeness", and the meaningful character of the "lectern", are in their essence absolutely identical.' [*Das Bedeutungshafte des "zeuglichen Fremdseins" und das Bedeutungshafte "Katheder" sind ihrem Wesenskern nach absolut identisch*]. By rendering this sentence, in absolute contradiction to Heidegger's statement, as: 'In the kernel of their essence, what is meaningful in "equipmental strangeness" and the "meaningful" lectern are *not* identical' (my emphasis, 82). See *Tool-Being: Heidegger and the Metaphysics of Objects* (Chicago: Open Court, 2002), 80–7.

19  What Heidegger calls at this stage of his work the 'environing world' (*Umwelt*) forms the context that allows a certain meaning to be co-given in the experience. The environment has the character of a world and the world worlds, as Heidegger renders it in the middle voice 'it worlds' (*es weltet*).

20  In a similar way Heidegger's linguistic-hermeneutical formulation of 'formal indication', which Heidegger formulated as a solution to Natorp's objections, is both indefinite and vague but still determinate. This sense of understanding, or hermeneutical intuition, does not seek to reject Husserl's model of reflection, but to deepen it in opposition to Natorp's criticisms. But this means avoiding the term reflection and, instead, reinterpreting intuition in terms of the historicity and pre-understanding that is, for the Heidegger of the 1920s, built into life. In this way Heidegger begins to develop the radical implications of Husserl's latent conceptions of fore-structures and horizons into a hermeneutic phenomenology. In the early 1920s the process of phenomenological-critical *Destruktion* is bound to preconception, or pre-delineation (*Vorzeichnung*), in the sense that it is guided by historically situated factical understanding where meanings point to contexts. Pure intuition, and even the phenomenological *Wesensschau*, as Heidegger argues in *Being and Time*, is founded upon the fore-structures of understanding and interpretation: fore-having (*Vorhabe*), fore-sight (*Vorsicht*) and fore-conception (*Vorgriff*). In this way experience, understood as involvement in the world, is structured in advance.

21  Since temporality pervades all lived-experience, all intentional objects are, for Husserl, temporal objects except those that are ideal objects.

22  Husserl, *Husserliana X: Vorlesungen zur Phänomenologie des Inneren Zeitbewusstseins* (The Hague: Martinus Nijhoff, 1966), 29. *The Phenomenology of Internal Time-Consciousness*, trans. James S. Churchhill, ed. Martin Heidegger (Bloomington: Indiana University Press, 1964), 51. *On the Phenomenology of the Consciousness of Internal Time (1893-1917)*, trans. John B. Brough (Springer Science + Business Media, BV, 1991), 31.

23 Yoko Ono, 'The World of a Fabricator', in Munroe, Alexandra with Jon Hendricks, *YES Yoko Ono* (New York: Harry N. Abrams and Japan Society, 2000), 285.
24 See Julia Robinson, 'From Abstraction to Model: George Brecht's Events and the Conceptual Turn in Art of the 1960s', *October* 127 (Winter, 2008): 77–108.
25 Gadamer, *Truth and Method*, 305, 367, 390 and 578.
26 Caputo, *Radical Hermeneutics*, 108–15. Gerald Bruns observes that *The Relevance of the Beautiful*, which discusses Duchamp and Dada, most certainly written as a response to Heidegger's rejection of modernism. See Bruns, *On the Anarchy of Poetry and Philosophy* (New York: Fordham University Press, 2007), 41.
27 Paul Patton and Terry Smith, *Jacques Derrida: Deconstruction Engaged: The Sydney Seminars* (Sydney: Power Publications, 2001), 23.
28 Ibid., 22.
29 Ibid., 15.

# Chapter 7

1 André Bazin, *What Is Cinema?*, vol. 1, trans. Hugh Gray (Berkeley: University of California Press, 1967), 13.
2 Ibid., 13.
3 Ibid., 12.
4 Ibid., 14.
5 Roland Barthes, *Camera Lucida: Reflections on Photography*, trans. Richard Howard (London: Fontana, 1984), 27.
6 Ibid., 28.
7 Mary Ann Doane, *The Emergence of Cinematic Time: Modernity, Contingency, the Archive* (Cambridge, MA: Harvard University Press, 2002), 95.
8 Ibid.
9 Michael Fried, *Why Photography Matters as Art as Never Before* (New Haven: Yale University Press, 2008), 103, Barthes, *Camera Lucida*, 70.
10 Fried, *Why Photography Matters*, 103, Barthes, *Camera Lucida*, 91.
11 Miriam Bratu Hansen notes a similar Proustian distinction in Kracauer and Benjamin's thoughts on the photographic image in *Cinema and Experience: Siegfried Kracauer, Walter Benjamin, and Theodor W. Adorno* (Berkeley: University of California Press, 2012), 31.
12 Fried, *Why Photography Matters*, 103.

13  Ibid., 104.
14  Walter Benjamin, 'A Small History of Photography' (1931), trans. Kingsley Shorter, in *One Way Street and Other Writings* (London: NLB, 1979), 243.
15  Ibid.
16  Siegfried Kracauer, *Theory of Film: The Redemption of Material Reality* (New York: Oxford University Press, 1960), 15.
17  Ibid., 20.
18  Walter Benjamin, 'On Some Motifs in Baudelaire', trans. Harry Zohn, in *Illuminations* (London: Fontana/Collins, 1982), 162–3.
19  Barthes, *Camera Lucida*, 76.
20  Doane, *The Emergence of Cinematic Time*, 94.
21  Marie-Françoise Plissart and Jacques Derrida, *Droit de regards* (Paris: Minuit, 1985); trans. David Wills as 'Right of Inspection', *Art & Text* 32 (Autumn 1989): 20–97, 34.
22  Ibid., 91.
23  Ibid.
24  Ibid.
25  In French the word 'ontology' and Derrida's neologism 'hauntology' are homophonic. They sound exactly the same when pronounced.
26  Benjamin, 'A Small History of Photography', 243.
27  Ibid.
28  Barthes, *Camera Lucida*, 90.
29  Roland Barthes, 'Rhetoric of the Image', in *Image Music Text*, trans. Stephen Heath (London: Fontana, 1984), 44.
30  Barthes, *Camera Lucida*, 95–6.
31  Ibid., 90.
32  *The Genius of Photography*. 'Paper Movies', S1 Ep. 4. 2007. BBC.
33  Stephen Heath, 'Repetition Time: Notes Around "Structural/Materialist Film"', in *Questions of Cinema* (London: Macmillan Press, 1981), 174 (First published in *Wide Angle* 2, no. 3 (1978): 4–11.), Heath's emphasis.
34  Ibid., 174.
35  Malcolm Le Grice, *Abstract Film and Beyond* (London: Studio Vista, 1977), 124.
36  Peter Wollen, *Readings and Writings: Semiotic Counter Strategies* (London: Verso, 1982), 217 n. 15.
37  In *Abstract Film and Beyond*, Le Grice erroneously relates in *Windmill II* 'that the camera motor speed is determined by the rate at which a windmill turns'. Watching the film, it is obvious that this is not the case.
38  Chris Welsby, 'Seven Days', *Luxonline*. Accessed 23 November 2019.

http://www.luxonline.org.uk/luxonline/artists/chris_welsby/seven_days.html.
39 Peter Gidal, *Materialist Film* (London: Routledge, 1990), 100.
40 Le Grice, *Abstract Film and Beyond*, 120.
41 Annette Michelson, 'Toward Snow', *Artforum* (June 1971), reprinted in Peter Gidal, ed., *Structural Film Anthology* (London: British Film Institute, 1976), 43.
42 Both Michelson and Deke Dusinberre essentially see the wavelength in Husserlian terms as a 'metaphor for the intentionality of consciousness', where the camera view simulates intentional directedness. See Michelson, 'Toward Snow', 40, Deke Dusinberre, '"The Ascetic Task" & "St George in the Forest"', in *A Perspective on English Avant-Garde Film: A Touring Exhibition Selected by David Curtis and Deke Dusinberre*, 41, Deke Dusinberre, 'The Ascetic Task: Peter Gidal's *Room Film 1973*', in Peter Gidal, ed., *Structural Film Anthology*, 110.
43 Le Grice, *Abstract Film and Beyond*, 120.
44 Peter Wollen '"Ontology" and "Materialism" in Film', in *Readings and Writings*, 197.
45 Also known as Owen Land.
46 Paul Sharits, 'Words per Page', *Afterimage* 4 (Autumn, 1972): 26–42. Reproduced on 'Paul Sharits / Mike Hoodbloom', unpaginated. Accessed 23 November 2019. http://mikehoolboom.com/?p=39.
47 Ibid.
48 Wollen, *Readings and Writings*, 198.
49 Craig Dworkin, *No Medium* (Cambridge, MA: MIT Press, 2013), 135.
50 Ibid., 136.
51 Le Grice, *Abstract Film and Beyond*, 95.
52 Ibid., 94.
53 Andy Warhol, Minneapolis Lecture, February 1968, cited in David Bourdon, *Warhol* (New York: Abrams, 1989), 188.
54 Ronald Tavel, quoted in David E. James, 'The Warhol Screenplays: An Interview with Ronald Tavel', *Persistence of Vision* 11 (1995): 51, cited in Douglas Crimp, *'Our Kind of Movie' The Films of Andy Warhol* (Cambridge, MA: MIT Press, 2012), 145, 161 n. 16.
55 The repetition in *Vexations* differs markedly from repetition in traditional Western classical music where, as Wim Mertens notes, repetition is associated with narrative and teleology. *Vexations* – and the music of the minimalist composers – is not directed towards a final climax, and Mertens describes this form as 'non-narrative', 'a-teleological' and, in general, non-dialectical. See Wim Mertens, *American Minimal Music: La Monte Young, Terry Riley, Steve Reich Philip Glass*, trans. J. Hautekiet (London: Kahn & Averill; New York: Alexander

Brou Inc), 16. African and Eastern music – which were being appropriated by Western modernism at the time of *Vexations* – are also very much a-teleological. Gregory Bateson utilises this model – which he in-turn derived from the work of the composer Colin McPhee – to describe the 'steady-state' value system of the Balinese as *non-schismogenic* – a concept relied upon by Delueze and Guattari in their formulation of the 'plateau', as an a-climactic continuous region of intensity.

56  Higgins, *A Dialectic of Centuries*, 43.
57  Cage, *For the Birds*, 153.
58  Cage, interviewed by Alan Gillmor and Roger Shattuck (1973), in Kostelanetz, *Conversing with Cage*, 48.
59  Cage, *Silence*, 93.
60  David J. Kangas, *Kierkegaard's Instant: On Beginnings* (Bloomington: Indiana University Press), 196.
61  See 'The Rotation Method: An Essay in the Theory of Social Prudence', in *Either /Or, Volume 1*, trans. David F. Swenson (Princeton: Princeton University Press, 1959), 279–96.
62  Kangas, *Kierkegaard's Instant*, 60; Kangas's emphasis.
63  Ibid., 56. As Kierkegaard puts it, 'boredom rests on the nothing that interlaces existence.' *Either/Or*, 2 vols, trans. Howard V. Hong and Edna H. Hong (Princeton: Princeton University Press, 1987), 1:291; *Søren Kierkegaards Skrifter*, published by the Søren Kierkegaard Research Centre in Copenhagen, 2:280, cited in Kangas, *Kierkegaard's Instant*, 56; Kierkegaard's emphasis.
64  Kangas, *Kierkegaard's Instant*, 197.
65  Ibid., 196.
66  Jussi Backman, 'All of a Sudden: Heidegger and Plato's Parmenides', *Epoche* 11, no. 2 (2007): 393–408.
67  On Derrida's frequent deployment of this phrase, see Geoffrey Bennington, 'A Moment of Madness: Derrida's Kierkegaard', *Oxford Literary Review*, 33, no. 1, The Unreadable (2011): 103–27. See Kierkegaard, *Philosophical Fragments or a Fragment of Philosophy*, trans. David F. Swenson (Princeton: Princeton University Press, 1962), 64.
68  Derrida, *The Gift of Death*, trans. David Wills (Chicago: University of Chicago Press, 1992), 65.
69  Derrida, *Given Time: I. Counterfeit Money*, trans. Peggy Kamuf (Chicago: University of Chicago Press, 1992), 9.
70  See Ray Brassier, *Nihil Unbound: Enlightenment and Extinction* (Basingstoke: Palgrave Macmillan, 2007), 116.

71 Thomas S. Kuhn, *The Structure of Scientific Revolutions*, 2nd edn Enlarged (Chicago: University of Chicago Press, 1970), 64.
72 Bruno Latour, 'What Is Iconoclash? Or Is There a World Beyond the Image Wars?' First published in *Iconoclash: Beyond the Image Wars in Science, Religion, and Art*, ed. Bruno Latour and Peter Weibel (Cambridge, MA: MIT Press, 2002). Reproduced in *On the Modern Cult of the Factish Gods* (Durham: Duke University Press, 2010), 67–97. Also see John Caputo, *The Insistence of God: A Theology of the Perhaps* (Bloomington: Indiana University Press, 2013).
73 See Quentin Meillassoux, *After Finitude: An Essay on the Necessity of Contingency*, trans. Ray Brassier (London: Bloomsbury, 2013).

# Chapter 8

1 The term 'poethics' is taken from Joan Retallack. It resonates with Caputo's terms 'theo-poetics' and 'cosmo-poetics'.
2 A mesostic poem is much like an acrostic text but the vertical phrase, or spine – which in Cage's poems often consist of proper names – runs down the middle rather than the edge. The term is attributed to Norman O. Brown.
3 See Liz Kotz, *Words to Be Looked At: Language in 1960s Art* (Cambridge, MA: MIT Press, 2007), 127.
4 Tyrus Miller, *Singular Examples: Artistic Politics and the Neo-Avant-Garde* (Evanston: Northwestern University Press, 2009), 70.
5 Cage, *I-IV*, 13.
6 Ibid., 15–16. The line 'It's because I'm in the position of writing a text that uses words' is omitted from the written text. It can be heard in the recording (6'50" in) on the cassette tape supplied with the book.
7 Cage, *Silence*, 39, 69, and *A Year from Monday*, 129.
8 John Cage, *Musicage: Cage Muses on Words, Art, Music*, ed. Joan Retallack (Hanover: Wesleyan University Press; University Press of New England, 1996), 214.
9 Ibid., 69.
10 Cage, *Empty Words*, 183. Cage writes: 'Implicit in the use of words (when messages are put across) are training, government, enforcement, and finally the military. Thoreau said that hearing a sentence he heard feet marching, Syntax, N. [Norman] O. Brown told me, is the arrangement of the army', 183.
11 There are two words in French that can be translated by the English word 'meaning': *sens* and *vouloir-dire*. The latter has connotations of volition as it

is etymologically linked to *voluntas*, and can be translated as 'meaning' or 'to mean' but has strong connotations towards 'want to say' or 'will to say'. Derrida translates *bedeuten*, the verbal form of the word Husserl uses for 'meaning' (*Bedeutung*) as *vouloir-dire*, a necessity since *sens* is reserved for the translation of the German word *Sinn*, and as Derrida explains in *Speech and Phenomena*, the French word *signification* presents problems because whereas in German and English one can say that a sign is without meaning (*bedeutungslos*), or that a sign is meaningful (*bedeutsame Zeichen*) to translate *Bedeutung* as *signification*, risks giving the sense of these expressions as the absurd 'non-signifying sign', and the redundant 'signifying sign'. Cf. *SP* 17–18.

12 Jacques Derrida, *Limited Inc.*, trans. Samuel Weber and Jeffrey Mehlman (Evanston: Northwestern University Press, 1988). Henceforth cited parenthetically in the text as *LInc*.

13 See Samuel Weber, *Mass Mediauras: Form Technics Media*, ed. Alan Cholodenko (Sydney: Power Publications, 1996), 139–40.

14 Rodolphe Gasché, *The Tain of the Mirror: Derrida and the Philosophy of Reflection* (Cambridge, MA: Harvard University Press, 1986), 127. Gasché's emphasis.

15 See Stanley Fish, *Doing What Comes Naturally: Change, Rhetoric, and the Practice of Theory in Literary and Legal Studies* (Durham: Duke University Press, 1989), 505.

16 Derrida, *The Beast and the Sovereign*, vol. 1, trans. Geoffrey Bennington (Chicago: University of Chicago Press, 2009), 33.

17 Derrida in his response in the afterword is clearly irritated by Graff's misconstrual of the notion of undecidability. What is named 'undecidable' here seems to be the product of (at least) two authors: Graff, Derrida and 'Some American critics' (Searle among them) that Graff credits with accusing Derrida of 'setting up a kind of "all or nothing" choice between pure realization of self-presence and complete freeplay or undecidability' (*LInc* 114). It could be said that the central theme of Derrida's reply (to John Searle's criticisms of 'Signature Event Context') in 'Limited Inc a b c ...' is the inevitable misreading and the shift that meaning takes when we attempt to understand each other. Thus, the shift in meaning of 'undecidability' is an example.

18 Julia Kristeva, *Revolution in Poetic Language*, trans. Margaret Waller (New York: Columbia University Press, 1984), 233.

19 Ibid., 211.

20 Elizabeth Grosz, *Sexual Subversions: Three French Feminists* (Sydney: Allen & Unwin, 1989), 69.

21 Jardine, *Gynesis*, 45.
22 See Julia Kristeva, *Desire in Language: A Semiotic Approach to Literature and Art*, trans. Thomas Gora, Alice Jardine and Leon S. Roudiez (New York: Columbia University Press, 1980), 168.
23 Judith Butler, 'Performative Agency', *Journal of Cultural Economy*, no. 3, issue 2 (2010): 147–61, 147.
24 Slavoj Žižek. 'The Real of Sexual Difference', in *Interrogating the Real*, ed. Rex Butler and Scott Stephens (London: Bloomsbury, 2005), 293–316.
25 Although Catherine Malabou argues that the deconstruction of sexual identity should not preclude the struggle for women's liberation, nor relinquish the term 'woman', which, for Malabou, refers to a 'subject overexposed to a specific type of violence', it is necessary to counter anti-essentialism with the same force as any counter to essentialism. Rather than a substantialist idea of essence, Malabou points us towards Hegelian and Heideggerian conceptions of essence which she renders as femininity's 'secret plasticity'. See Catherine Malabou, *Changing Difference: The Feminine and the Question of Philosophy*, trans. Carolyn Shread (Cambridge: Polity Press, 2011), 93.
26 Joan Retallack, *The Poethical Wager* (Berkeley: University of California Press, 2003), 16.
27 Ibid., 3.
28 Retallack (Talk), 'John Cage's Anarchic Harmony'. Accessed 28 November 2019. See Pierre Bourdieu, *Practical Reason: On the Theory of Action*, trans. Gisele Sapiro, ed. Brian McHale (Cambridge: Polity Press, 1998), 7–8.
29 Retallack, 'Introduction: Conversations in Retrospect', in *Musicage*, xv.
30 Derrida, *Taking Chances*, 2. Quentin Meillassoux makes the point that the notion of chance is dependent on the principle of sufficient reason. Thus, for Meillasoux, chance differs from contingency because the latter is non-totalizable. He employs the example of the *clinamen* to make this point. See *After Finitude: An Essay on the Necessity of Contingency*, trans. Ray Brassier (London: Bloomsbury, 2009), 99–101.
31 This indeterminate reading has been at the centre of, as Derrida says, 'a classical philological problem'. Derrida, *Taking Chances*, 7. Natania Meeker points out that in the early editions, including the *Oblongus* and *Quadratus* manuscripts from the ninth and tenth centuries, the lines in question are transcribed as: '*libera per terras unde haec animantibus exstat, unde est haec, inquam, fatis avulsa voluptas, per quam progredimur quo ducit quemque voluntus.*' The generally accepted rendering is: '*libera per terras unde haec animantibus exstat, unde est haec, inquam, fatis avolsa voluntas, per quam progredimur quo ducit quemque voluptas.*'

See Natania Meeker, *Voluptuous Philosophy: Literary Materialism in the French Enlightenment* (New York: Fordham University Press, 2006). Also see Cyril Bailey, *The Greek Atomists and Epicurus* (Oxford: Clarendon Press, 1928).
32 Retallack, *The Poethical Wager*, 12. Retallack's emphasis.
33 Niall Lucy, *Debating Derrida* (Melbourne: Melbourne University Press, 1995), 24. Lucy's emphasis.
34 Rainer, 'Looking Myself in the Mouth', 47.

# Bibliography

Aristotle. *Nicomachean Ethics Book Six, English and Greek*. Translated by L. H. G. Greenwood. Cambridge: Cambridge University Press, 1909.
Austin, J. L. *How to Do Things with Words*. 2nd edn. Oxford: Clarendon Press, 1975.
Backman, Jussi. 'All of a Sudden: Heidegger and Plato's Parmenides', *Epoche* 11, no. 2 (2007): 393–408.
Badiou, Alain. *Handbook of Inaesthetics*. Translated by Alberto Toscano. Stanford: Stanford University Press, 2005.
Barthes, Roland. *Camera Lucida: Reflections on Photography*. Translated by Richard Howard. London: Fontana, 1984.
Barthes, Roland. *Image, Music, Text*. Translated by Stephen Heath. New York: Hill and Wang, 1977.
Barthes, Roland. *S/Z*. Translated by Richard Miller. 1st American edn. New York: Hill and Wang, 1974.
Bazin, André. *What Is Cinema?* Vol. 1. Translated by Hugh Gray. Berkeley: University of California Press, 1967.
Beistegui, Miguel de. *Thinking with Heidegger: Displacements*. Bloomington: Indiana University Press, 2003.
Belgrad, Daniel. *The Culture of Spontaneity: Improvisation and the Arts in Postwar America*. Chicago: University of Chicago Press, 1998.
Benjamin, Walter. 'A Small History of Photography' (1931). Translated by Kingsley Shorter. In *One Way Street and Other Writings*, 240–57. London: NLB, 1979.
Benjamin, Walter. 'On Some Motifs in Baudelaire'. In *Illuminations*, translated by Harry Zohn, 157–202. London: Fontana/Collins, 1982.
Bennington, Geoffrey. 'A Moment of Madness: Derrida's Kierkegaard', *Oxford Literary Review* 33, no. 1, The Unreadable (2011): 103–27.
Bernstein, Jay. *The Fate of Art: Aesthetic Alienation from Kant to Derrida and Adorno*. Cambridge: Polity Press, 1992.
Blom, Ina. 'Theories of Fluxus: Boredom and Oblivion'. In *The Fluxus Reader*, edited by Ken Friedman, 63–90. Chichester: Academy Edition, 1998.
Bourdieu, Pierre. *Practical Reason: On the Theory of Action*. Cambridge: Polity Press, 1998.
Brassier, Ray. *Nihil Unbound: Enlightenment and Extinction*. Basingstoke: Palgrave Macmillan, 2007.

Brecht, George. *Chance-Imagery*. ubuclassics, 2004. Accessed 3 May 2008. http://www.ubu.com/historical/gb/brecht_chance.pdf.

Breton, André. *Manifestoes of Surrealism*. Translated by Richard Seaver and Helen R. Lane. Ann Arbor: University of Michigan Press, 1972.

Bruns, Gerald L. *Heidegger's Estrangements: Language, Truth, and Poetry in the Later Writings*. New Haven: Yale University Press, 1989.

Bruns, Gerald L. *The Material of Poetry: Sketches for a Philosophical Poetics*. Athens: The University of Georgia Press, 2005.

Bruns, Gerald L. *On the Anarchy of Poetry and Philosophy a Guide for the Unruly*. New York: Fordham University Press, 2006.

Bruns, Gerald L. 'Poethics: John Cage and Stanley Cavell at the Crossroads of Ethical Theory'. In *John Cage: Composed in America*, edited by Marjorie Perloff and Charles Junkerman, 206–25. Chicago: University of Chicago Press, 1994.

Butler, Judith. *Bodies That Matter: On the Discursive Limits of "Sex"*. New York: Routledge, 1993.

Butler, Judith. *Excitable Speech: A Politics of the Performative*. New York: Routledge, 1997.

Butler, Judith. 'Performative Acts and Gender Constitution: An Essay in Phenomenology and Feminist Theory', *Theatre Journal* 40, no. 4 (1988): 519–31.

Butler, Judith. 'Performative Agency', *Journal of Cultural Economy* 3, no. 2 (2010): 147–61.

Butler, Judith. 'Précis of *Senses of the Subject*', *Philosophy and Phenomenological Research* 96, no. 1 (January 2018): 214.

Butler, Judith and Cayle Salamon. 'Learning to See', *Philosophy Today* 61, no. 2 (Spring 2017): 319–37.

Cage, John. *A Year from Monday: New Lectures and Writings*. London: Marion Boyars, 1968.

Cage, John. 'An Interview with John Cage', Michael Kirby and Richard Schechner, *Tulane Drama Review* 10, no. 2 (Winter 1965): 50–72.

Cage, John. *Composition in Retrospect*. Cambridge: Exact Change, 1993.

Cage, John. *Empty Words: Writings '73-'78*. 1st edn. Middletown: Wesleyan University Press; Marion Boyars, 1979.

Cage, John. *I-IV*. Charles Eliot Norton Lectures, 1988–89. Cambridge, MA: Harvard University Press, 1990.

Cage, John. *Musicage: Cage Muses on Words, Art, Music*. Edited by Joan Retallack. Hanover: Wesleyan University Press: University Press of New England, 1996.

Cage, John. *Silence: Lectures and Writings*. London: Calder & Boyars, 1968.

Cage, John and Geoffrey Barnard. *Conversation without Feldman*. Sydney: Black Ram Books, 1980.

Cage, John and Daniel Charles. *For the Birds*. Boston: M. Boyars, 1981.
Caputo, John D. *Against Ethics: Contributions to a Poetics of Obligation with Constant Reference to Deconstruction*. Bloomington: Indiana University Press, 1993.
Caputo, John D. *The Insistence of God: A Theology of the Perhaps*. Bloomington: Indiana University Press, 2013.
Caputo, John D. *The Mystical Element in Heidegger's Thought*. Rev. reprint. New York: Fordham University Press, 1986.
Caputo, John D. *Radical Hermeneutics: Repetition, Deconstruction, and the Hermeneutic Project*. Bloomington: Indiana University Press, 1987.
Carlisle, Clare. 'The Question of Habit in Theology and Philosophy: From Hexis to Plasticity', *Body & Society* 19, nos. 2–3 (2013): 30–57.
Chion, Michel. *Audio-Vision: Sound on Screen*. Translated by Claudia Gorbman. New York: Columbia University Press, 1994.
Chion, Michel. *Guide to Sound Objects: Pierre Schaeffer and Musical Research*. Translated by John Dack and Christine North, 1983. Paris: Éditions Buchet, 2009.
Collingwood, R. G. *The Idea of Nature*. Oxford: At the Clarendon Press, 1945.
Conty, Arianne. 'They Might Have Eyes That They Might Not See: Walter Benjamin's Aura and the Optical Unconscious', *Literature & Theology* 27, no. 4 (December 2013): 472–86.
Coomaraswamy, Ananda K. *The Transformation of Nature in Art*. New York: Dover Publications, 1934.
Coomaraswamy, Ananda K. 'Why Exhibit Works of Art?' *The Journal of Aesthetics and Art Criticism* 1, no. 2/3 (Autumn 1941): 27–41.
Crimp, Douglas. *'Our Kind of Movie' The Films of Andy Warhol*. Cambridge, MA: MIT Press, 2012.
Crooks, Edward, James. 'John Cage's Entanglement with the Ideas of Commaraswamy'. PhD diss., University of York, 2011.
Dastur, Françoise. 'Heidegger's Freiburg Version of the Origin of the Work of Art'. In *Heidegger toward the Turn: Essays on the Work of the 1930s*, edited by James Risser, 110–42. New York: State University of New York Press, 1999.
Davis, Bret W. *Heidegger and the Will: On the Way to Gelassenheit*. Evanston: Northwestern University Press, 2007.
Derrida, Jacques. *The Beast and the Sovereign*, Vol. 1. Translated by Geoffrey Bennington. Chicago: University of Chicago Press, 2009.
Derrida, Jacques. *Dissemination*. Translated by Barbara Johnson. London: Athlone, 1981.
Derrida, Jacques. 'Economimesis'. Translated by R. Klein, *Diacritics* 11, no. 2, The Ghost of Theology: Readings of Kant and Hegel (Summer 1981): 3–25.
Derrida, Jacques. *Edmund Husserl's Origin of Geometry: An Introduction*. Translated by John P. Leavey. Lincoln: University of Nebraska Press, 1989.

Derrida, Jacques. 'Force of Law: The "Mystical Foundation of Authority"'. Translated by Mary Quaintance, *Cardozo Law Review* 11 (1990): 920–1045.

Derrida, Jacques. *The Gift of Death*. Translated by David Wills. Chicago: University of Chicago Press, 1992.

Derrida, Jacques. *Given Time: I. Counterfeit Money*. Translated by Peggy Kamuf. Chicago: University of Chicago Press, 1992.

Derrida, Jacques. *Limited Inc*. Translated by Samuel Weber and Jeffrey Mehlman. Evanston: Northwestern University Press, 1988.

Derrida, Jacques. 'My Chances/ Mes Chances: A Rendezvous with Some Epicurean Stereophonies'. In *Taking Chances: Derrida, Psychoanalysis, and Literature*, edited by Joseph Smith and William Kerrigan, 1–32. Baltimore: Johns Hopkins University Press, 1984.

Derrida, Jacques. *Of Grammatology*. Translated by Gayatri Chakravorty Spivak. 1st American edn. Baltimore: Johns Hopkins University Press, 1976.

Derrida, Jacques. *Positions*. Translated by Alan Bass. Chicago: University of Chicago Press, 1981.

Derrida, Jacques. *The Problem of Genesis in Husserl's Philosophy*. Translated by Marian Hobson. Chicago: University of Chicago Press, 2001.

Derrida, Jacques. *Spectres of Marx: The State of Debt, the Work of Mourning, and the New International*. Translated by Peggy Kamuf. New York and London: Routledge, 1994.

Derrida, Jacques. *Speech and Phenomena, and Other Essays on Husserl's Theory of Signs*. Translated by David B. Allison. Evanston: Northwestern University Press, 1973.

Derrida, Jacques. *The Truth in Painting*. Translated by Geoff Bennington and Ian McLeod. Chicago: University of Chicago Press, 1987.

Derrida, Jacques. *Writing and Difference*. Translated by Alan Bass. Chicago: University of Chicago Press, 1978.

Descombes, Vincent. *Modern French Philosophy*. Translated by L. Scott-Fox and J. M. Harding. Cambridge: Cambridge University Press, 1980.

Dilthey, Wilhelm. *Poetry and Experience*. Edited by Rudolf A. Makkreel and Frithjof Rodi. Princeton: Princeton University Press, 1985.

Doane, Mary Ann. *The Emergence of Cinematic Time: Modernity, Contingency, the Archive*. Cambridge, MA and London: Harvard University Press, 2002.

Doris, David. 'Zen Vaudiville: A Medi(T)Ation in the Margins of Fluxus'. In *The Fluxus Reader*, edited by Ken Friedman, 91–135. Chichester: Academy Edition, 1998.

Duchamp, Marcel. *The Essential Writings of Marcel Duchamp: Salt Seller, Marchand Du Sel*. Edited by Michel Sanouillet and Elmer Peterson. London: Thames & Hudson, 1975.

Duchamp, Marcel and Pierre Cabanne. *Dialogues with Marcel Duchamp*. Translated by Ron Padgett. London: Thames and Hudson, 1971.

Dworkin, Craig. *No Medium*. Cambridge, MA: MIT Press, 2013.

Dworkin, Craig and Kenneth Goldsmith, eds. *Against Expression: An Anthology of Conceptual Writing*. Evanston: Northwestern University Press, 2010.

Dyson, Frances. *Sounding New Media: Immersion and Embodiment in the Arts and Culture*. Berkeley: University of California Press, 2009.

Dyson, Frances. 'Transmitter Bodies: Aurality, Corporeality, Cuts and Signals', *NMA*, no. 8 (1990): 14–19.

Eckhart, Meister. *The Complete Mystical Works of Meister Eckhart*. Translated by Maurice O'C. Walshe. New York: The Crossroads Publishing Company, 1979.

Eckhart, Meister. *Deutsche Predigten und Traktate*. Edited and translated by Josef Quint. Munich: Carl Hanser, 1963.

Eckhart, Meister. *Meister Eckhart* by Franz Pfeiffer. Translated by C. de B. Evans. London: John M. Watkins, 1956.

Engström, Andreas and Åsa Stjerna. 'Sound Art or *Klangkunst*? A Reading of the German and English Literature on Sound Art', *Organised Sound* 14, no. 1 (2009): 11–18.

Ernst, Max. 'On Frottage' (1936). In Herschel B. Chipp, *Theories of Modern Art: A Source Book by Artists and Critics*, 428–31. Berkeley: University of California Press, 1968.

Fish, Stanley. *Doing What Comes Naturally: Change, Rhetoric, and the Practice of Theory in Literary and Legal Studies*. Durham: Duke University Press, 1989.

Fontana, Bill. 'The Relocation of Ambient Sound: Urban Sound Sculpture', *Leonardo* 20, no. 2 (1987): 143–7.

Forti, Simone. *Handbook in Motion*. Halifax: Nova Scotia College of Art and Design, 1974.

Foster, Hal. *The Return of the Real: The Avant-Garde at the End of the Century*. Cambridge, MA: MIT Press, 1996.

Fried, Michael. *Why Photography Matters as Art as Never Before*. New Haven: Yale University Press, 2008.

Gadamer, Hans-Georg. *Philosophical Hermeneutics*. Translated by David E. Linge. Berkley: University of California Press, 2004.

Gadamer, Hans-Georg. *The Relevance of the Beautiful and Other Essays*. Translated by Nicholas Walker. Cambridge: Cambridge University Press, 1986.

Gadamer, Hans-Georg. *Truth and Method*. Translated by Joel Weinsheimer and Donald G. Marshall. 2nd rev. edn. London: Continuum, 2006.

Gann, Kyle. *No Such Thing as Silence: John Cage's 4' 33"*. New Haven: Yale University Press.

Gasché, Rodolphe. *Idea of Form: Rethinking Kant's Aesthetics*. Palo Alto: Stanford University Press, 2003.

Gasché, Rodolphe. *Inventions of Difference: On Jacques Derrida*. Cambridge, MA: Harvard University Press, 1994.

Gasché, Rodolphe. *The Tain of the Mirror: Derrida and the Philosophy of Reflection*. Cambridge, MA: Harvard University Press, 1986.

Gidal, Peter. *Materialist Film*. London: Routledge, 1990.

Gombrich, E. H. *Art and Illusion: A Study in the Psychology of Pictorial Presentation*. 3rd edn. London: Phaidon, 1968.

Graham, John D. *System and Dialectics of Art*. New York: Delphic Studios, 1937.

Grosz, Elizabeth. 'Habit Today: Ravaisson, Bergson, Deleuze and Us', *Body & Society* 19, nos. 2–3 (2013): 217–39.

Grosz, Elizabeth. *Sexual Subversions: Three French Feminists*. Sydney: Allen & Unwin, 1989.

Groys, Boris. *Art Power*. Cambridge, MA: MIT Press, 2008.

Groys, Boris. 'Not Aesthetics or Anti-aesthetics but Poetics'. In *Beyond the Aesthetic and the Anti-aesthetic*, edited by James Elkins and Harper Montgomery, 135–8. University Park: Pennsylvania State University Press, 2013.

Haacke, Hans. *Hans Haacke: For Real: Works 1959–2006*. Edited by Matthias Flèugge and Robert Fleck. Düsseldorf: Richter, 2006.

Haar, Michel. *Heidegger and the Essence of Man*. Translated by William Mc Neill. Albany: State University of New York Press, 1993.

Haar, Michel. *The Song of the Earth: Heidegger and the Grounds of the History of Being*. Translated by Reginald Lilly. Bloomington: Indiana University Press, 1993.

Haladyn, Julian Jason. *Boredom and Art: Passions of the Will to Boredom*. Winchester: Zero Books, 2015.

Halprin, Ann and Yvonne Rainer. 'Yvonne Rainer Interviews Ann Halprin', *Tulane Drama Review* 10, no. 2 (Winter 1965): 142–67.

Hansen, Miriam Bratu. *Cinema and Experience: Siegfried Kracauer, Walter Benjamin, and Theodor W. Adorno*. Berkeley: University of California Press, 2012.

Harman, Graham. *Tool-Being: Heidegger and the Metaphysics of Objects*. Chicago: Open Court, 2002.

Hayles, N. Katherine. 'Chance Operations: Cagean Paradox and Contemporary Science'. In *John Cage: Composed in America*, edited by Marjorie Perloff and Charles Junkerman, 226–41. Chicago: University of Chicago Press, 1994.

Heath, Stephen. *Questions of Cinema*. London: Macmillan Press, 1981.

Heidegger, Martin. *Aus Der Erfahrung Des Denkens, 1910–1976*. Frankfurt: Vittorio Klostermann, 2002.

Heidegger, Martin. *The Basic Problems of Phenomenology*. Translated by Albert Hofstadter. Rev. edn. Bloomington: Indiana University Press, 1988.

Heidegger, Martin. *Basic Questions of Philosophy: Selected 'Problems' of 'Logic'*. Translated by Richard Rojcewicz and André Schuwer. Bloomington: Indiana University Press, 1994.

Heidegger, Martin. *Basic Writings from Being and Time (1927) to the Task of Thinking (1964)*. Translated by David Farrell Krell. 1st edn. New York: Harper & Row, 1977.

Heidegger, Martin. *Being and Time*. Translated by John Macquarrie and Edward Robinson. Oxford: Basil Blackwell, 1962.

Heidegger, Martin. *Beiträge Zur Philosophie (Vom Ereignis)*. Frankfurt: Vittorio Klostermann, 1989.

Heidegger, Martin. *Besinnung*. Frankfurt: Vittorio Klostermann, 1997.

Heidegger, Martin. *Contributions to Philosophy: (from Enowning)*. Translated by Parvis Emad and Kenneth Maly. Bloomington: Indiana University Press, 1999.

Heidegger, Martin. *Die Geschicte Des Seyns*. Frankfurt: Vittorio Klostermann, 1998.

Heidegger, Martin. *Die Grundprobleme Der Phänomenologie*. Frankfurt: Vittorio Klostermann, 1975.

Heidegger, Martin. *Discourse on Thinking: A Translation of Gelassenheit*. Translated by John M. Anderson and E. Hans Freund. New York: Harper & Row, 1969.

Heidegger, Martin. *Einführung in die phänomenologische Forschung*. Edited by Friedrich-Wilhelm von Herrmann. Frankfurt: Vittorio Klostermann, 1994.

Heidegger, Martin. *The End of Philosophy*. Translated by Joan Stambaugh. Chicago: The University of Chicago Press, 2003.

Heidegger, Martin. *Four Seminars*. Translated by Andrew Mitchell and Francois Raffoul. Bloomington: Indiana University Press, 2003.

Heidegger, Martin. *The Fundamental Concepts of Metaphysics: World, Finitude, Solitude*. Translated by William McNeill and Nicholas Walker. Bloomington: Indiana University Press, 1995.

Heidegger, Martin. *Grundfragen Der Philosophie: Ausgewählt 'Probleme' Der 'Logik'*. Frankfurt: Vittorio Klostermann, 1984.

Heidegger, Martin. *Hölderlins Hymnen 'Germanien' und 'Der Rhein'*. Frankfurt: Vittorio Klostermann, 1980.

Heidegger, Martin. *Hölderlin's Hymns 'Germania' and 'The Rhine'*. Translated by William McNeill and Julia Ireland. Bloomington: Indiana University Press, 2014.

Heidegger, Martin. *Holzwege*. Frankfurt: Vittorio Klostermann, 1977.

Heidegger, Martin. *Introduction to Metaphysics*. Translated by Richard F. H. Polt and Gregory Fried. New Haven: Yale University Press, 2000.

Heidegger, Martin. *Introduction to Phenomenological Research*. Translated by Daniel O. Dahlstrom. Bloomington: Indiana University Press, 2005.

Heidegger, Martin. *Mindfulness*. Translated by Parvis Emad and Kenneth Maly. London: Continuum, 2006.

Heidegger, Martin. *Nietzsche: Ersterband*. Frankfurt: Vittorio Klostermann, 1996.

Heidegger, Martin. *Nietzsche: Zweiterband*. Frankfurt: Vittorio Klostermann, 1997.
Heidegger, Martin. *Nietzsche*: vol. I: *The Will to Power as Art*. Translated by David Farrell Krell. San Francisco: Harper and Row, 1979.
Heidegger, Martin. *Nietzsche*: vol. IV: *Nihilism*. Translated by David Farrell Krell. San Francisco: Harper and Row, 1982.
Heidegger, Martin. *Off the Beaten Track*. Translated by Julian Young and Kenneth Haynes. Cambridge: Cambridge University Press, 2002.
Heidegger, Martin. *On the Way to Language*. Translated by Peter D. Hertz. San Francisco: Harper & Row, 1982.
Heidegger, Martin. *Ontology: The Hermeneutics of Facticity*. Translated by John Van Buren. Bloomington: Indiana University Press, 1999.
Heidegger, Martin. *Pathmarks*. Edited by William McNeill. Cambridge: Cambridge University Press, 1998, includes 'What Is Metaphysics?' (1929), translated by David Farrell Krell, and 'Postscript to "What Is Metaphysics?"' (1943), translated by McNeill.
Heidegger, Martin. *Phänomenologie Der Anschauung Und Des Ausdrucks*. Frankfurt: Vittorio Klostermann, 1993.
Heidegger, Martin. *Phenomenology of Intuition and Expression: Theory of Philosophical Concept Formation*. Translated by Tracy Colony. London: Continuum, 2010.
Heidegger, Martin. *Poetry, Language, Thought*. Translated by Albert Hofstadter. New York: Harper & Row, 1975.
Heidegger, Martin. *The Principle of Reason*. Translated by Reginald Lilly. Bloomington: Indiana University Press, 1991.
Heidegger, Martin. *The Question Concerning Technology, and Other Essays*. Translated by William Lovitt. New York: Garland Pub., 1977.
Heidegger, Martin. *Sein und Zeit*. [GA 2] Tübingen: Max Niemeyer, 1957.
Heidegger, Martin. *Towards the Definition of Philosophy: With a Transcript of the Lecture Course 'on the Nature of the University and Academic Study'*. Translated by Ted Sadler. New Brunswick: Athlone Press, 2000.
Heidegger, Martin. *Unterwegs Zur Sprache*. Pfullingen: Günther Neske, 1975.
Heidegger, Martin. *Vorträge Und Aufsätze*. 10th edn. Stuttgart: Klett-Cotta, 2004.
Heidegger, Martin. *Was Heisst Denken?* Tübingen: Max Niemeyer, 1977.
Heidegger, Martin. *What Is Called Thinking?* Translated by J. Glenn Gray. New York: Harper Colophon Books, 1968.
Held, Klaus. 'Husserl's Phenomenological Method'. Translated by Lanei Rodemeyer. In *The New Husserl a Critical Reader*, edited by Donn Welton, 3–31. Bloomington: Indiana University Press, 2003.
Higgins, Dick. *A Dialectic of Centuries: Notes Towards a Theory of the New Arts*. New York: Printed Editions, 1978.

Higgins, Dick. 'Fluxus: Theory and Reception'. In *The Fluxus Reader*, edited by Ken Friedman, 217–36. Chichester: Academy Editions, 1998.

Higgins, Hannah, *Fluxus Experience*. Berkeley: University of California Press, 2002.

Husserl, Edmund. *Cartesian Meditations: An Introduction to Phenomenology*. Translated by Dorion Cairns. Dordrecht: Kluwer Academic, 1995.

Husserl, Edmund. *Erfahrung und Urteil: Untersuchungen zur Genealogie der Logik*. Edited by Ludwig Landgrebe. Prague: Academia, 1939.

Husserl, Edmund. *Experience and Judgment: Investigations in a Genealogy of Logic*. Translated by James S. Churchill and Karl Ameriks. Edited by Ludwig Landgrebe. Evanston: Northwestern University Press, 1973.

Husserl, Edmund. *Husserliana I: Cartesianische Meditationen und Pariser Vorträge*. The Hague: Martinus Nijhoff, 1950.

Husserl, Edmund. *Husserliana III/1: Ideen zu Einer Reinen Phänomenologie und Phänomenologischen Philosophie*. The Hague: Martinus Nijhoff, 1976.

Husserl, Edmund. *Husserliana X: Vorlesungen zur Phänomenologie des Inneren Zeitbewusstseins*. The Hague: Martinus Nijhoff, 1966.

Husserl, Edmund. 'Husserl's Letter to Hofmannsthal – Phenomenology and Pure Art'. Translated by Sven-Olov Wallenstein. *Site* 26–7 (2009): 2–.

Husserl, Edmund. *Ideas: General Introduction to Pure Phenomenology I (Ideas I)*. Translated by William Ralph Boyce Gibson. London: George Allen & Unwin, 1969.

Husserl, Edmund. *Logical Investigations*, Vol. 1. Translated by John Niemeyer Findlay. London: Routledge, 2001.

Husserl, Edmund. *Logical Investigations*, Vol. 2. Translated by John Niemeyer Findlay. London: Routledge, 2001.

Husserl, Edmund. *Logische Untersuchungen*, Zweiter Theil. Halle: Max Niemeyer, 1901.

Husserl, Edmund. *On the Phenomenology of the Consciousness of Internal Time (1893–1917)*. Translated by John B. Brough. Dordrecht: Springer Science + Business Media, BV, 1991.

Husserl, Edmund. *Phantasy, Image Consciousness, and Memory, 1898–1925*. Translated by John B. Brough. Dordrecht: Springer, 2005.

Husserl, Edmund. *The Phenomenology of Internal Time-Consciousness*. Translated by James S. Churchill. Edited by Martin Heidegger. Bloomington: Indiana University Press, 1964.

Ihde, Don. *Listening and Voice: Phenomenologies of Sound*. 2nd edn. Albany: State University of New York Press, 2007.

Jardine, Alice. *Gynesis: Configurations of Woman and Modernity*. Ithaca: Cornell University Press, 1985.

Jay, Martin. *Songs of Experience Modern American and European Variations on a Universal Theme*. Berkeley: University of California Press, 2005.

Joseph, Brandon W. *Random Order: Robert Rauschenberg and the Neo-Avant-Garde*. Cambridge, MA: MIT Press, 2007.

Kahn, Douglas. *Noise, Water, Meat: A History of Sound in the Arts*. Cambridge, MA: MIT Press, 1999.

Kane, Brian. 'L'objet Sonore Maintenant: Pierre Schaeffer, Sound Objects and the Phenomenological Reduction', *Organised Sound* 12, no. 1 (2007): 15–24.

Kangas, David J. *Kierkegaard's Instant: On Beginnings*. Bloomington: Indiana University Press, 2007.

Kant, Immanuel. *The Critique of Judgement*. Translated by Paul Guyer. Cambridge: Cambridge University Press, 2000.

Kierkegaard, Søren. *Philosophical Fragments or a Fragment of Philosophy*. Translated by David F. Swenson. Princeton: Princeton University Press, 1962.

Kierkegaard, Søren. 'The Rotation Method: An Essay in the Theory of Social Prudence'. In *Either /Or, Volume 1*. Translated by David F. Swenson, 279–96. Princeton: Princeton University Press, 1959.

Kim-Cohen, Seth. *In the Blink of an Ear: Towards a Non-Cochlear Sonic Art*. New York: Continuum, 2009.

Kisiel, Theodore J. *The Genesis of Heidegger's Being and Time*. Berkeley: University of California Press, 1993.

Kockelmans, Joseph J., ed. *Phenomenology: The Philosophy of Edmund Husserl and Its Interpretation*. Garden City: Anchor Books, 1967.

Kostelanetz, Richard. *Conversing with Cage*. New York: Limelight Editions, 1988.

Kotz, Liz. 'Post-Cagean Aesthetics and the Event Score' (2001). In *John Cage*, edited by Julia Robinson, 101–40. Cambridge, MA: MIT Press, 2011.

Kotz, Liz. *Words to Be Looked At: Language in 1960s Art*. Cambridge, MA: MIT Press, 2007.

Krell, David Farrell. *Daimon Life: Heidegger and Life-Philosophy*. Bloomington: Indiana University Press, 1992.

Kristeva, Julia. *Desire in Language: A Semiotic Approach to Literature and Art*. Translated by Thomas Gora, Alice Jardine and Leon S. Roudiez. New York: Columbia University Press, 1980.

Kristeva, Julia. *Revolution in Poetic Language*, Translated by Margaret Waller. New York: Columbia University Press, 1984.

Kuhn, Thomas S. *The Structure of Scientific Revolutions*. 2nd edn. Enlarged. Chicago: University of Chicago Press, 1970.

LaBelle, Brandon. *Background Noise: Perspectives on Sound Art*. New York: Continuum International, 2006.

Latour, Bruno. *On the Modern Cult of the Factish Gods*. Durham: Duke University Press, 2010.

Le Grice, Malcolm. *Abstract Film and Beyond*. London: Studio Vista, 1977.

Lévinas, Emmanuel. *Alterity and Transcendence*. Translated by Michael B. Smith. New York: Columbia University Press, 1999.

Lévinas, Emmanuel. 'Intuition of Essences'. Translated by Joseph J. Kockelmans. In *Phenomenology: The Philosophy of Edmund Husserl and Its Interpretation*, edited by Joseph J. Kockelmans, 83–105. Garden City: Anchor Books, 1967.

LeWitt, Sol. 'Paragraphs on Conceptual Art'. In *Conceptual Art: A Critical Anthology*, edited by Alexander Alberro and Blake Stimson, 12–6. Cambridge, MA: MIT Press, 1999.

LeWitt, Sol. 'Sentences on Conceptual Art'. In *Conceptual Art: A Critical Anthology*, edited by Alexander Alberro and Blake Stimson, 106–7. Cambridge, MA: MIT Press, 1999.

Lomas, David, with Jeremy Stubbs. *Simulating the Marvellous, Psychology – Surrealism – Postmodernism*. Manchester: Manchester University Press, 2013.

Lories, Danielle. 'Remarks on Aesthetic Intentionality: Husserl or Kant', *International Journal of Philosophical Studies* 14, no. 1 (2006): 31–49.

Lucy, Niall. *Debating Derrida*. Melbourne: Melbourne University Press, 1995.

Lumsden, Simon. 'Habit and the Limits of the Autonomous Subject', *Body & Society* 19, nos. 2–3 (2013): 58–82.

Lyotard, Jean François. *Driftworks*. Translated by Joseph Maier. New York: Semiotext(e), 1984.

Malabou, Catherine. *Before Tomorrow: Epigenesis and Rationality*. Translated by Carolyn Shread. Cambridge: Polity Press, 2016.

Malabou, Catherine. *Changing Difference: The Feminine and the Question of Philosophy*. Translated by Carolyn Shread. Cambridge: Polity Press, 2011.

Malabou, Catherine. *The Future of Hegel: Plasticity, Temporality and Dialectic*. Translated by Lisabeth During. London: Routledge, 2005.

Malpas, Jeff E. *Heidegger's Topology: Being, Place, World*. Cambridge, MA: MIT Press, 2006.

Maritain, Jacques. *Art and Scholasticism: With Other Essays*. Translated by J. F. Scanlan. London: Sheed & Ward, 1946.

Meeker, Natania. *Voluptuous Philosophy: Literary Materialism in the French Enlightenment*. New York: Fordham University Press, 2006.

Meillassoux, Quentin. *After Finitude: An Essay on the Necessity of Contingency*. Translated by Ray Brassier. London: Bloomsbury, 2013.

Mendez, Mathew. '"A Power of Sonorous Paradoxes . . .": Passivity, Singularity, and Indifference in Jean François Lyotard's Readings of John Cage', *Cultural Politics* 9, no. 2 (2013): 170–87.

Metz, Christian. 'Aural Objects'. Translated by Georgia Gurrieri. *Yale French Studies*, no. 60, Cinema/Sound (1980): 24–32.

Miller, Tyrus. *Singular Examples: Artistic Politics and the Neo-Avant-Garde*. Evanston: Northwestern University Press, 2009.

Morris, Robert. *Continuous Project Altered Daily: Writings of Robert Morris*. New edn. Cambridge, MA: MIT Press, 1995.

Morris, Robert. 'Notes on Dance', *Tulane Drama Review* 10, no. 2 (Winter 1965): 179–86.

Motherwell, Robert, ed. *The Dada Painters and Poets: An Anthology*. Cambridge, MA: The Belknap Press of the Harvard University Press 1989.

Motherwell, Robert, Dore Ashton and Joan Banach. *The Writings of Robert Motherwell*. The Documents of Twentieth-Century Art. Berkeley: University of California Press, 2007.

Motte, Warren F. *Oulipo: A Primer of Potential Literature*. Lincoln: University of Nebraska Press, 1986.

Munroe, Alexandra with Jon Hendricks. *YES Yoko Ono*. New York: Harry N. Abrams and Japan Society, 2000.

Nancy, Jean-Luc. *A Finite Thinking*. Edited by Simon Sparks. Stanford: Stanford University Press, 2003.

Nancy, Jean-Luc. *The Birth to Presence*. Translated by Brian Holmes et al. Stanford: Stanford University Press, 1993.

Ono, Yoko. *Grapefruit: A book of Instructions + Drawings by Yoko Ono*. New York: Simon & Schuster, 2000.

Palombini, Carlos. 'Schaeffer's Sonic Object: Prolegomena' (1999). Accessed 27 November 2019. http://compmus.ime.usp.br/sbcm/1999/papers/Carlos_Palombini.html

Patton, Paul and Terry Smith. *Jacques Derrida: Deconstruction Engaged: The Sydney Seminars*. Sydney: Power Publications, 2001.

Perloff, Marjorie and Charles Junkerman, eds. *John Cage: Composed in America* Chicago: University of Chicago Press, 1994).

Piper, Adrian. *Out of Order, Out of Sight: Selected Writings in Meta-Art, 1968–1992*, Vols. 1 and 2. Cambridge, MA: MIT Press, 1996.

Rainer, Yvonne. 'Looking Myself in the Mouth' (1981). In *John Cage*, edited by Julia Robinson, 35–48. Cambridge, MA: MIT Press, 2011.

Reich, Steve. *Writings About Music*. Halifax: The Press of Nova Scotia College of Art and Design, 1974.

Retallack, Joan. *The Poethical Wager*. Berkeley: University of California Press, 2003.

Richter, Hans. *Dada: Art and Anti-art*. Translated by David Britt. London: Thames and Hudson, 1997.

Robinson, Julia. 'From Abstraction to Model: George Brecht's Events and the Conceptual Turn in Art of the 1960s', *October* 127 (Winter 2008): 77–108.

Ronell, Avital. *The Telephone Book: Technology, Schizophrenia, Electric Speech*. Lincoln: University of Nebraska Press, 1989.

Rorty, Richard. *Contingency, Irony and Solidarity*. Cambridge: Cambridge University Press, 1989.

Ross, Alison. *The Aesthetic Paths of Philosophy: Presentation in Kant, Heidegger, Lacoue-Labarthe, and Nancy*. Stanford: Stanford University Press, 2007.

Rubin, William S. *Dada, Surrealism and Their Heritage*. New York: The Museum of Modern Art, 1968.

Safer, Craig. 'Fluxus as Laboratory'. In *The Fluxus Reader*, edited by Ken Friedman, 136–51. Chichester: Academy Editions, 1998.

Sante, Luc. *Evidence*. 1st edn. New York: Farrar, Straus and Giroux, 1992.

Schaeffer, Pierre. 'Acousmatics' excerpt from *Traité des objets musicaux*. Paris: Éditions du Seuil, 1966, in *Audio Culture: Readings in Modern Music*. Edited by Christoph Cox and Daniel Warner. Translated by Daniel W. Smith, 76–81. New York: Continuum, 2004.

Schaeffer, Pierre. *Solfège De L'objet Sonore*. Translated by Livia Bellagamba. Paris: Institut National de l'Audiovisuel, 1998.

Schafer, R. Murray. *The Soundscape: Our Sonic Environment and the Tuning of the World*. Rochester: Destiny Books, 1993.

Staten, Henry. *Wittgenstein and Derrida*. Lincoln: University of Nebraska Press, 1984.

Taminiaux, Jacques. *The Metamorphoses of Phenomenological Reduction*. 1st edn. Milwaukee: Marquette University Press, 2004.

Taminiaux, Jacques. *Poetics, Speculation, and Judgment: The Shadow of the Work of Art from Kant to Phenomenology*. Translated by Michael Gendre. Albany: State University of New York Press, 1993.

Vallega-Neu, Daniela. 'Diseminating Time: Durations, Configurations, and Chance', *Research in Phenomenology* 47 (2017): 1–18.

Vattimo, Gianni. *Art's Claim to Truth*. Translated by Luca D'Isanto. New York: Columbia University Press, 2008.

Vattimo, Gianni. *The End of Modernity*. Translated by Jon R. Snyder. Cambridge: Polity Press, 1988.

Weber, Samuel. *Mass Mediauras: Form, Technics, Media*. Sydney: Power Publications, 1996.

Welton, Donn. *The Other Husserl: The Horizons of Transcendental Phenomenology*. Bloomington: Indiana University Press, 2000.

Wilden, Anthony. *System and Structure: Essays in Communication and Exchange*. London: Tavistock, 1977.

Windelband, Wilhelm. *History of Philosophy: With Especial Reference to Formation and Development of Its Problems and Conceptions*. Translated by James H. Tufts. New York: Macmillan, 1914.

Wollen, Peter. *Readings and Writings: Semiotic Counter Strategies*. London: Verso, 1982.
Young, La Monte, ed. *An Anthology of Chance Operations*. New York: La Monte Young and Jackson Mac Low, 1963.
Young, La Monte, ed. 'Lecture 1960', *Tulane Drama Review* 10, no. 2 (Winter 1965): 73–83.
Zahavi, Dan. *Husserl's Phenomenology*. Stanford: Stanford University Press, 2003.
Zahavi, Dan. *Self-Awareness and Alterity: A Phenomenological Investigation*. Evanston: Northwestern University Press, 1999.
Ziarek, Krzysztof. 'After Aesthetics: Heidegger and Benjamin on Art and Experience', *Philosophy Today* 41, no. 1 (Spring 1997): 199–208.
Ziarek, Krzysztof. 'Art, Power, and Politics: Heidegger on *Machenschaft* and *Poiēsis*', *Contretemps* 3, no. July (2002): 175–86.
Ziarek, Krzysztof. 'Beyond Critique? Art and Power'. In *Adorno and Heidegger: Philosophical Questions*, edited by Iain Macdonald and Krzysztof Ziarek, 105–23. Stanford: Stanford University Press, 2008.
Ziarek, Krzysztof. *The Force of Art*. Stanford: Stanford University Press, 2004.
Ziarek, Krzysztof. *The Historicity of Experience: Modernity, the Avant-Garde, and the Event*. Evanston: Northwestern University Press, 2001.
Žižek, Slavoj. *Interrogating the Real*. Edited by Rex Butler and Scott Stephens. London: Bloomsbury, 2005.

# Index

abstract expressionism
    and automatism   15, 16
    and existentialism   18
Ackerman, Chantal   155
action painting   6, 16, 18
Ader, Bas Jan   64
Albers, Josef   114, 90 n.4
*alētheia*   4, 73, 74
Amacher, Maryanne   67, 68
anthropocentrism   2, 8, 28, 52, 56, 68, 81, 97, 102, 107, 109, 146
Antin, Eleanor   145
Aquinas, St Thomas   29, 99
Aristotle   12, 29, 100, 116, 154, 177 n.2
Arp, Jean (Hans)   1, 20, 179 n.30
as-structure of experience   120, 128
Augustine, St.   29
Austin, J. L.   165–6, 168, 172
automatic writing   15–18, 23, 24, 26
automatism
    in abstract expressionism   15–20, 28
    and Breton   13, 14, 26
    and Motherwell   15–17
    and Oulipo   22–24
    and Pollock   16, 19, 20, 29
    in surrealism   6, 13–17, 20, 26, 178 n.9
avant-garde art   2, 4, 6, 12, 31, 91, 131, 132, 145, 171

Backman, Jussi   155, 195 n.66
Badiou, Alain   156
Baldessari, John   1, 64, 143–4, 145
Banes, Sally   183 n.25
Barthes, Roland
    *Camera Lucida*   137, 138, 142
    death of the author   27
    'The Photographic Message'   136, 137
    photographic reference   140
    on photography   135–8, 140, 142
    *punctum*   137, 139, 142
    temporality of the photograph   142
    'The Third Meaning'   137
Bass, Alan   164
Bataille, George   23, 171
Bazin, André
    non-human agency of photography   135–6
    ontological equivalence of photographic image   40, 135–7, 140
Baziotes, William   16, 178 n.13
beautiful, the
    and Derrida   102–6, 109, 111
    and favour   89, 110
    and Heidegger   80, 89, 111
    and Kant   8, 46, 101–11
    and Plato   112
Becher, Bernd and Hilla   64, 144–5
Beistegui, Miguel de   184 n.45
Belgrad, Daniel   18–19, 178 n.22
Benjamin, Walter   135, 139–40, 141–2, 192 n.11
Bennington, Geoffrey   195 n.67
Bergson, Henri   29, 76, 139
Bernstein, J. M   185 n.3
Boulez, Pierre   52
Bourdieu, Pierre   28, 174
bracketing, *see epochē*
Brassier, Ray   156, 195 n.70
Brecht, George
    chance and automatism   20, 22, 25, 29, 64, 114
    'Chance Imagery'   20, 29, 179 n.28
    and Fluxus   1, 8, 20, 114, 115, 128–31
    Fluxus event scores   8, 128–9
    influence of Dada   19
    irrelevant process   22, 25, 57, 59
    New School of Social Research   115, 151
    *Three Chair Events*   130–1
Brentano, Franz   120, 125
Breton, André   13–15, 17–18, 23, 26
Broodthaers, Marcel   64

Brown, Norman O.   196 n.2, n.10
Bruns, Gerald L 91
Burroughs, Wiiliam S.   1, 28, 180 n.46
Busa, Peter   16
Butler, Judith   172–3

Cabanne, Pierre   21
Cage
   and Aquinas   99–101
   and chance operations   1, 2, 5–7, 22, 25, 27, 48–54, 56–8, 91, 95–6, 159, 160–2, 169, 170, 174, 176
   and change   7, 51, 56, 57, 91, 93, 95
   and *I Ching*   22, 52, 58, 161
   and Coomaraswamy   94, 99–101
   and Eckhart   7, 50, 91, 93–8, 99, 102, 112, 162
   and Fluxus   113–15, 128
   *For the Birds*   57, 95, 114
   *4'33"*   54–6, 65, 67, 128, 133, 83 n.14
   *Imaginary Landscape No. 4*   52
   indeterminacy   1, 7, 53–4, 57, 62, 91, 109, 170
   mesostic poems   160, 196 n.2
   *Music for Changes*   52
   New School of Social Research   60, 115, 151
   non-intention   2, 16, 27, 48, 50, 52–6, 64, 67, 69, 95, 96, 109, 159, 160, 168–70, 176
   Norton lectures   56, 160
   and Rauschenberg's White paintings   55
   and Reich   58–9
   and self-expression   51–2, 68, 93, 99, 162, 176
   *Silence*   152
   and silence   54–6, 114, 162
   *Silent Prayer*   55, 183 n.14
   and Suzuki   51–2, 55, 94, 99
   and Zen Buddhism   51–2, 55, 56, 91, 93–6, 102, 151–2
calculative thinking   76, 81
Caputo, John D.   96, 113, 132
Cartesianism   3, 33, 67, 77, 78–9, 81, 82, 119, 122
chance and non-intention
   in art   1, 2, 6, 9, 11–12, 13, 15, 19–22, 25–9, 50, 58, 60–1, 64, 71–2, 91, 129, 165

   in Cage   1, 2, 5–7, 22, 25, 27, 29, 48–54, 56–8, 64, 69, 91, 93, 95–6, 109, 113, 159–62, 169, 170, 174, 176
   in dada   1, 2, 6, 12, 19–21, 29, 58
   in dance   1, 59–60
   and Derrida   5, 8, 173
   in film   1, 146–7
   in Fluxus   1, 114, 129
   in music   1, 48, 51–6, 57, 58–9
   in photography   1, 8, 135–6, 138–41, 143–5
   in poetry and literature   23–4, 160–2, 167–9, 175, 176
   in surrealism   1, 2, 12–15, 20, 23, 24, 58
Charles Daniel   51, 56, 57, 95, 114, 151, 187 n.5
Chillida, Eduardo   4, 90
*I Ching*   22, 52, 58, 161
Chion, Michel   43, 44
collage   1, 9, 14, 20
Collingwood, R. G.   189 n.23
complexity   54, 56–8
conceptual art   22, 35–6, 60, 64, 117, 129
constraint, the   6, 22–6, 28, 29, 60, 91, 144, 161, 171
context   39, 65–8, 131, 132–3, 165, 166
contingency
   and art   50, 51, 58, 62, 91, 129
   and Cage   51, 91
   in cinema   156
   and Derrida   6, 133, 170
   and the flux   113, 114
   and indexicality   8, 137–8, 140
   and Kant   8, 104, 107, 108
   and photography   138, 139, 143–5
   and projection   13
   and the swerve   174
   systems in music   1
   systems in photography   143–51
   systems in process art   62
Coomaraswamy, Ananda K.   94, 99–101
Cox, Christoph   27, 35
Cozens, Alexander   13
Crooks, Edward, James   100
Cunningham, Merce   1, 59

dada   1, 2, 6, 12, 19, 20, 21, 58, 192 n.26
Dali, Salvador   15

dance   1, 59–60, 183 n.25
Daoism   16, 94, 95
*Dasein*   76, 78, 86, 87, 89, 94, 96, 152–4
Davis, Bret W.   50, 89, 91, 94, 96, 188 n.14
Derrida
　and absolute past   141
　'Afterword: Toward An Ethic of Discussion'   168–70, 173
　arche-writing   118, 127
　and Austin   165–6, 168, 172
　and Barthes   140
　*The Beast and the Sovereign*   169
　and chance, non-intention   5, 8, 173
　and consciousness   126, 127, 141, 163–5
　and decision   155, 160, 168, 169–70
　*Deconstruction Engaged*   133
　and destinerrance   105, 173–4
　'Differance'   141, 164
　différance   118, 127, 155, 170, 180 n.46
　dissemination   105, 167
　*Dissemination*   167
　'Economimesis'   7, 101–2, 108
　and errant beauty   104–7, 111
　and ethics   2, 8, 168–71, 175, 176
　'Force of Law'   169–70
　and form   45, 46
　'Form and Meaning'   45
　and the gift   155
　*The Gift of Death*   155
　*Given Time*   155
　*Of Grammatology*   116–19
　hauntology   8, 140–2, 193 n.25
　and Heidegger   4, 5, 32, 47
　and Husserl   6, 8, 32, 45, 46, 115, 118–19, 123–7, 132, 141, 163–4
　and ideality   122–4, 126, 127, 164
　and indeterminacy   170, 173
　and intention   163–8, 175, 176
　and internal time consciousness   125–6
　and iterability   8, 159, 165–7, 170, 176
　and Kant   101–8, 111–12
　and Kierkegaard   155, 160, 195 n.67
　'Limited Inc a b c …'   165–8, 170, 175
　'My Chances'   173–4
　*The Origins of Geometry*   123–7
　*Positions*   170, 175, 176
　'Right of Inspection'   140–1
　and Searle   165, 167, 168, 172, 197 n.17
　'Signature Event Context'   165–6, 172, 197 n.17
　*Specters of Marx*   141
　'Speech and Phenomena'   124–7, 141, 163–4
　supplement   127
　trace   4, 5, 28, 118, 127, 133, 134, 136, 141, 156, 159, 173
　and truth   4
　*The Truth in Painting*   7, 105–7
　undecidability   5, 167, 169, 170, 197 n.17
de Saussure, Ferdinand   118
Descartes, Rene   74, 110, *see also* Cartesianism
detachment–(*Abgescheidenheit*)   7, 50, 95–7, 155, 188 n.14
Dewey, John   16, 29
Dibbets, Jan   145
Dilthey, Wilhelm   76–8
Dine, Jim   115
Doane, Mary Ann   138, 140,
Duchamp, Marcel   1, 6, 21, 23, 25, 29, 35, 36, 50, 59, 60, 62, 129, 130, 190 n.4, 192 n.26
Dunn, Robert   59–60, 183 n.25
Dürer, Albrecht   46
Dworkin, Craig   150
Dyson, Frances   33

Eckhart, Meister
　and Angelus Silesius   99
　and Cage   7, 50, 91, 93, 94–8, 102
　detachment   95–6
　*Gelassenheit*   96–8
　the Ground   94
　and habit   29
　and Heidegger   7, 94, 96–8, 112
　and Kierkegaard   154
ego, the   2, 6, 17, 26, 28, 51, 64, 69, 92, 110, 162, 167
Emerson, Ruth   1, 60, 183 n.25
empiricism   37, 115–18, 123
*epochē*, the
　and the aesthetic judgment   179 n.44
　and Cage   7, 8, 27, 48, 50, 95, 113, 162
　of the chance operation   8, 25–7, 48, 50, 65, 69, 95, 113, 159, 161, 162

and Derrida   159, 169
and Husserl   39, 40, 46
and photography   8
and poetics   159, 161
and Schaeffer   40
Ernst, Max   12, 13
estrangement   2, 4, 67, 83, 90
ethics   2, 8, 159–62, 165, 167–71, 175, 176
Evans, C. de B.   94
event, the   2, 3, 4
event scores   8, 127–31
everyday, the   2, 4, 28, 34, 67, 83, 86, 87, 96, 97, 115, 128–31, 175
existentialism   16, 18
experience
   contextured   132–4
   demise of   116
   primary and secondary   8, 116–17, 124, 127, 130
expression
   in art   2, 3, 11, 18, 21, 26, 27, 60, 61
   and Cage   51–2, 68, 93, 99, 162, 176
   and Derrida   107, 123–4, 126, 163–4, 175, 176
   and Heidegger   77, 79, 88
   and Husserl   123–4, 126, 163–4

favour–*Gunst*   46, 89, 111
Fichte, Johann Gottlieb   111
Fischer, Konrad   145
Fish, Stanley   169
Fluxus   1, 8, 20, 22, 91, 113–18, 127–32, 155
Fontana, Bill   66–8
Forti, Simone   1, 60
Foucault, Michel   27, 28
Frankenthaler, Helen   18
Freud, Sigmund   139–41, 174
Fried, Michael   138–9
Friedman, Gene   59
fusion of horizons   131–2

Gadamer, Hans-Georg
   fusion of horizons   131–2
   on lived experience (*Erlebnis*)   76
   on modern art   4, 90
   'The Phenomenological Movement'   181
   *Truth and Method*   76, 131–2

Gann, Kyle   188 n.21
Gasché, Rodolphe   103, 168
*Gegnet*   68
German Idealism   110–11, 123
Gestalt   16, 84
Gidal, Peter   145, 148, 150
Gombrich, E. H.   13
Graff, Gerald   165, 169, 170, 173, 179 n.17
Graham, Dan   1, 64
Graham, John D   15–16
Greenberg, Clement   35
Grooms, Red   115
Grosz, Elizabeth   171

Haacke, Hans   62–5, 145
Haar, Michel   92, 110
habit   19–21, 26, 29, 37, 47, 49, 51, 54, 60, 84, 161, 187 n.10
Halprin, Ann   1, 60
Hansen, Al   115
Hansen, Miriam Bratu   192 n.11
Harman, Graham   191 n.18
Hayles, N. Katherine   56–7
Heath, Stephen   145
Hegel, Wilhelm Friedrich   19, 74, 79, 80, 81, 82, 111, 198 n.25
Heidegger
   and aesthetics   73–4, 80–2, 88–92
   and art   3–5, 7, 28, 72–4, 79–80, 82, 84–5
   *Basic Problems of Phenomenology*   74, 154
   *Basic Questions of Philosophy*   81, 84, 92
   *Being and Time*   76, 78, 87, 186 n.12
   The Black Notebooks   186 n.13
   and boredom   8, 152–5
   *Country Path Conversations*   86, 97, 98, 184 n.44, 188 n.16
   *Destruktion*   32, 73–4
   *Discourse on Thinking*   86, 97, 98, 184 n.44, 188 n.16
   early lectures   76–8, 120–1
   *The End of Philosophy*   82
   *The Fundamental Concepts of Metaphysics*   152–5
   *Gelassenheit*   7, 68, 91, 94, 96–8, 154–5, 164
   *Introduction to Metaphysics*   80, 83, 87

*Hölderlin's Hymns 'Germania' and*
   *'The Rhine'* 79
and Husserl   27, 29, 31–2, 35, 47, 48,
   50, 77, 120
and Kant   46, 88–9, 110–11
and Leibniz   98–9
and letting   3–4, 5, 7, 27, 50, 67–8,
   72, 73, 84, 86, 87, 89–91, 97,
   98, 110, 157
and lived experience
   (*Erlebnis*)   75–9, 81–3
non-willing thinking   3, 5, 7, 72, 89,
   91, 98, 112, 154, 164
'The Origin of the Work of Art'   5,
   72–3, 74, 75, 79, 83, 84–5, 87,
   88, 90, 185 n.4
and phenomenology   31, 35, 48,
   67, 76, 78
*Phenomenology of Intuition and*
   *Experience*   77
and place   67–8
*The Principle of Reason*   98–9, 111
representational thinking   3, 5,
   50, 68, 75, 76, 81, 97, 111,
   112, 124, 175
resoluteness   3, 28, 86–7, 89, 154
*Seminare: Platon-Aristoteles-*
   *Augustinus*   155
and temporality   152–4
*Towards the Definition of*
   *Philosophy*   77, 121
and truth   4, 5, 72–5, 79, 81, 82,
   85, 86, 88
'What is Metaphysics'   152
and the will   5, 7, 32, 69, 72,
   82–91, 164
will to power   74, 82–3, 88, 90
'The Will to Power as Art'   72, 74, 75,
   80–3, 86, 88–90, 110–12
will to will   82–3, 89
and wonder   83–4
Held, Klaus   42
Heraclitus   113
hermeneutics   31, 32, 35, 47, 113, 114,
   131, 132, 191 n.20
Higgins, Dick
   and chance   1, 22, 64
   criticism of Cage   114
   'Danger and Boredom'   151
   and Fluxus   114, 115

'Fluxus: Theory and
   Reception'   131–2
and Gadamer's fusion of
   horizons   131–2
and phenomenology   119
on Satie   151
Higgins, Hannah   115–17, 127, 190 n.7
Hjelmslev, Louis   118
Hofstadter, Albert   85, 185 n.4, 186 n.15
Hölderlin, Friedrich   79, 90
Huebler, Douglas   1, 145
Hugnet, Georges   13
Hume, David   29
Husserl
   his aestheticism   44–8
   *Cartesian Meditations*   46, 122
   constitution   46, 48, 120, 122,
      128, 130, 141
   eidetic reduction   7, 35, 38–40, 46, 47
   *epochē*   39, 40, 46
   *Experience and Judgment*   42
   form   45, 46
   horizons   2, 32, 48, 68, 121–2, 131–2,
      141, 191 n.20
   ideality   122–4, 126, 127, 164
   *Ideas I*   38–9, 45, 46
   ideation (*Wesensschau*)   40, 191 n.20
   intentionality   2, 42, 92, 120–
      2, 128, 163
   internal time consciousness   125–6
   'Letter to Hofmannsthal'   45
   *Logical Investigations*   121, 123–5
   natural attitude, natural
      standpoint   25, 27, 39, 46,
      50, 95, 113
   *Phantasy, Image Consciousness, and*
      *Memory, 1898–1925*   46
   *The Phenomenology of Internal Time*
      *Consciousness*   125
   pre-delineation   48, 121,
      122, 191 n.20
   presuppositions   7, 25–8, 47,
      48, 50, 64
   transcendental reduction   25, 117,
      127, 155, 187 n.10

Ihde, Don   6, 31–4, 48
indeterminacy
   and Cage   1, 7, 53–4, 57, 62,
      91, 109, 170

and Derrida  170, 173
and destinerrance  105, 173–4
indexical sign  8, 137–8, 140, 163
Indiana, Robert  150
intention
and communication  71, 99, 131
and conviction  5, 28, 91
and ethics  8, 161, 169, 175–6
and expression  159, 163, 176
hegemony of  3, 11, 176
and intentionality  2, 163
and iterability  166–7
and Kant  8, 107–9
and limited responsibility  174–5
and meaning  33, 117, 159,
162–4, 168
intentionality  2, 42, 92, 120–2,
125, 128, 163
irrationalism  11, 14, 76, 103, 175

James, William  19, 29, 76
Jardine, Alice  116, 171, 172
Jay, Martin  186 n.9
Johns, Jasper  19, 60
Jones, Joe  129
Joyce, James  171

Kahn, Douglas  188 n.21
Kammerer, Paul  2
Kamrowski, Gerome  16, 178 n.13
Kane, Brian  37, 38, 41,
Kangas, David, J.  154
Kant, Immanuel
contingency  104, 107–8
*Critique of Judgement*  102–12
*Critique of Reason*  111
favour (*Gunst*)  46, 89, 110, 111
free beauty  104–7
intention  107–8
purposiveness without
purpose  101–10, 112
reason  103, 104, 106, 109, 111
taste  46–7, 105–7, 111, 179 n.44
Kaprow, Allan  19, 115
Kerner, Justinus  13
Kierkegaard, Søren  29, 113, 154–5
Kim-Cohen, Seth  27, 32, 35–6,
47, 180 n.3
Klee, Paul  4, 90
knowing  3, 33, 73, 85–6, 90, 92, 134

Knowles, Alison  115, 129, 190 n.7
Kotz, Liz  196 n.3
Kracauer, Siegfried  135, 139,
Krell, David Farrell  185 n.4, 186 n.7
Kren, Kurt  146, 148
Kristeva, Julia  171, 172
Kuhn, Thomas S.  156

LaBelle, Brandon  65, 66, 115
Land, Owen  194 n.45
Landow, George  149
Lask, Emil  76, 77
Latour, Bruno  156
Le Grice, Malcolm  146–51
Leibniz, Gottfried Wilhelm  29,
98, 110, 111
Leiris, Michel  23
Leonardo da Vinci  12, 13, 17, 18
LeWitt, Sol  1, 64, 65
Lionnais, François le  23
Lomas, David  17–18
Lories, Danielle  46
Lorrain Claude  13
Lucretius  173, 174
Lucy, Niall  175
Lyotard, Jean François  69, 120

McDowell, John Herbert  59, 60
Maciunas, George  113, 114, 129
Mac Low, Jackson  1, 160, 168, 176
Malabou, Catherine  19, 29, 198 n.25
Mallarmé, Stéphane  171
Malpas, Jeff. E.  184 n.45
Maritain, Jacques  100, 101
Matta (Echaurren), Roberto  16
Maxfield, Richard  1, 114
Meeker, Natania  198–9 n.31
Meillassoux, Quentin  156, 196
n.73, 198 n.30
Meinong, Alexius  125
Mendez, Mathew  97
Merleau-Ponty, Maurice  19, 29, 119,
172, 180 n.2
mesostics  160, 196 n.2
Messer, Thomas  63
Metz, Christian  37
Miller, Tyrus  160
mimesis  101–2, 107, 109
Mitchell, W.J.T.  116
Moholy-Nagy, Lázló  114

Monet, Claude 18
Morris, Robert 1, 60–1, 65, 91, 128
Motherwell, Robert 15–19
*musique concrète* 34, 37, 43, 65

Nancy, Jean-Luc 4, 87
National Socialism 79, 186 n.13
Natorp, Paul 77, 120, 191 n.20
neo-Kantianism 38, 76, 77, 120
New School of Social
 Research 60, 115, 151
Nietzsche, Friedrich
 art as applied physiology 74,
 and Cartesian subjectivity 82
 completion of
  metaphysics 74, 87–8, 111
 creator genius 82
 the grand style 89
 and Kant 88, 110
 self-overcoming of aesthetics 88
 *Rausch* 88, 89
 will-to-power 74, 82
non-intention, *see* chance and
 non-intention
non-willing
 and *Gelassenheit* 98, 154, 164
 and letting 5
 and not-willing 89
 and resoluteness 3
 and 'The Origin of the Work of Art'
 and thinking 7, 50, 72, 91, 112

Oldenburg, Claes 115
Ono, Yoko 60, 128, 129
ontology 3, 8, 31–6, 40, 45, 73, 78, 79,
 83, 96, 113, 116, 117, 135, 136,
 140, 149, 150, 192 n.25
optical unconscious 135, 139, 140, 142
ordinary, the 4, 60, 84–5, 115, 128, 129,
 131, 132, 143, 144, 150
other, the, otherness 2, 33, 72, 83, 84, 92,
 126, 141, 156
Oulipo 1, 6, 23–4, 28

Palombini, Carlos 42, 43
Panteli, Lucy 148
Partisan Review 18
Patterson, David Wayne 188 n.21
Peirce, Charles Sanders 137–8
perception

 and acousmatic reduction 34, 39
 and as-structure 120–2
 bare, naked, direct 6, 34, 56,
  115, 116, 119
 and constitution 119–20, 122, 127, 130
 and Derrida 45, 133
 and ideality 45
 and immediacy 32, 33, 75, 77, 115,
  120, 123–5, 127–8, 132, 133
 and intentionality 42, 120–2, 128
 and meaning 122–3, 127
 and musicality 34, 44
 and pre-delineation 121–2
 and pres-absence 8, 122, 157
 reconfiguring the patterns of 113
 and silent presence 45
 as sound in itself 56
 of temporal intentional objects 125–6
performative 165–6, 177
Pfeiffer, Franz 94
phenomenology
 and aesthetic
  presuppositions 44–7, 48, 50
 and art 6, 8, 32, 127
 and Cage 48
 and Derrida 32, 45, 115, 118–19,
  124–7, 132–4
 and discursive description 119–20
 and *epochē* 7, 8, 25–7, 39–40, 45–6,
  48, 50, 65, 159, 161
 first and second (Ihde) 31–2, 47, 48
 forestructures of experience 121–2,
  128, 191 n.20
 and givenness 4, 6, 25, 38,
  48, 121, 123
 and Heidegger 27, 29, 31–2, 35, 47,
  48, 50, 77, 120
 and horizons 2, 32, 48, 67, 68, 121–2,
  130–2, 141, 191 n.20
 and ideality 122–4, 126, 128, 156, 164
 and ideation (*Wesensschau*) 40
 and intentionality 2, 42, 92, 120–2,
  125, 128, 163
 internal time-consciousness 125–6
 and lived experience 44, 45, 76, 155
 and presuppositionlessness 5, 7,
  25–8, 38, 44, 47, 48, 50, 58, 64,
  65, 68, 92, 123, 144
 Natorp's critique of 120
 post- 118

and presence 45, 115, 119–20, 122, 124, 126–8, 131, 133, 141, 164, 165, 170
and Schaeffer 34–5, 37–9, 47
and sound 31, 34–5, 37–44
'third' 32
transcendental 25, 31, 50, 117–18, 155, 163
photography 135–45
Piper, Adrian 1, 64
place 67–8
plastic automatism 6, 17–20, 28
plasticity 19, 29
Plato 33, 45, 73, 74, 83, 100, 112, 116, 154, 155, 168
Pliny 12
Plissart, Marie-François 140
poethics 159, 168, 174
poetics 174, 175
poetry 1, 13, 17, 21, 24, 76, 79, 90, 161, 166, 168
*poiesis* 3, 91
Pollock, Jackson 15, 16, 19, 20, 29, 61, 178 n.13
post-aesthetics 66, 72
post-structuralism 118
Pound, Ezra 160
pre-delineation 48, 121, 122, 191 n.20
probability 57, 58
process art 1, 7, 22, 49, 50, 61, 62–5
process philosophy 16
protention 48, 120, 125, 126, 132, 141, 142
Proust, Marcel 138–9, 140, 192 n.11
*punctum* 137, 139, 142
purposiveness without purpose 101–5, 107–10, 112
purposive purposefulness 7, 97, 99, 102–3, 109, 112
Putnam, Hilary 116, 117
Pythagoras 36, 40

Queneau, Raymond 22–4

Raban, William 147
Rainer, Yvonne 60, 176, 183 n.25, 188 n.14
Rauschenberg, Robert 19, 55, 66
Ravaisson, Félix 29
Ray, Charles 145

readymade 1, 21, 62, 129, 130
real, the 2, 5, 6, 14, 38, 49, 116, 118, 119, 135, 156–7, 161, 173
Reich, Steve 59, 61–2, 63, 65
releasment (*Gelassenheit*)
 Cage 91, 96, 114, 159, 162
 Eckhart 94–8, 154–5
 Heidegger 7, 68, 91, 94, 96–8, 154–5, 164
repetition
 Cage 54, 151, 161
 Derrida–presence depends upon 4, 124, 127, 133, 141, 166
 Dick Higgins 151
 Duchamp 21
 Erik Satie *Vexations* 151–2
Retallack, Joan 8, 28, 161, 174
retention 48, 120, 125–7, 130, 132, 133, 141, 142
Reverdy, Pierre 14
Richter, Gehard 145
Richter, Hans 20, 21
Rickert, Heinrich 77
Ricoeur, Paul 29
Riffaterre, Michael 17
Robinson, Julia 192 n.24
romanticism 13, 15, 71, 75, 76, 89
Ronell, Avital 15, 186 n.16
Rorschach Hermann 13, 17
Rorty, Richard 4
Rosenberg, Alfred 79
Rosenberg, Harold 18
Rosenberg, Jim 161
Rosler, Martha 64, 145
Ross, Alison 107–8
Rubin, William S. 179 n.30
Ruscha, Ed 1, 64, 143–4

Safer, Craig 114
Sante, Luc 143
Satie, Erik 151–2
Schaeffer, Pierre
 acousmatic listening 36–7, 39, 67
 acousmatic reduction 32, 35, 39, 40
 aucology 43–4
 five stages of musical research 43
 and Husserl's phenomenology 34, 35, 37, 40–3, 48
 *musique concrète* 34, 37, 43, 65

    in opposition to Cage   34–5, 44, 47–9, 65, 68, 113
    and presuppositions   36, 44, 47, 48
    reduction to pure musicality   34, 39, 40, 43, 44, 49
    sonic reserch   7, 35, 36, 39, 47, 48, 68
    sound oblect   37, 40, 42–4, 47, 65
    *Traité des objets musicaux*   42, 44
Schafer, R. Murray   184 n.41
Scheffler, Johann, *see* Angelus Silesius
Schelling, Friedrich Eilhlem Joseph   111
Schleiermacher, Friedrich   76
Schopenhauer, Arthur   88, 110
Searle, John R.   165, 167, 168, 172, 197 n.17
Sharits, Paul   149–50
Silesisus, Angelus   98, 104, 109, 112
Smith, Terry   133, 134
Snow, Michael   147, 149
sound   6–7, 27, 31–7, 39–45, 47, 48, 50, 51, 53, 55, 56, 58, 59, 61, 62, 65–9, 93, 96, 113, 144, 162
sound Art   32, 35–6, 66
sound-in-itself   35–6, 47
spacing   5, 127, 134, 167, 173, 176
Spinoza, Baruch   29
Stella, Frank   60
structural and structural-materialist cinema   145–51
subject, the   28, 31, 33, 67, 68, 73, 74, 78, 82, 88, 97, 110, 111, 126, 127, 154, 155, 171–3
subjectivism   2, 3, 4, 7, 8, 22–5, 27, 28, 33, 37, 41, 47, 48, 50, 51, 53, 54, 57, 58, 64, 69, 73, 75, 77, 79, 82–4, 88, 89, 97, 110, 111, 117, 123, 136, 138, 145, 146, 161, 163, 171, 189 n.35
Summers, Elaine   1, 59–60
supplement   127
surrealism   1, 2, 6, 12–17, 20, 22–4, 58
Sussman, Eve   1
Suzuki, Teitaro Daisetz   51–2, 55, 94, 99
swerve, the   173, 174

Taminiaux, Jacques   39, 110
taste   5, 7, 13, 21, 25, 26, 46, 47, 48, 51, 53, 54, 58, 68, 76, 105–6, 107, 111, 161, 162, 179 n.44
Tavel, Ronald   151

*technē*   3, 12, 83–4, 91
temporality   66, 120, 125–7, 142, 148, 152–5, 191 n.21
time   8, 54, 56, 65, 125–6, 135, 136, 141, 142, 147–51, 152–5
transcendental reduction   25, 117, 127, 155, 187 n.10
truth   3–5, 11, 38, 72–5, 79, 81, 82, 85, 86, 88, 92, 136, 156, 157, 171
Tudor, David   54, 128
Tzara, Tristan   1, 6, 21, 23

uncanny, the (*Unheimlich*)   2, 67, 83
unconcealment   4, 73, 74–5, 84, 86, 87, 110
undecidability   170, 197 n.17

van Gogh, Vincent   4
Vassar College   55
Vattimo, Gianni   81

Wagner, Richard   74, 80, 82, 89
Warhol, Andy   150–1, 152, 155
Weber, Samuel   197 n.13
Webern, Anton   55
Welsby, Chris   146–7
Whitehead, Alfred North   16
Whitman, Robert   115
Wieland, Joyce   148
Wilden, Anthony   180 n.46
will   7, 23, 45, 64, 68, 69, 72, 82, 86, 88, 89, 94–8, 110, 111, 154, 162
willing   3, 7, 72, 73, 85–90, 97, 102, 109, 163–5, 170–4
will to Power   74, 82, 88, 89
will to Will   82, 83, 89
Windelband, Wilhelm   77, 189 n.23
Wolff, Christian   1, 52
Wollen, Peter   146, 149, 150
wonder   83–5

Xenakis, Iannis   57

Yorck von Wartenburg, Paul Graf   77
Young, Julian   85, 186 n.15
Young, La Monte   1, 128, 172

Zen Buddhism   16, 51, 55, 56, 91, 93–6, 102, 129, 150–2
Ziarek, Krzysztof   72, 185 n.3
Žižek, Slavoj   173

www.ingramcontent.com/pod-product-compliance
Lightning Source LLC
Chambersburg PA
CBHW072108010526
44111CB00037B/2048